# DEMAND FOR MONEY

# DEMAND FOR MONEY

## An Analysis of the Long-Run Behavior of the Velocity of Circulation

## Michael D. Bordo
## Lars Jonung

Routledge
Taylor & Francis Group

LONDON AND NEW YORK

Originally published in 1987 by Cambridge University Press

Published 2004 by Transaction Publishers

Published 2017 by Routledge
2 Park Square, Milton Park, Abingdon, Oxon OX14 4RN
711 Third Avenue, New York, NY 10017, USA

*Routledge is an imprint of the Taylor & Francis Group, an informa business*

Library of Congress Catalog Number: 2003053730

Library of Congress Cataloging-in-Publication Data

Bordo, Michael D.
    Demand for money : an analysis of the long-run behavior of the velocity of circulation / Michael D. Bordo and Lars Jonung ; with a new introduction by the authors.
        p. cm.
    Rev. ed. of: The long-run behavior of the velocity of circulation / Michael D. Bordo, Lars Jonung. c1987.
    Includes bibliographical references and index.
    ISBN 0-7658-0961-3 (alk. paper)
        1. Circular velocity of money—Econometric models.   2. Demand for money—Econometric models.   3. Money supply—Econometric models.
    I. Jonung, Lars.   II. Title.

HG226.6.B67 2003
332.4'01—dc21                                                           2003053730

ISBN 13: 978-0-7658-0961-2 (pbk)

# Contents

# Introduction to the Transaction Edition[1]

In 1987, we published *The Long-Run Behavior of Velocity: The International Evidence*.[2] There we presented evidence that the income velocity of money for five countries for which we had good data—the United States, Canada, the United Kingdom, Sweden, and Norway—displayed a U-shaped pattern from the 1870s to the 1970s. Similar patterns were found for a number of other countries. Velocity went through three stages: first it declined, then it fluctuated around a fairly flat section, and finally it rose. Next, we developed and tested an explanation for this long-run pattern, emphasizing the role of institutional variables. We hypothesized that the decline was due to a process of monetization, whereby the growth in the demand for money holdings outpaced that of real income, thus inducing a fall in velocity. The rise was attributed to financial sophistication, the development of close substitutes for money, and to improved economic security and stability. The turning point, that is, the low point of the velocity curve, marks the phase where these two institutional forces roughly balance each other.

As there were no available measures of the institutional changes that we considered, we constructed a set of proxy variables. These were then incorporated into the arguments of a standard money demand function.[3] In our empirical work we found support for the institutional approach based on four types of evidence: an econometric study of the long-run velocity function for the five countries for which we had adequate data, a cross-section study of about eighty countries in the post-World War II period, a case study of the monetization process in Sweden prior to 1914, and an examination of the time series properties of velocity.

Following the publication of our book, we updated the empirical work through the 1980s in Bordo and Jonung (1990). We also used co-integration techniques in a joint paper with Pierre Siklos which confirmed the earlier findings up to 1992 in Bordo, Jonung and Siklos (1997).

ix

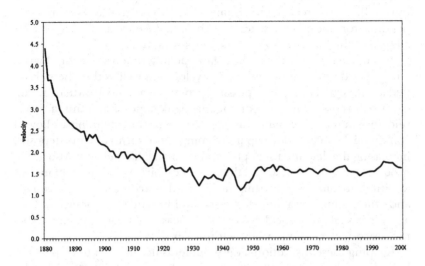

Chart 1. Income velocity of money (*V*2) in the United States, 1880-2000

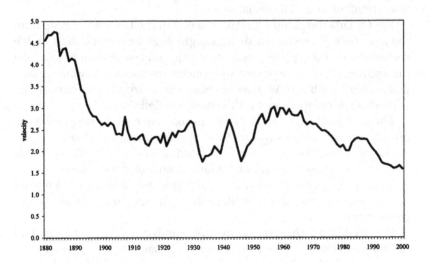

Chart 2. Income velocity of money (*V*2) in Canada, 1880-2000

employment and high growth, based on fine tuning, to a price-level-stability or inflation target oriented framework, with central banks more independent from the political system than before. Price stabilization was gradually given a higher priority than full employment.

It is unclear a priori how these far-reaching financial, technological and policy developments influenced velocity as well as the assets classified as money. Deregulation possibly promoted a rapid growth of financial assets as substitutes for commercial bank deposits and thus a rise in velocity. On the other hand, financial liberalization might have allowed commercial banks to develop more competitive forms of bank deposits, increasing the demand for deposits, and thus a fall in velocity. Also, these processes could have changed the proper empirical definition of money in different countries blurring the line of demarcation between money and other assets with a high degree of liquidity (that is "moneyness"). As a result, it might be difficult to construct measures of velocity comparable to those calculated for periods before 1975.

Keeping these institutional developments in mind, let us inspect the behavior of the income velocity of money displayed in Charts 1-5 for the period 1880-2000 adopting an M2-definition of money. The following conclusions emerge. For the United States there is a continuation of the fairly stable and flat trend in M2 velocity observed since the 1950s (Chart 1). This is so despite far-reaching financial innovations, episodes of inflation, disinflation, and financial stress.

For Canada the pattern is similar to that in the United States up until the late 1960s after which it shows a slight negative trend (Chart 2). We conjecture that this pattern reflects a major reclassification of financial institutions.[5] What were previously termed trust companies were reclassified as chartered banks. We have not been able to adjust the historical data to completely compensate for this change in definition.

For the UK, like Canada, there is a problem in constructing a continuous M2 measure of velocity for 1975-2000, reflecting two changes in the definition of broad money from M2 to sterling M3 in the 1970s and to M4 in the 1980s. These changes were made to encompass the liabilities of a wider set of financial intermediaries. Unfortunately, The Bank of England has not adjusted the data preceding these changes to eliminate the discontinuity (Chart 3).[6]

For Sweden, a U-shaped velocity curve stands out when the observation period is extended (Chart 4). Here the curve was adjusted for changes in the commercial banking data by a level shift in 1955. Similarly for Norway, we have clear confirmation of our original hypothesis of a U-shaped velocity curve (Chart 5). In the post-World War II period there is a slight rise in the trend of velocity.

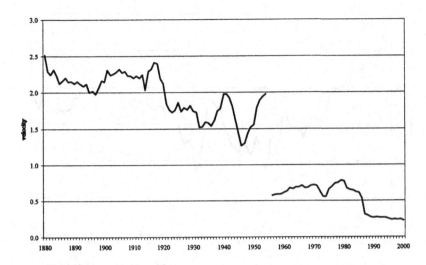

Chart 3. Income velocity of money (*V2*) in the United Kingdom, 1880-2000

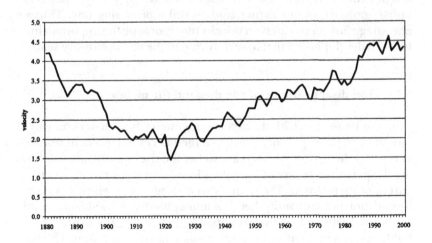

Chart 4. Income velocity of money (*V2*) in Sweden, 1880-2000

Chart 5. Income velocity of money (*V*2) in Norway, 1880-2000

To sum up, this most casual inspection of the long run behavior of velocity covering close to a century and a quarter of data seems to be roughly consistent with what we found earlier. We suggest that the institutional approach of our earlier study is still a promising one. Thus we encourage further research on velocity incorporating the important institutional developments that have occurred in the past twenty-five years.

## ii.    The disappearance of the demand for money

In the 1960s and 1970s the demand for money (the income velocity of money) and the supply of money emerged as central topics in research and policy discussion. This was a result of the rise of monetarism following the perceived failure of prevailing Keynesian stabilization policies to curtail rising inflation. The monetarist message, as developed in the reformulation of the quantity theory of money by Milton Friedman and others in the 1950s and 1960s, was initially one stressing the existence of a stable *long-run* relationship between money and prices/nominal income through a stable long-run money demand (velocity) function. In the short run, however, monetary policy was associated with long and variable lags. Changes in the money stock influenced both output and prices in the short run with no clear division into real and nominal effects. This was a major argument for the monetarist stress on a rule-bound monetary policy aimed at minimizing policy-induced disturbances.

In spite of this stress on the long run, the monetarist message was applied to the framing of short-run stabilization policies. This renaissance for money eventually influenced the actual conduct of central banks. The U.S. Federal Reserve, the Bank of England, the Bank of Canada as well as central banks in other countries started to use the short-run demand for money function as a key element in their monetary policy framework. Based on forecasts of the money demand function, central banks set short-term interest rates to achieve their desired stock of money target.

The strategy of monetary targeting ran into difficulties in the 1980s. A key reason was evidence of significant instability in the short-run money demand functions.[7] These shifts caused large errors in the monetary control process. The factors that produced this result included the increase in the rate of inflation in the 1970s, followed by disinflation as well as important deregulatory steps in the financial system in the U.S. and other advanced nations. The experience of monetary targeting led to serious concern over the proper monetary aggregates to target in the short run and also over the proper specification of the money demand function. As a consequence, interest in the demand for money waned. Central banks abandoned monetary aggregate targeting and the use of the short-run demand function as an input in the monetary policy process.[8]

Since the second half of the 1980s many central banks, the Bank of Canada and Bank of New Zealand being pioneers, have used a different approach to conduct monetary policy. They now target the inflation rate directly, with an interest rate (the overnight commercial borrowing rate) as their instrument of control. In the US as well as in other countries the real economy and financial stability may also influence the interest rate target. In many countries central banking practice today is about setting the rate of interest on the basis of forecasts of the future behavior of inflation.[9]

Central banks have thus moved from using monetary aggregates to influence the rate of inflation and the real economy to the direct targeting of the inflation rate by setting the relevant short-term rate of interest. To put this point in terms of the standard macroeconomic textbook framework; the traditional IS-LM system where money demand and money supply jointly determine the rate of interest has been pushed aside, thus dispensing with money demand and money supply analysis. Instead, the central bank sets an interest rate, given a forecast of the future rate of inflation and output. Now the supply of money has become infinitely elastic, a residual with no explicit role in the transmission mechanism. This strategy does not require estimating either the short-run demand for money function, or the supply function for money. However, the macroeconomic model underlying current monetary policymaking implicitly includes the supply of and demand for base (reserve) money, which are determined endogenously. They need not to appear explicitly in the analysis, however.[10]

Today, inflation targeting without any explicit reference to the demand for and supply of money is the common approach to monetary policy making. However, the ECB, the central bank of the euro area, is an exception in the sense that one of the two pillars of the ECB's monetary policy strategy gives an explicit role to the money supply and thus to the demand for money. The use of the money supply by the ECB is at present a subject of controversy.[11] Many commentators are of the opinion that the ECB regards inflation targeting as the main pillar, but uses monetary aggregates as indicators of potential inflationary problems.

Reflecting these changes in the prevailing monetary policy strategy, the theory of the demand for money has changed little in the past quarter of a century.[12] After ruling out a stable short-run money demand function and after implicitly downplaying the role of money in the framework for monetary policy analysis, a logical next step appears to be to eliminate money fully from monetary analysis. Some monetary theorists have actually taken this step by establishing a monetary theory without money—a step that we suspect will prove to be less constructive in the long run.[13]

Empirical work on the demand for money has continued, however. Recent research gives a mixed picture. Several contributions are based on a distinction between the long run (low frequencies) and the short run relationship (high frequencies) between money and prices. Here money has made a return in the sense that recent results indicate that for low frequencies—say, observations lasting for three to five years—"inflation is always and everywhere a monetary phenomenon," that is there is a strong link between the growth rate in the money supply and the rate of inflation. This strand of work basically reinforces earlier quantity theory interpretations concerning the role of money in periods of high inflation. For periods of low inflation, the correlation between money and prices tends to disappear. There is too much "noise" in the relationship for it to be statistically significant.[14]

Studies applying co-integration (error correction) techniques to examine the characteristics of the demand for money function have been published in the past decade. These studies, with their focus on long run equilibrium relationships confirm traditional views that money demand is a stable function in the long run of a scale variable (income or wealth) and an opportunity cost (a rate of interest).[15] This approach also suggests that our institutional proxies are important determinants of long run velocity.[15] Other studies have re-examined the characteristics of the short-run demand for money. Here the evidence is mixed.

### iii. The return of the demand for money?

Let us conclude by presenting a forecast of the future of money demand analysis. It is our impression that the attention the economics profession and of policymakers pay to the supply and demand for money is a function of the rate of inflation. The higher the rate of inflation, the more attention is given to monetary aggregates and the demand for money. The high and variable inflation of the 1970s and 1980s led first to wide acceptance of the monetarist view that inflation is everywhere and always a monetary phenomenon. This influenced  monetary policy making, leading to the adoption by central bankers first of monetary targeting, next to monetary contraction, followed by disinflation, and subsequently to the present low inflation environment. This process in turn led to instability in the demand for money which discredited  monetary targeting and  set the stage for the advent of inflation targeting.

We are presently, in the early years of the twenty-first century, living through a period of low and stable inflation. This non-inflationary environment, we believe, contributes to the weak link observed between money and the price level and thus to disinterest in money supply and money demand analysis. If inflation (or deflation) would appear in the future as a major policy issue among advanced countries, the analysis of the demand for money and thus of velocity may re-emerge as a lively research area.

Still—regardless of the level of inflation—we believe that it remains important to study how ongoing institutional changes such as financial innovations and regulatory developments influence our concept of money and the demand for and supply of money. We hope that this reprint of our work may contribute to such an interest.

Michael D. Bordo

Lars Jonung

### Notes

1. We are grateful to Karel Havik, Angela Redish, David Willoughby, and Geoffrey Wood for help with data for the velocity charts in this introduction. We have benefited significantly from the comments by Eoin Drea, Oliver Dieckmann, Sylvester Eijffinger, Vitor Gaspar, David Laidler, Lars E O Svensson, and Geoffrey Wood.
2. See Bordo and Jonung (1987).
3. Velocity (V) defined as the ratio of nominal income (Y) to the money stock (M) is also the inverse of the demand for money defined as the ratio of the money stock to nominal income (often referred to as Cambridge K).Thus

there is a close link between money demand analysis and the study of velocity.

4. We defined M2 as the sum of currency demand and time deposits. It was the only money measure available for all the five countries and for the entire period we originally studied.

5. We have used data from Metcalf, Redish, and Shearer (1998) to construct Chart 2.

6. For helpful elucidation on the intricacies of recent British monetary aggregates we thank David Willoughby. We have not adjusted the data in Chart 3 for a large downward shift in the level of velocity in 1955.

7. See, for example, Goldfeld (1976) and Judd and Scadding (1982).

8. King (2002) quotes a former governor of the Bank of Canada as remarking "we didn't abandon the monetary aggregates, they abandoned us."

9. The theory of inflation targeting has been developed in a number of recent studies, see for example Svensson (1999) for a brief survey of the field. The roots of inflation targeting may be traced back to Knut Wicksell's theory of price level determination and his monetary policy rule of price level stabilization. In Wicksell's model money and credit are determined endogenously as a result of the interaction between the real rate and the interest rate (the bank rate) set by the central bank.

10. Laidler (1999) remarks that the Bank of Canada has adopted a forecast model that does not even include any monetary aggregate. Several central bankers have remarked recently on the disappearance of money from monetary policy making. See, for example, King (2002) and Meyer (2001).

11. See, for example, chapter 5 in Issing et al. (2001) in defence of the ECB's strategy. For a sample of the critique of the strategy see Svensson (2000) and Gerlach ( 2003).

12. See Laidler (1993) for a summary of the field of money demand studies – a survey that still remains of current interest.

13. This is done predominantly in work by Woodford (1997, 2003). In response to this 'new consensus' concerning the irrelevance of money, Nelson (2003) and Leeper and Rousch (2003) continue to stress the role of monetary aggregates and thus of the demand for money in monetary policy making. See also McCallum (2001).

14. See for example De Grauwe and Polan (2001) and Fischer, Sahay, and Vegh (2002).

15. Siram (2001) surveys recent money demand studies. See also Ball (1998, 2002) for the U.S. evidence. Velocity has acquired a new role in the rapidly expanding literature on the contributions of financial development to economic growth. Beginning with Raymond Goldsmith's (1969) work, M/Y, (the inverse of velocity) an important proxy for the growth of the financial system, has been used as a measure of financial development and maturity. This approach is consistent with our interpretation that the fall in velocity is associated with a decline of the barter economy and the rise of commercial banking.

# References

Ball, L. (1998), "Another Look at Long Run Money Demand," *NBER Working Paper Series*, No. 6597.

Ball, L. (2002), "Short Run Money Demand," *NBER Working Paper Series*, No. 9235.

Bordo, M.D, and L. Jonung (1987), *The Long-Run Behavior of Velocity: The International Evidence*, Cambridge University Press.

Bordo, M.D. and L. Jonung (1990), "The Long-Run Behavior of Velocity: The Institutional Approach Revisited," *Journal of Policy Modeling*, pp. 165-197.

Bordo, M.D., L Jonung and P. Siklos (1997), "The Common Development of Institutional Change as Measured by Income Velocity of Money: A Century of Evidence from Five Industrialized Countries," *Economic Inquiry*, October, pp. 710-724.

DeGrauwe, P. and M. Polan (2002), "Is Inflation Always and Everywhere a Monetary Phenomenon?" CEPR discussion paper, no 2841.

Fischer, S., R. Sahay and C. A. Végh (2002), "Modern Hyper- and High Inflations," *Journal of Economic Literature*, pp. 837-880, September.

Friedman, M. (1963), *Inflation: Causes and Consequences*, Asia Publishing House, Bombay.

Gerlach, S. (2003), "The ECB's Two Pillars," *CEPR Discussion Paper Series*, No. 3689.

Goldfeld, S.M. (1976), "The Case of Missing Money," *Brookings Papers on Economic Activity*, pp. 683-730.

Goldsmith, R. (1969), *Financial Structure and Development*, Yale University Press, New Haven.

Issing, O., V. Gaspar, I. Angeloni and O. Tristani (2001), "Monetary Policy in the Euro Area: Strategy and Decision-making at the European Central Bank," Cambridge University Press.

Judd, J.P. and J. L. Scadding (1982), "The Search for a Stable Money Demand Function," pp. 993-1023, *Journal of Economic Literature*.

King, M. (2002), "No Money, No Inflation – The Role of Money in the Economy," pp. 162-177, summer, *Bank of England Quarterly Review*.

Laidler, D. (1993), *The Demand for Money: Theories, Evidence and Problems*," 4th edition, Donnelley Publishing Corp., New York.

Laidler, D. (1999), "The Quantity of Money and Monetary Policy," working paper 99-5, Bank of Canada, Ottawa.

Leeper, E. M. and J. E. Rousch (2003), "Putting 'M' Back in Monetary Policy," International finance discussion papers, Federal Reserve Board, no 761, April.

McCallum, B.T. (2001), "Monetary Policy Analysis in Models without Money," *Federal Reserve Bank of St Louis Review*, pp 1-15.

Metcalf, C., A. Redish, and R. Shearer (1998), "New Estimates of the Canadian Money Stock, 1871-1967," pp. 104-124, *Canadian Journal of Economics*.

Meyer, L. H. (2001); "Does Money Matter?" The Homer Jones Memorial Lecture, *Federal Reserve Bank of St. Louis Review*, pp. 145-60.

Nelson, E. (2003), "The Future of Monetary Aggregates in Monetary Policy Analysis," *Journal of Monetary Economics*, pp. 1029-1059, July.

Siklos, P. (1993), "Income Velocity and Institutional Change: Some New Time Series Evidence, 1870-1986," pp. 377-92, August, *Journal of Money, Credit and Banking*.

Sriram, S. S. (2001), "A Survey of Recent Empirical Money Demand Studies," *IMF Staff Papers*, Vol. 47, No. 3, IMF, Washington, DC.

Svensson, L. E. O. (1999), "Inflation Targeting as a Monetary Policy Rule," *Journal of Monetary Economics*, pp. 606-654.

Svensson, L. E. O. (2000), "*What is Wrong with the Eurosystem's Money-Growth Indicator, and What Should the Eurosystem Do about It?*" Briefing paper for the Committee on Economic and Monetary Affairs (ECON) of the European Parliament.

Woodford, M. (1997), "Doing without Money: Controlling Inflation in a Post Monetary World," No. 6188, NBER Working Paper Series.

Woodford, M. (2003), *Interest and Prices: Foundations of a Theory of Monetary Policy*, Princeton University.

# Foreword

The income velocity of money – a measure of the demand for money balances – is the ratio of the money value of income to the average money stock that the nonbank public holds in a given period. Why the magnitude of that ratio has changed over broad sweeps of time is the subject of this study by Michael Bordo and Lars Jonung. Their interpretation of the historical behavior of velocity affords readers a perspective in an international setting on slow-moving economic, social, and political forces that interact with the decisions that households and firms make about how much money to hold. Their work demonstrates that historical analysis, buttressed by statistical data and econometric estimation techniques, can enrich theoretical formulations.

The background for the Bordo and Jonung investigation is the vast literature on the demand for money. Many econometric studies cover relatively brief time spans, usually recent decades. In such studies it is appropriate to focus on explanatory variables likely to change over short periods that can account satisfactorily for movements in money demand. Two variables are typically included in short-run demand-for-money functions: a scale variable, often permanent income – the expected future value of income – and the opportunity cost of holding money – yields on assets other than money. Since the institutional framework of the economy is subject to slow change, variables reflecting it are omitted.

Earlier studies of long runs of annual data also omitted institutional variables because these variables are not readily found. Instead those studies assigned a crucial role to permanent income in explaining the behavior of velocity. For example, in the United States the velocity ratio fell in the nineteenth century and well into the twentieth century. The fall seemed to be associated with the growing size of permanent income. As the level of expected income rose, it appeared that the public chose to increase even more the sums of money it found convenient to hold. The permanent income elasticity of demand for money was said to be higher than unity. Money according to this view was a luxury good, the percentage change in demand for which increased by more than the percentage increase in income.

A difficulty with this explanation arose in the post–World War II period, when the velocity ratio did not fall but increased despite the continued growth in permanent income. However, it was possible to account for the changed behavior of the ratio by noting that more stable economic conditions in the postwar world had led the public to reduce the sums of money it held relative to income. Even for the prewar period, the early finding of a high permanent income elasticity of demand for money was modified by a later finding that the elasticity was not a constant but had fallen over time.

It was at this point that Bordo and Jonung began their investigation. In their research they first established that there was a well-defined pattern of velocity behavior in many industrialized countries for which long time series of money and income data are available. The pattern is U-shaped, with an initial declining segment, an intermediate flat segment, followed by a rising segment of the velocity ratio. Bordo and Jonung offer a unified explanation of the pattern. In the first segment, institutional change involving the increasing use of money in transactions, assisted by the geographical spread of bank offices, accounts for larger money holding and hence the decline in the velocity ratio. The monetization process eventually is completed, and the stable segment of the velocity curve results. In the post–World War II period, economic, political, and social developments fostered financial innovations and improvements in economic security that produced the rising segment of the velocity curve.

The authors support their explanation of the velocity pattern by reference to four kinds of evidence:

1. They incorporate into velocity functions for five countries, first estimated individually and then pooled and estimated as one entity, variables reflecting the institutional changes they have posited. They show that these imaginatively constructed variables add to the explanatory power of the relationships when compared to the results based solely on standard variables (real income and interest rates) and that the institutional variables reduce the permanent income elasticity of demand for money to below unity.

2. A case study of the Swedish monetization process before World War I details monetization's effects on velocity. The institutional variables examined that reflect monetization include the proportion of the labor force employed outside of agricul-

ture, the ratio of population to the number of bank offices, and the degree of variation of prices for identical goods between various regions within Sweden.

3. The explanation of the velocity pattern is generally confirmed when applied to cross-section data for about eighty countries since the 1950s classified according to stage of financial development as reflected in level of per capita real income. For low-income countries, falling velocity is observed. For high-income countries, with the exception of Italy, Germany, and Japan, velocity is rising. The exceptions with falling velocity, the authors suggest, may be responding to postwar rebuilding of their financial systems disrupted in the aftermath of "losing" the war. For middle-income countries, velocity is relatively constant, except that in high-inflation countries, such as Brazil, Israel, and Chile, velocity rises. Expectations of future higher inflation rates can account for rising velocity in those countries.

4. An investigation of the time series properties of velocity for the five countries with a century or so of data shows that, although past changes in velocity cannot be used to predict future changes, changes in the determinants of velocity isolated in the study can in every country be used to predict future changes. There is no conflict between the random walk hypothesis of velocity change and the institutional approach used by Bordo and Jonung.

This study offers valuable insights into the effects of the evolution of institutions, the nature of monetary regimes, and the response of the demand for money to changing historical developments. I salute the authors for their contribution to monetary economics.

*National Bureau of Economic Research, New York*     ANNA J. SCHWARTZ

# Preface

This book has taken a long time to write. We initiated work on it in 1976, and it has subsequently developed through a series of articles. During the last decade we have received help and support from a large number of sources.

We owe a special debt to Anna Schwartz for her encouragement, her useful suggestions, and her careful editing of the manuscript. We also wish to thank the following for helpful comments and suggestions at various stages of our work: Roy Batchelor, Dallas Batten, Ehsan Choudhri, Michael Darby, Dean Dutton, Hans Genberg, Philip Graves, Rodney Jacobs, Benjamin Klein, David Laidler, Axel Leijonhufvud, James Lothian, Allan Meltzer, Johan Myhrman, Charles Nelson, Joseph Ostroy, Soo Bin Park, Ron Shearer. The usual disclaimer holds.

We are indebted to the following for able and conscientious research assistance: Alvaro Aguiar, Tarmo Haavisto, Kim McPhail, Ivan Marcotte, Ronald Meng, Sharon Michaud, Fernando Santos, Lennart Söderlund, Glen Voigt. We owe a special vote of thanks to Ingemar Dahlstrand for excellent drafting of all the charts as well as for insightful econometric work.

We would also like to thank participants of seminars on various aspects of this work: the Arne Ryde symposium of 1977 at Frostavallen in Sweden, and seminars at Carleton University, the University of Western Ontario, UCLA, the European Econometric Society, the Western Economic Association, the Graduate Institute of International Studies in Geneva, the University of Arizona, the University of South Carolina, the University of Lund, and the Bank of Japan. We would like to thank the following institutions and universities for support: Carleton University, the University of Lund, the University of South Carolina, and the Federal Reserve Bank of St. Louis.

For financial assistance, without which this book would not have been written, we would like to thank the Canada Council for research grants for the period 1977–80 and the Jan Wallander Foundation of the Svenska Handelsbanken for generous support for the years

1981–6. A stipend from the PK-banken enabled Lars Jonung to take a partial leave of absence to complete the book.

We acknowledge the following journals, in which some of this material has appeared: *The Scandinavian Journal of Economics, Explorations in Economic History,* and *Economic Inquiry.*

Finally, we want to stress that this book is truly the product of international cooperation.

Michael D. Bordo                           Lars Jonung
*University of South Carolina*             *University of Lund*

# CHAPTER 1

# Introduction

## 1.1   Purpose of the study

The purpose of this study is to present and empirically test a coherent framework explaining the secular behavior of the income velocity of money. Annual time series of velocity for a number of countries over the last century display a U-shaped pattern. In addition, in the post–World War II period, velocity of a large number of countries, classified by level of economic development, exhibits a similar U-shaped pattern.

Existing theories can explain each section of the velocity curve – the falling, flat, and rising parts – but the overall pattern is not consistent with any one prevailing theory. In this book we offer a comprehensive explanation for velocity's secular behavior. The explanation is to a large degree an extension and development of the approach of the Swedish economist Knut Wicksell, who stressed the role of substitution between monetary assets. This approach, which emphasizes institutional variables, is then incorporated into the arguments of the traditional long-run money demand (or velocity) function, namely a scale variable and rates of return on assets alternative to money.

Four types of empirical evidence provide strong confirmation of our approach: econometric studies of the long-run velocity function for five countries – the United States, Canada, the United Kingdom, Sweden, and Norway; a cross-section study of about eighty countries in the postwar period; a case study of the Swedish monetization process in the fifty years preceding World War I; and an examination of the time series properties of velocity.

In contrast to standard macrostudies of the demand for money, or velocity, we focus on institutional factors. For two reasons, these factors have rarely been incorporated in studies of the demand for money. First, since most studies deal with shorter time periods, they assume (implicitly or explicitly) that institutional factors are constant. Second, empirical measures of institutional developments are difficult to construct.

This study draws on both monetary theory and economic history.

1

Although our approach is a macro one, the empirical regularities we highlight lend themselves to theorizing on the microfoundations of the exchange mechanism and of the monetary system.

## 1.2     Plan of the study

Chapter 2 presents evidence of a U-shaped pattern of velocity for a number of industrial economies in the past 100 years and reviews existing theories of the long-run behavior of velocity. No one theory is able to explain the secular pattern described. Chapter 3 presents a coherent explanation of the U-shaped pattern based on the concept of substitution between different monetary assets induced by institutional forces. This explanation is inspired by the work of Knut Wicksell.

Chapter 4 contains a series of econometric tests of the hypothesis presented in Chapter 3. The secular fall in velocity is explained by monetization and the growth of banking, the secular rise by financial sophistication and improved economic stability. Evidence for each of five countries treated separately and then pooled and treated as one entity is examined here. Chapter 5 studies in greater detail than Chapter 4 the Swedish monetization process and its effects on velocity over the period 1871–1913. Evidence on the monetization process is derived from the growth of commercial banking, changes in labor market contracts, and developments in commodity markets.

Chapter 6 continues the investigation of the hypothesis in Chapter 3 using IFS data for about eighty countries for the period since the 1950s. According to our explanation, for low-income countries velocity should fall, for high-income countries it should rise, and for middle-income countries it should be roughly constant. With two major exceptions, this pattern is confirmed. First, velocity is falling in Italy, Germany, and Japan but rises in all other high-income countries. Second, velocity rises in high-inflation countries such as Brazil, Israel, and Chile when, according to our approach, velocity for these upper middle-income countries is expected to be roughly constant.

Chapter 7 explores the time series properties of velocity, demonstrating that velocity over the past century for the five countries examined in Chapter 4 displays a random walk without drift. A random walk implies that changes in velocity cannot be predicted from past velocity changes, but it does not imply that past changes in other variables deemed important determinants of velocity cannot be used in prediction. Our finding that previous changes in the institutional and traditional determinants of velocity isolated in Chapter 4 can be used to predict future changes in velocity reconciles the stochastic behavior of velocity with our approach. Finally, Chapter 8 summarizes the results and discusses their implications.

# CHAPTER 2

# Evidence and theories of the long-run behavior of velocity

## 2.1    The secular picture

The long-run behavior of the income velocity of money (*V*2) from the 1870s to the 1970s in the United States, Canada, the United Kingdom, Sweden, and Norway is displayed in Charts 2.1 through 2.5. The velocity curves are calculated using a broad definition of money, *M*2, where *M*2 is defined as the sum of currency, demand, and time deposits. *M*2 is the only monetary aggregate available over the entire data period and for the five countries covered by the charts. National income is measured by NNP at market prices for the United States and the United Kingdom, by GNP at market prices for Canada, and by GDP at market prices for Sweden and Norway. (For sources of the data used see Appendix 1A.)

The five charts show that velocity has exhibited a secular U-shaped pattern over the past century in the five countries, most prominently in Sweden, Norway, Canada, and the United States. The dating of the turnaround differs, however, across countries. There are also considerable cyclical fluctuations in the velocity curves; specifically, the depressions of the 1920s and 1930s are commonly reflected in substantial declines in velocity.

Velocity was falling in the United States prior to the mid-1940s, when the turnaround occurred (Chart 2.1). It has displayed an upward trend since then. The depression in the 1930s is associated with a sharp fall in velocity. The Canadian curve (Chart 2.2) has great similarities with the American one, with a turnaround in the 1940s after a sharp cyclical downturn around 1930. For the United Kingdom, velocity falls from around 1910 onward, with a turnaround occurring in the mid-1940s (Chart 2.3). Prior to World War I, however, there is a weak upward trend.[1] The U-shaped pattern is clearest for Sweden

---

[1] Capie and Webber (1985) present new revised estimates of the UK money supply for 1870–1982 that suggest that the measure of velocity used here is slightly biased downward from 1870 to 1914. Their velocity curve displays a flat trend from 1870 to 1914 followed by the same pattern shown in Chart 2.3. New estimates by Collins (1983) of the UK money supply and velocity for the period 1844–80 show that velocity declined in a manner similar to that of the other countries examined in this study, although at an earlier period.

4

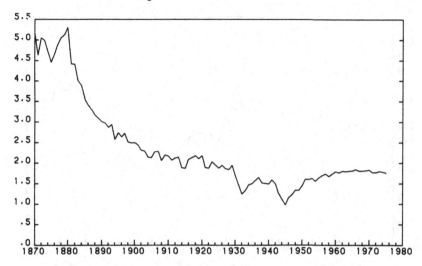

Chart 2.1. Income velocity of money (*V*2) in the United States, 1870–1975. (*Source:* Appendix 1A.)

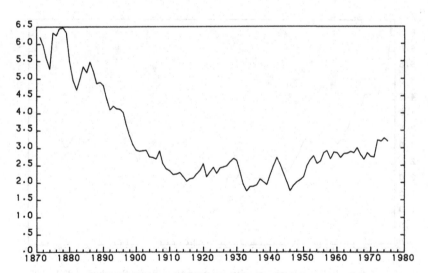

Chart 2.2. Income velocity of money (*V*2) in Canada, 1870–1975. (*Source:* Appendix 1A.)

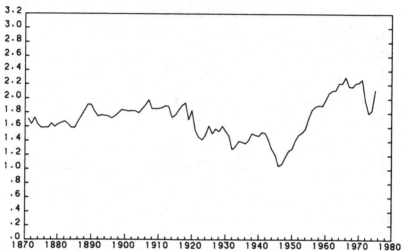

Chart 2.3. Income velocity of money (V2) in the United Kingdom, 1870–1975. (*Source:* Appendix 1A.)

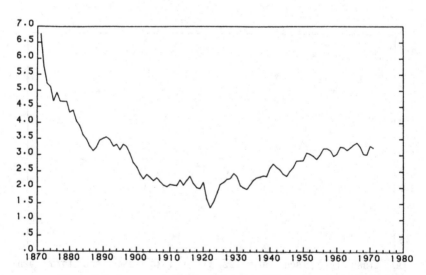

Chart 2.4. Income velocity of money (V2) in Sweden, 1871–1971. (*Source:* Appendix 1A.)

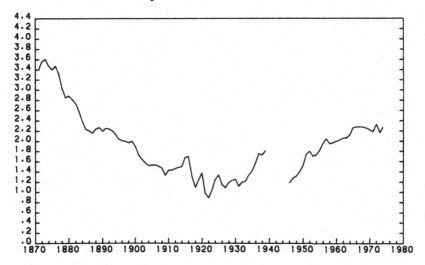

Chart 2.5. Income velocity of money (*V*2) in Norway, 1870–1974. (*Source:* Appendix 1A.)

(Chart 2.4); the bottom was reached in 1922, which was a year of deep depression. Norway (Chart 2.5) and Sweden exhibit similar patterns until 1939, when World War II interrupts the data series for the former, allowing the conjecture that had Norway not been involved in the war, its velocity would have continued to behave in the Swedish mode.

To sum up, for these five countries, for which good data covering long periods are available, velocity follows a U-shaped curve.

Lack of data generally prevents the study of the secular experience of most other countries. However, acceptable data on velocity exist for a few countries other than the five just discussed. Charts 2.6 through 2.13 cover the experience of Australia, Denmark, Finland, France, Germany, Holland, Italy, and Japan. With the exception of France, an *M*2 definition of the money stock has been used to maintain comparability with the first five charts. (For the data used see Appendix 1A.)

The Danish velocity curve (Chart 2.6) displays a pattern similar to the Swedish and Norwegian curves. The fall in velocity is pronounced prior to World War I, but the postwar rise is limited. The Finnish data suggest a fall in velocity prior to the liberation of Finland from Russia in 1919, a rapid rise in the early 1920s followed by a fall, and a secular rise after the mid-1940s interrupted by a fall in the 1950s

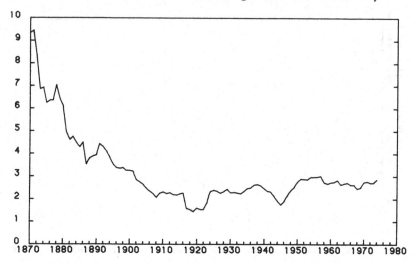

Chart 2.6. Income velocity of money (*V*2) in Denmark, 1870–1974. (*Source:* Appendix 1A.)

(Chart 2.7). The income velocity of money in Germany falls prior to 1914 (Chart 2.8). The two world wars are excluded due to lack of reliable data. After World War II, velocity shows a downward trend. In Holland, income velocity exhibits a pronounced secular decline until World War I, a postwar rise followed by a decline until World War II, and a strong upward trend after World War II (Chart 2.9). Sections of this pattern conform closely to sections for other countries.

Italy shows a continuous fall in velocity for the entire period 1870 –1975 interrupted by a sharp rise after World War II (Chart 2.10). The velocity curve of Japan (Chart 2.11) displays some similarity to those of Germany and Italy. It falls secularly from the 1890s to the 1980s interrupted by a shift upward of the curve following World War II. (For further discussion of the post–World War II pattern of velocity of these three countries, see Chapter 6.) The income velocity of money in Australia (Chart 2.12) suggests a U shape with a triple bottom: a fall until the mid-1890s, a rise until the 1920s, then a fall to 1932, a rise until the war, then a wartime fall, and a secular upward trend thereafter. The income velocity of France during the period 1870–1969, based on an *M*1 definition (since consistent *M*2 series were not available for most of the period), displays a falling trend prior to World War I, followed by a brief rise in the early 1920s and then a

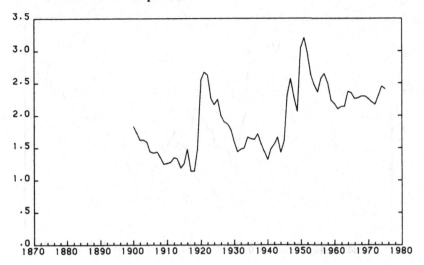

Chart 2.7. Income velocity of money (*V*2) in Finland, 1900–1975. (*Source:* Appendix 1A.)

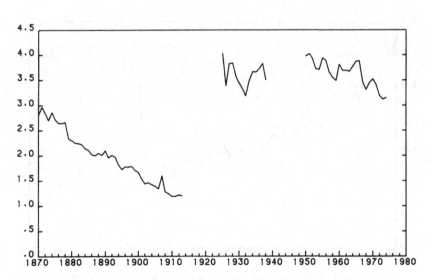

Chart 2.8. Income velocity of money (*V*2) in Germany, 1870–1974. (*Source:* Appendix 1A.)

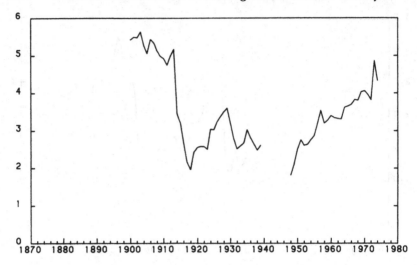

Chart 2.9. Income velocity of money (*V*2) in Holland, 1900–1974. (*Source:* Appendix 1A.)

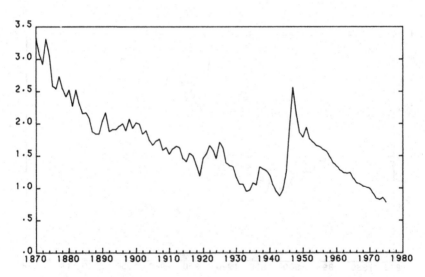

Chart 2.10. Income velocity of money (*V*2) in Italy, 1870–1975. (*Source:* Appendix 1A.)

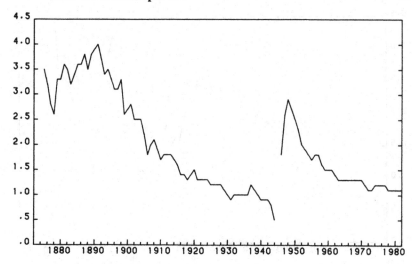

Chart 2.11. Income velocity of money (*V*2) in Japan, 1875–1982. (*Source:* Appendix 1A.)

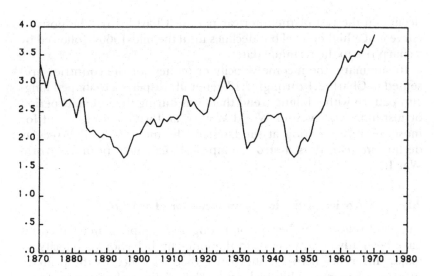

Chart 2.12. Income velocity of money (*V*2) in Australia, 1870–1970. (*Source:* Appendix 1A.)

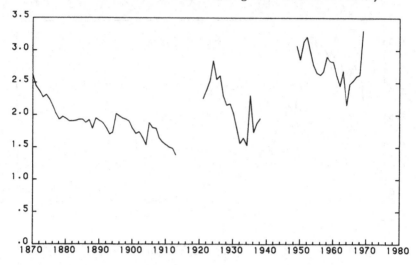

Chart 2.13. Income velocity of money (*V*1) in France, 1870–1969. (*Source:* Appendix 1A.)

decline in the rest of the interwar period (Chart 2.13). The postwar curve is at a higher level but declines until the mid-1960s, followed by a sharp rise to the terminal date.

In summary, the income velocity of money for the countries presented in Charts 2.1 through 2.13 generally displays a U-shaped long-run pattern with a falling trend that ends during the interwar period or just immediately after World War II, and with a rising trend for most countries starting at the latest in the mid-1940s. The secular decline in velocity is a strong empirical regularity prior to World War I.

## 2.2     Theories of the long-run behavior of velocity

In recent years a number of competing and complementary theories have been advanced to explain the long-run behavior of velocity. A major difference between alternative theories concerns the primary function of money. Those who view the medium-of-exchange function of money to be of central importance focus on technological and other variables that influence the payments process, whereas those who view money primarily as an asset focus on variables that affect the fraction of its portfolio the community decides to hold in the form of money balances.

Investigators have used different empirical definitions of velocity corresponding to differing views on the functions of money. Irving Fisher and his followers were concerned with the behavior of transactions velocity, $V_t$, the ratio of the volume of transactions to the money stock.[2] However, problems in the measurement of transactions, especially the treatment of intermediate and financial transactions, led to the widespread adoption of income velocity, $V_y$,[3] that is, the ratio of national income to a narrow money definition (the sum of currency and demand deposits = $M1$). By contrast, economists who stress the asset function of money have preferred to use an income velocity concept based on a broader definition of money also including time deposits ($M2$).

For most countries it has been difficult to separate the data on deposits into demand and time deposit components for the period before World War I.[4] Consequently, the discussion of long-run velocity behavior is based on the $M2$ definition. (Evidence for the post–World War II period, when both $M1$ and $M2$ definitions of money exist, is considered in Chapter 6.)

In this section we survey a number of theories of the long-run behavior of velocity. First, we examine explanations that stress the role of money as an asset, then explanations that stress the medium-of-exchange function. Finally, we note recent studies of the stochastic properties of velocity and the assertion that velocity is a random walk. We focus here on U.S. monetary studies since the pioneering work in this field originated in that country.

### 2.2.1. Explanations stressing the role of money as an asset

*The role of income:* Friedman and Schwartz (1963), in their *A Monetary History of the United States, 1867–1960,* examined data on the income velocity of money using a broad money definition ($M2$). They observed a steadily declining trend in velocity until shortly after World War II, when velocity began to rise (Chart 2.1). Their explanation for the decline in velocity, based on Friedman's (1959) estimate of the permanent income (wealth) elasticity of the demand for real cash balances of 1.8, was that money can be regarded as a luxury good. Thus

---

[2] Snyder (1924) in the 1920s, and Garvy (1959) and Garvy and Blyn (1970) in recent years. Also see Lieberman (1977).
[3] See Selden (1956), Friedman (1971), and Friedman and Schwartz (1982, Chapter 2).
[4] For the United States the demarcation begins in 1914, whereas data on $M2$ go back to the 1830s. See Friedman and Schwartz (1970). For the United Kingdom see Capie and Webber (1985). For Canada see Patterson and Shearer (1985).

the demand for money would rise with the growth of real income, imparting a secularly declining trend to velocity.[5] Friedman and Schwartz then explained the postwar rise in velocity as a temporary phenomenon that reflected improved expectations about economic stability in the post–World War II period.

Since the publication of *A Monetary History*, several pieces of evidence have called into question Friedman and Schwartz's interpretation. First, velocity for the United States and for other countries has continued to rise since 1960, disproving its supposed temporary nature. Second, estimates of the permanent income elasticity of the demand for money for other countries are considerably lower than for the United States, and for the United States the elasticity over time appears to decline to close to unity in the postwar period.[6] Third, there is evidence that permanent income may be serving as a proxy for other, more pertinent determinants of velocity, and that when such variables are introduced into a regression explaining velocity, the estimate of the income elasticity is reduced significantly. These variables, presented in Chapter 4, stress the role of institutional factors, including monetization and financial development, as explanations of the trend of velocity. Indeed Tobin (1965), in a review of *A Monetary History*, attributed the fall in velocity in the United States from 1880 to 1915 to the spread of commercial banking.[7] Finally, Friedman and Schwartz (1982) have more recently explained the secular fall in United States velocity from 1870 to 1905 as due primarily to growing financial sophistication.

*Interest rates:* Traditionally, the demand for money is regarded as a function of interest rates, representing the opportunity cost of holding money rather than other assets in the portfolio. The work of Latané (1954, 1969) stressed movements in long-term interest rates as the primary determinant of long-run movements in velocity in the United States over the period 1919–52. His results were criticized by Friedman and Schwartz (1963) for their failure to explain movements in the velocity of $M2$ in the 1930s and in the twenty-five years preceding World War I. Subsequently, several studies of the long-run demand for money (see, e.g., Brunner and Meltzer (1963); Meltzer (1963); Chow (1966); Laidler (1966)) concluded that both interest rates and

---

[5] Friedman and Schwartz's approach follows Warburton's (1949) explanation for a secular decline in his measure of velocity from the beginning of the nineteenth century. Selden (1956) also presents evidence for the luxury good explanation.
[6] See Laidler (1985).
[7] Also see Graves (1978), Stauffer (1978), and Mayor and Pearl (1984).

wealth (permanent income) are important determinants of the demand for money and hence velocity.[8]

Klein (1973) presented evidence supporting Latané's original regression. In addition to permanent income and both short- and long-term interest rates as measures of alternative rates of return, Klein found the ratio of high-powered money to money ($H/M$) a significant determinant of velocity in the United States in the period 1880–1968.[9] According to Klein, the own-rate of return on money, which on price theoretic grounds should be included in the demand-for-money function, would vary inversely with $H/M$. Moreover, $H/M$ can be decomposed into the banking system's reserve–deposit ratio ($R/D$) and the public's currency–money ratio ($C/M$). Thus, improved monetary stability in the United States in the post–Civil War period lowered both $R/D$ and $C/M$, in turn raising the own-rate of return on money and thus reducing velocity.[10]

Nevertheless, although various interest rates are important determinants of velocity, they do not fully explain the long-run movements in velocity surveyed in the previous section. The fall in velocity occurred during periods of rising as well as of falling rates, as originally pointed out by Friedman and Schwartz (1963). Similarly, the rise in velocity occurred during periods of rising as well as falling interest rates. Long-run movements in interest rates are also closely associated with periods of secular inflation and deflation. Consequently, one should expect velocity to fall (or rise more slowly) during periods of deflation and to rise (or fall more slowly) during periods of inflation. Such a consistent pattern cannot be discerned from the evidence in Charts 2.1 through 2.13.

Recent work on the demand for money in open economies has included as explanatory variables measures of the rates of return on foreign currencies and foreign securities (see Miles (1978); Arango and Nadiri (1981); Brittain (1981); Bordo and Choudhri (1982); McKinnon (1982); Cuddington (1983)). Both portfolio balance models and theories of currency substitution posit important roles for foreign variables under flexible exchange rates, although the empirical evidence for advanced countries is mixed. Arguments similar to those made for domestic interest rates can be advanced, suggesting that for-

---

[8] For surveys of the literature see Goldfeld (1973), Fase and Kure (1975), Fisher (1978), and Laidler (1985).

[9] Also included is the ratio of measured to permanent income to account for the business cycle.

[10] Indeed Klein's results emphasizing a falling currency–money ratio as the key determinant of a declining velocity amplify Tobin's emphasis on the spread of commercial banking.

eign rates of return would not be significant determinants of the secular behavior of velocity in a period largely characterized by fixed exchange rates.

*The expected rate of inflation:* Traditionally, the expected rate of inflation can be regarded as the opportunity cost of holding money in terms of real assets. The expected rate of inflation has generally been a significant explanatory variable in money demand studies covering periods of rapid rates of inflation. Most studies in this field deal with the post–World War I German and other European hyperinflations and the experience of several Latin American countries in recent decades (Cagan (1956); Laidler (1985)).

Occasionally, measures of the expected inflation rate have been entered as determinants of the demand for money in situations involving controls on money and capital markets where published interest rates do not reflect the proper opportunity cost of holding money (Khan (1980)). However, the expected rate of inflation would not likely account for the long-run movements in velocity displayed in Charts 2.1 through 2.13. During most of the periods covered, the rate of inflation was stable or low, giving rise to low and stable expected changes in the price level. Consequently, it is unlikely that the expected rate could have contributed to large secular changes in velocity. Moreover, if the explanation were to hold, we would expect periods of falling velocity to be associated with secular deflation. Such a pattern is observable in the period 1870–96, but velocity continued to fall in the subsequent pre–World War I period when the price trend was reversed.

*Financial developments:* Financial developments encompass two different processes discussed in the literature: the growth of the financial sector and the development of money substitutes. We consider each in turn.

*Growth of the financial sector:* In the face of the mounting evidence against the luxury good hypothesis discussed previously, Friedman and Schwartz (1982), after comparing trends of velocity in the United States and the United Kingdom, concluded that the relatively steeper decline in United States velocity than that of the United Kingdom from 1870 to 1905 (Charts 2.1 and 2.3) can be explained by growing financial sophistication in the United States. They noted that by 1870 the United Kingdom possessed a highly developed financial system. The system was virtually fully monetized, with a vast proliferation of commercial bank branches and a well-developed money market. By contrast, a significant fraction of the U.S. banking system was still in its adolescence. In the next thirty years the monetization process was virtually completed, and the commercial banking network spread across the country. Thus, by 1905 the two countries had achieved similar levels of financial development and similar levels of velocity.

To account for the financial development of the United States, Friedman and Schwartz adjusted their U.S. money supply series by a constant 2.5 percent times the number of years to 1905, on the assumption that financial development occurred at a steady rate. This procedure has the effect of reducing considerably the trend of U.S. velocity before 1905 − making it similar to that of the United Kingdom − and also of reducing the U.S. income elasticity of the demand for money to a figure closer to one.[11]

Numerous studies in economic history have focused on various aspects of the growth of the financial sector. Thus Cameron (1967, 1972), Barkai (1973), Riley and McCusker (1983), Saint Marc (1983), and Komlos (1986) have examined the process of monetization and expansion of the commercial banking system in a number of countries. Tobin (1965) and Timberlake (1974) mentioned monetization as contributing to the secular decline in the U.S. velocity. Goldsmith (1969, 1985), following Gurley and Shaw (1960), provides evidence of secular advance in various measures of financial sector growth for a considerable number of countries.[12]

*Development of money substitutes:* A popular explanation in the 1950s and 1960s for the postwar rise in velocity was that the development of new substitutes for money reduced the demand for money (Gurley and Shaw (1960); Smith (1960)). The effects of money substitutes on the demand for money and velocity, it was argued, would manifest themselves in two ways. The first way was by raising the in-

[11] Friedman and Schwartz have been criticized by Goodhart (1982) and Mayer (1982) for using this dummy-variable technique instead of trying to account directly for increasing financial sophistication by such proxy variables as are used in Chapters 4 and 5.

[12] An alternative approach to financial development is that of Klein (1977). According to him, the long-run demand for money, and hence velocity, has been affected by improvements in the quality of money. Following Friedman (1956), he defines an improvement in quality as an increase in the flow of services derived from a given stock of real cash balances. Using price predictability (measured by price variability) as a measure of quality, he finds that increased price predictability raises the demand for money and reduces velocity in the United States over the period 1880–1976. However, Laidler (1980) finds Klein's quality variable to be insignificant after 1976.

terest elasticity of the money demanded (changing the slope of the velocity curve). However, this effect would be captured by the interest rate variable in a demand-for-money function. The second way was by reducing the demand for money at any given interest rate (shifting the velocity curve). This effect would occur if the new assets were of higher quality than existing money substitutes or if they offered a new service flow competitive with those provided by monetary assets.[13]

Although the growth of savings-and-loans shares in the postwar United States probably reduced the demand for money (Friedman and Schwartz (1963)), other evidence does not support the first effect (see Cagan and Schwartz (1975); Feige and Pearce (1977); Hafer and Hein (1982)). Moreover, Cagan and Schwartz (1975) and Laidler (1985) argue that the new financial assets may satisfy asset motives previously met by demand deposits, freeing demand deposits to satisfy only medium-of-exchange and precautionary motives.

Since the mid-1970s, the tendency of conventional narrow ($M1$) money demand equations to systematically overpredict actual money balances in the United States has led to a focus on financial innovation as a key determinant of money demand. Financial innovation, as a consequence both of deregulation of the U.S. financial system and of an acceleration of inflation in the late 1970s, has been modeled through the use of time trends, dummy and shift variables, interest rate ratchets, and the introduction of rates of return on various financial instruments (Judd and Scadding (1982); Roley (1985)). Although many studies were able to explain the experience of the late 1970s, all have encountered difficulty in explaining an unprecedented decline in the velocity of $M1$ during the early 1980s. According to Schwartz (1985), the recent experience of money demand instability may be characteristic of other periods in monetary history during which new financial instruments emerged as monies. Thus, in the transition period, while the public is learning to accept the new instrument (e.g., deposits in the early nineteenth century), the velocity of the old instrument (e.g., currency) exhibits instability.

An alternative explanation for the recent unstable behavior of the short-run demand for money in the United States is that the short-run money demand function based on the conventional partial adjustment mechanism is misspecified (see Chow (1966)). According to Laidler (1982, 1984), in the short run with an exogenous money supply, it is difficult to conceive of the community as a whole adjusting its actual holdings of real cash balances to a new desired level when faced

---

[13] See Friedman and Schwartz (1963, pp. 659–60).

with a change in one of the arguments of the demand for money as suggested by the Chow approach. Instead, Laidler contended that in the short run, individuals hold real cash balances as a "buffer stock" before they rearrange their portfolios.

### 2.2.2. Explanations stressing the role of money as a medium of exchange

*Transactions velocity:* Irving Fisher (1911) viewed money's key role as that of a medium of exchange facilitating transactions. He therefore expected velocity to rise secularly, reflecting technological improvements in the payments process. Economists at the Federal Reserve Bank of New York measured the movements of transactions velocity, like Fisher, focusing on improvements in the payments technology as the key determinants of the long-run behavior of velocity. Thus Garvy (1959) and Garvy and Blyn (1970) emphasized the substitution of commercial bank deposits for deposits at mutual savings banks, the growing share of output that passes through the market, and the substitution of bank money for trade credit as determinants of the decline in velocity in the United States from 1880 until World War II. To explain the rise in velocity since World War II, these investigators suggested that technological changes in the payments process and in the corporate management of cash balances had made money an inferior asset in the community's portfolio.

Using demand deposit debits plus currency transactions as a measure of transactions, Lieberman (1977) found that this measure outperformed national income, permanent income, and wealth as a scale variable in the demand-for-money function for the United States in the post–World War II period. In addition, an exponential decay term that Lieberman included in the money demand function as a proxy for technical change in the payments process was significant.

Finally, the inventory-theoretic approach of Baumol (1952) and Tobin (1956) implies economies of scale in the holding of money; that is, the income elasticity of money demand should be less than one; in the original Baumol (1952) version it is equal to one-half. Like the Fisher approach, this theory predicts a secularly rising trend for velocity. An income elasticity of the demand for narrow money significantly less than one for the postwar period supports the presence of such economies of scale (Lieberman (1980); Laidler (1985)).[14]

---

[14] However, Meltzer (1963), using cross-section data, finds an elasticity of unity. Brunner and Meltzer (1967) argue that allowing for a variable brokerage fee in the Baumol–Tobin model brings into question the case for economies of scale in cash management.

*The development of the exchange economy:* Hicks (1967), Clower (1969), and a number of general equilibrium theorists such as Townsend (1983) focus on payments arrangements that reduce transactions costs in the development of the exchange economy. According to Clower (1969), in the transition from a rudimentary barter stage to a more advanced market economy, payments media with the lowest transactions costs are chosen. Thus the process of economic development is associated with a progressive shift from barter toward superior forms of money – commodity money, fiduciary money, and finally to trade credit – with an associated reduction in transactions costs at each stage. Such a shift implies a rise in the velocity of each respective definition of the "proper" money stock.[15]

### 2.2.3.   The stochastic properties of velocity

Gould and Nelson (1974) questioned the predictive content of Friedman and Schwartz's long-run time series on U.S. velocity. According to Gould and Nelson, the discussion by Friedman and Schwartz of meaningful patterns in the long-run movement of velocity, and of deviations from trend taken directly from the time series, presumes that future velocity behavior can be extrapolated from velocity history. Gould and Nelson examined the stochastic structure of velocity to determine whether a statistical basis can be found for extrapolative predictions. Zero autocorrelation of the first differences of velocity as well as an insignificant coefficient on the trend term led them to conclude that velocity is a random walk without drift.

Subsequently, Stokes and Neuberger (1979) demonstrated that the Gould and Nelson result is highly period sensitive. They noted that the 1867–1960 period covered by Friedman and Schwartz combines three distinct historical periods: 1867–79 – the Greenback episode; 1940–60 – World War II and the subsequent rise in velocity; and the rest. A reexamination of the evidence for the homogeneous period, 1880–1940, led Stokes and Neuberger to reverse Gould and Nelson's results: Velocity is not a random walk, and the trend has a significant negative coefficient. Other recent contributions to the debate include Gould et al. (1978) and Nelson and Plosser (1982). See Chapter 7 for additional evidence on this question.

In summary, a salient theme of the literature on the long-run behavior of velocity is the importance attached by many writers to the role

---

[15] See Townsend (1983) for an extension and for evidence consistent with this approach.

of institutional and technical changes in the financial sector. In the next chapter we show how many of these developments can be integrated in a coherent way into an extension of Knut Wicksell's theory of the behavior of velocity.

# CHAPTER 3

# The institutional approach

Two movements in the income velocity of money require explanation: the long-run fall and the subsequent secular rise. Chapter 2 revealed that none of the theories of velocity gave a full account of the secular U-shaped behavior of velocity. In this chapter we propose an explanation for this pattern stressing the influence of institutional factors. According to our approach, the downward trend is attributable to the process of monetization, and the upward trend to two developments: increasing financial sophistication and improved economic stability.

We begin by analyzing the factors associated with the long-run fall and then those associated with the secular rise. The horizontal section of the velocity curve then marks a transition period, when the factors associated with the downward trend are roughly counterbalanced by those associated with the upward trend.

## 3.1 The institutional explanation

As indicated, the downward trend in velocity is explained by the monetization process. This process consists of two interrelated developments: (1) the growing use of "money" for settling transactions at the expense of a decline in barter and payments in kind, occurring simultaneously with an expansion of markets and decline of production for own consumption; and (2) the rise of a commercial banking system supplying the public with notes and deposit facilities. These two developments might be expected to promote a more rapid growth in the demand for money than in nominal income and to dominate other secular influences on velocity.

The upward trend in velocity is explained by increasing financial sophistication and improved economic security and stability. Financial sophistication as defined here refers to both (1) the emergence of a large number of close substitutes for money, such as bonds, common stocks, and other financial assets, that reduce the demand for money as an asset; and (2) the development of various methods of economizing on money balances, such as the use of credit cards, the transfer of funds by telegraph, by telephone, or electronically, and modern cash management techniques that reduce the transactions demand for money.

The rubric of growing economic security and stability encompasses many of the aspects of the modern welfare state, including unemployment benefits, public insurance schemes, old age pensions, and various government-provided health programs, as well as macroeconomic policies aimed at minimizing business cycle fluctuations and maintaining full employment. These developments reduce the returns on holding money as a contingency reserve and as a store of value.

The institutional developments mentioned produce changes in the quality of the service flows yielded by money and other assets that induce a series of substitutions between assets yielding monetary and nonmonetary services. Thus, in the process of economic development there is substitution into money in the form of bank notes and deposits, replacing earlier arrangements for payments and for storing wealth. Eventually, new substitutes for money develop over time, inducing portfolio holders to switch out of money into the new assets.

According to our approach, both sets of institutional variables operate at the same time, but the monetization effect first dominates, causing velocity to decline. Later, the influence of financial sophistication and economic security and stability is stronger than the monetization process, causing velocity to rise. The relative strength of these two sets of forces determines the dating of the turning point of velocity.

Our suggested institutional approach does not preclude the influence on velocity of the standard determinants of velocity found in the money demand literature, that is, real income and interest rates. Rather, the institutional factors should be regarded as additional explanatory variables with significant effects on the long-run ratio of income to money. Empirical tests reported in Chapters 4 through 6 reveal the extent to which accounting for institutional factors improves or reduces the explanation for the long-run behavior of velocity provided by the traditional determinants.

Elements of our explanation are found in the literature. The institutional approach that we suggest is inspired by and builds upon Knut Wicksell's work on velocity. Wicksell was among the first to consider the effects of the rise of bank-produced substitutes for metallic money on the transactions velocity of that money. As shown in Chapter 2, various studies in economic history have emphasized the process of monetization as an aspect of the growth of commercial banking (Cameron (1967, 1972); Barkai (1973); Riley and McCusker (1983); Saint Marc (1983); Komlos (1986)). Tobin (1965) and Timberlake (1974) mentioned monetization as contributing to the secular decline in the U.S. velocity. Friedman and Schwartz (1963) suggested that improved stability in the U.S. economy in the postwar period produced an upward movement in velocity, albeit a temporary one. Other economists noted that vertical integration, improved cash management techniques, and changes in the payments technology should raise velocity. As far as we know, however, none have suggested a consistent explanation for the secular U-shaped pattern of velocity similar to the institutional approach proposed here.

## 3.2     Knut Wicksell on the growth of banking and the velocity of hard cash

We regard the proposed explanation of the secular behavior of the income velocity of money as inspired by Knut Wicksell's analysis of the transactions velocity of metallic money. This analysis occupies a central position in Wicksell's monetary theory, particularly in *Interest and Prices*, as well as in *Lectures on Political Economy*, Vol. 2.[1] Wicksell also discussed changes in velocity in a number of other places, notably in a speech at the annual meeting of the *Bankmannaförening* (Association of the Employees of the Commercial Banks) in 1902. Here Wicksell dealt more explicitly with the Swedish monetary situation, explaining how the spread of bank notes in Sweden had influenced velocity.

Wicksell's analysis of velocity revolves around the development of credit as a substitute for "money" – "money" being defined by him as "hard cash," that is, as equal to metallic currency. Gold was the metallic currency in the pre-1914 gold standard, the institutional setting that Wicksell was considering. Bank notes and bank deposits were thus not regarded as money but as close substitutes for hard cash. The growth of such assets as well as of other types of credit influenced the velocity of hard cash. In Wicksell's words: "The influence of credit [i.e., notes and bank deposits] on currency, may, under all circumstances, be regarded as accelerating the circulation of money. . . . The occasions on which credit actually replaces money . . . may, quite simply, be regarded as special cases of the general acceleration of circulation; for instead of a purely physical transfer of money we have a

---

[1] See Chapter 6 in *Interest and Prices* (Wicksell (1936)) and Part 3 in *Lectures 2* (Wicksell (1935)).

virtual, i.e., a merely imaginary or possible transfer, but of the same effectiveness."[2]

Thus the growth of substitutes for metallic currency implies that a given amount of hard cash can form the basis for a larger volume of transactions than previously was the case. As a consequence of this expansion of money substitutes, virtual velocity will increase.

This argument may be summarized in the following manner. Let $T$ denote the volume of transactions per period, and $G$ the amount of metallic currency held by the nonbank public, where $G$ is equivalent to Wicksell's definition of money. The ratio of $T$ to $G$ then represents the transactions velocity of money according to Wicksell:

$$V_g = T/G \qquad \text{transactions velocity of hard cash (=gold)}$$
(3.1)

In a pure cash economy with no credit and no banks, actual velocity will be equal to the physical velocity of the metallic money in use, since every transaction is settled with hard cash. When credit in the form of bank notes and bank deposits is introduced, this picture will change. Let $D$ represent the amount of bank notes and deposits used as means of payment. Then the transactions velocity of the sum of notes and deposits can be expressed in the following way:

$$V_d = (T/G) \cdot (G/D) \qquad \text{transactions velocity of notes and deposits}$$
(3.2)

that is, as the product of the transactions velocity of hard cash, and the ratio of hard cash to notes and deposits. The introduction of notes and deposits replacing gold in transactions will cause a rise in virtual velocity ($=T/G$), assuming that the replaced gold is transfered to the banking system.[3] In the extreme case, the public holds no gold and uses only bank money, which makes virtual velocity equal to infinity. This is the case of Wicksell's "pure credit system" – the polar case of the pure cash economy – where the public has no monetary use of gold.

Wicksell discussed in detail the effects on virtual velocity of various

---

[2] *Lectures 2*, p. 67.
[3] Generally speaking, a more rapid growth in the volume of transactions ($T$) than in the amount of gold held by the public ($G$) raises virtual velocity. Thus Wicksell's argument is consistent with a growing volume of gold in the hands of the public so long as the volume of transactions is expanding at a faster rate, presumably due to the use of bank money for settling transactions to a larger extent than previously. However, the tenor of Wicksell's analysis of virtual velocity suggests that he envisaged an actual decline in the volume of gold held by the nonbank public. See Part 3 in *Lectures 2*.

institutional arrangements for granting credit. Credit given between private individuals without the intervention of financial intermediaries, that is, "simple credit," "has only a very limited influence as a substitute for money tending to accelerate the velocity of circulation."[4] The appearance of "organized credit," specifically in the form of commercial banking, will have far-reaching effects, however. The major part of Wicksell's analysis of velocity actually deals with the growth of banks, which he regarded as "the heart and centre of modern currency systems."[5]

Through the development of banking, gold is gradually replaced by bank credit, that is, by notes and deposits. Wicksell envisioned a system where all gold eventually ends up in the vaults of the banking system as reserves.[6] He argued that the reserve–deposit ratio of the banking system would decline over time as the result of two factors. First, "the law of large numbers," and, second, transactions between customers of the same bank would be settled through bookkeeping transfers from one account to another, reducing the demand for gold as reserves by the banks.

Returning to expression (3.2), this means that the ratio of $G$ to $D$ can be regarded as the reserve ratio of the banking system. Wicksell expected this ratio to approach zero over time, and gold to lose all its monetary use in the future. Then the "ideal" banking system would operate without any metallic currency, and virtual velocity would be infinitely large.[7] Wicksell pointed to a number of obstacles to the realization of the "ideal bank" but hoped that they would eventually be eliminated. According to him the demonetization of gold through the replacement of bank-produced monies "would undoubtedly be a very great national saving."[8]

Wicksell's discussion here may be compared with the analysis of commodity versus fiduciary money. Gold represents commodity money, and bank notes and bank deposits fiduciary money. The progressive substitution of fiduciary money for commodity money – which is the essence of Wicksell's theory of velocity – represents a gain for society as a whole. Resources previously used for the production of gold for monetary use may now be released for other purposes.[9] Wicksell's

---

[4] Ibid., p. 70.
[5] Ibid., p. 73.
[6] Ibid., p. 84.
[7] Ibid., p. 85.
[8] Ibid., p. 123.
[9] On this point see also Johnson (1969). The demonetization of gold is actually a necessary condition for a central bank to adopt Wicksell's norm of price stabilization. Only if the central bank is able to control the domestic money stock is the norm feasible.

major argument is that the gradual replacement of gold by bank notes and bank deposits will raise the virtual velocity of hard cash. He also suggested other institutional developments that influenced the public's holdings of currency, notes, and deposits. The transition from a barter economy to a monetary economy – that is, monetization – would increase the demand for currency and for bank-produced means of payment.[10] When discussing the problem of empirically testing the quantity theory, he stated that "commercial progress" induced a more efficient use of existing media of exchange, implying that technological and financial innovations influenced the velocity of notes and deposits.[11]

Wicksell analyzed the effects of the rise of bank-produced substitutes for metallic money on the transactions velocity of metallic money. With his velocity concept replaced by the income velocity of a broad money definition encompassing notes and deposits ($M2$), Wicksell's analysis suggests that the growth of commercial banking and the process of monetization in the nineteenth century – the period considered by him – would cause a fall in this velocity, assuming that the volume of bank-produced money grew faster than nominal income. (This *fall* in the income velocity of broad money thus took place simultaneously with a *rise* in the transactions velocity of gold [virtual velocity]). Similarly, Wicksell's argument concerning improved efficiency of the use of money due to "commercial progress" can be extended to mean a rise in the income velocity of money ($M2$) once commercial bank expansion and monetization cease to influence velocity.

Knut Wicksell was examining velocity behavior at the turn of the century with the European institutional framework in mind. Roughly a decade later, the American economist Irving Fisher (1911) analyzed, apparently independently of Wicksell, the behavior of velocity in a manner similar to Wicksell's. Fisher considered the transactions velocity of currency as well as of bank deposits, focusing on the role of technological factors. He presented a detailed account of developments that contributed to a long-run rise in transactions velocity, combined with a host of data on the behavior of various velocities. His approach was influential, in particular in the United States, prior to the Keynesian revolution.[12,13]

---

[10] *Lectures 2*, pp. 66 and 145.
[11] Ibid., p. 145.
[12] See, e.g., Tobin (1985).
[13] The work of Wicksell and Fisher builds upon earlier contributions by Mill, Jevons, and Newcomb, among others. On this point see, e.g., Holtrop (1929) and Hegeland (1951).

To sum up, Wicksell's work provides insights that we build upon to explain the secular pattern of the income velocity of money (M2) shown in Chapter 2. In discussing the rise in the transactions velocity of hard cash, Wicksell stressed the role of institutional changes and substitution in the transition from metallic currency and barter to bank monies. Our approach includes the expansion of commercial banking and the process of monetization to account for the fall of the income velocity of money (where money is defined as the sum of the notes and bank deposits held by the nonbank public). To explain the subsequent secular rise of velocity, we also incorporate the appearance of substitutes for bank monies such as bonds, stocks, and social security provisions, as well as government compensation schemes and stabilization policies to minimize macroeconomic fluctuations. Our explanation also covers a later phase in the development of the monetary system than Wicksell experienced and thus was able to consider.

# CHAPTER 4

# The institutional approach: The long-run econometric evidence

Econometric tests of the institutional approach are presented in this chapter. These tests cover the monetary experience of the United States, Canada, the United Kingdom, Sweden, and Norway, since fairly good data are available for these five countries from the 1870s onward. Generally, lack of data for most other countries for long periods of time prevents testing our approach elsewhere.

This chapter is organized as follows. First, various operational measures of institutional developments are considered. Second, these measures are included in a number of regressions to test their influence on velocity in each country. Finally, time series data are pooled for all five countries, and regression tests similar to those for the individual countries are run.

## 4.1  Measures of institutional developments across countries

Quantitative measures of monetization, financial sophistication, and economic stability must be constructed to test for the influence of these variables on velocity. Such factors are generally hard to quantify, however, making it difficult to find all-inclusive measures. For this reason we adopt a number of proxy variables, all of which are available for the five countries.

The process of monetization can be measured in a number of ways (see Chapter 5). As an economy develops, the composition of output shifts from home production toward market production. This movement implies a shift from sectors with low ratios of intermediate transactions such as agriculture, forestry, and fishing to sectors with higher ratios such as commerce and industry. These shifts lead to an increased use of currency, notes, and deposits.

Economic development is also accompanied by a shift of the labor force from agriculture and other primary sectors to commercial activities, manufacturing, and services. This change in the composition of the labor force, reflected by a rise in the share of the labor force in nonagricultural pursuits, serves in this chapter as the measure of the monetization process (for additional measures see Chapter 5.)

As a measure of the spread of commercial banking we use the currency—money ratio, where currency is defined to include both coinage and bank notes. Early commercial bank monetary liabilities consisted primarily of note issues; later, as the banking habit developed, deposits gradually eclipsed note issues as the principal share of bank liabilities. At the same time there was a gradual reduction in the public's use of hard currency relative to both bank notes and deposits. Both of these forces tended to reduce the currency—money ratio as commercial banking spread. Later the volume of deposits grew at a more rapid rate than the note issue.[1] The indicators of monetization and the spread of commercial banking discussed here are available for all countries and are used in the regressions.

An alternative measure of the spread of commercial banking is the number of inhabitants per bank office. This indicator might be expected to decline as the use of commercial bank notes and deposits became more frequent. It was not possible, however, to obtain adequate data for this variable for the United States and Norway. Legal restrictions in some countries on the extent of branch banking also limit the use of this proxy variable.

In Sweden the number of inhabitants per bank office declined from thirty thousand in 1871 to around forty-five hundred in 1922; that is, it reached a low at the same time velocity reached its turning point. See Chart 2.4 and also Chapter 5. However, the number of inhabitants per bank office does not exhibit a consistent upward trend in Sweden after the 1920s.

Possible additional proxies for monetization include the share of noncash wages to cash wages, the number of bank accounts per capita, and the ratio of taxes paid in kind to those paid in money. The behavior of these variables in Sweden in the period 1871–1913 is de-

---

[1] A number of biases may affect the use of the currency—money ratio. First, for Canada before 1913 and Sweden before 1900, the currency series used consist entirely of notes (chartered bank and Dominion notes for Canada and commercial bank and *Riksbank* notes for Sweden) since it was not possible to obtain data on coinage held by the public. To the extent that one would expect to observe substitution between coinage and bank money in general in the early stages of economic development as well as between bank notes and deposits, this omission would tend to make the currency—money ratio higher than a true measure of the spread of commercial banks.

The limited evidence for other countries suggests, however, that the volume of coinage changed little compared to the volume of notes and deposits, minimizing the possible extent of bias. In addition, since World War I, one would expect the ratio to be a misleading proxy for the spread of commercial banking because rising income taxes should have led to a rise in the demand for currency relative to bank deposits. See Cagan (1965) for U.S. evidence and Macesich (1962) for Canadian evidence relating the income tax to the currency—money ratio.

scribed in Chapter 5, which examines in detail the pre-1914 monetization process in Sweden.

Melitz and Correa (1970) used a measure of urbanization as a proxy for monetization, and Timberlake (1974) used the ratio of small denominations to all denominations of currency. (See also Chandavarkar (1977) for a discussion of measures of monetization.) However, such measures generally have two drawbacks. First, they are not readily available for all the five countries. Second, some of them cover only a part of the time span studied here; for instance, in Sweden, before the outbreak of World War I, most wages in industry had been converted to pure money wages, and the payment of taxes in kind, which was prevalent in early times, disappeared in the nineteenth century.

It is common knowledge that a country's financial structure undergoes development during economic growth. From his examination of various measures of financial development in quantitative comparisons of financial structures, Goldsmith (1969, pp. 158–9) drew two conclusions that are of interest for this study. First, he showed that financial sophistication in a number of advanced Western economies had increased secularly since the Industrial Revolution. Second, over the same period the relative share of national assets held by commercial banks had generally declined implying that a given volume of the money stock could "support a larger financial superstructure."[2] These findings are consistent with our emphasis on financial sophistication as a determinant of the secular rise in the income velocity of notes and deposits.

There are considerable difficulties, however, in finding suitable measures of the degree of financial sophistication. A major reason is the lack of comprehensive and continuous statistics on the composition of national wealth for long stretches of time. Still, a few indicators may be proposed. We adopt as a proxy for financial development one that Goldsmith (1969) suggested: the ratio of total nonbank financial assets to total financial assets. For the United States and Canada, where central bank and government financial institutions are more recent phenomena than in Europe, we also use the ratio of total private nonbank financial assets to total private financial assets.

For a country like Sweden, which financed its industrialization by

---

[2] However, Goldsmith (1985, p. 44) found that the financial interrelations ratio (his measure of financial development), which exhibited a secular upward trend for six developed countries (two of which are considered in this chapter – the United States and the United Kingdom) from the mid-nineteenth century to after World War I, has subsequently shown considerable variation. This, he argued, largely reflects the consequences of several episodes of inflation.

considerable foreign borrowing, the ratio of holdings of government securities by the nonbank public within the country either to the volume held by foreigners or to the national income, could also be regarded as a proxy for financial sophistication. As the domestic capital market expanded, the ratio declined. Eventually, in the 1920s Sweden became a net capital exporter. This development is consistent with the dating of the turning point of velocity in the early 1920s.

Finally, we use as a proxy for the influence of growing economic stability a six-year moving standard deviation of the annual percent change in real income per capita. The construction of this variable was suggested by Klein (1977) in his analysis of the long-run U.S. demand for money. It is a measure of future uncertainty about the behavior of real income. It is constructed on the assumption that the more variable past movements in real income have been, the more uncertain the future will be.

## 4.2.    The econometric evidence

The econometric tests are conducted in three steps. First, a benchmark long-run velocity function is estimated for each of the five countries. This function summarizes the standard determinants of velocity: a measure of real income and a measure of the opportunity cost of holding money, that is, the rate of interest. It also includes a cycle variable. Second, we add to the benchmark equation a number of proxy variables for monetization, financial sophistication, and growing economic security. (For the data sources see Appendix 1B.) Finally, we compare the estimates of the benchmark and the extended velocity function and assess the effects of the institutional variables.

The benchmark velocity function, derived from a semilogarithmic long-run demand-for-money function,[3] is of the following form:

[3] Equation (1) is derived from the long-run demand-for-money function:

$$\log(M/PN) = A_0 + A_1 \log(Y/PN)^\mathrm{p} + A_2 i + e \tag{1}$$

where $M/PN$ is real cash balances per capita, $(Y/PN)^\mathrm{p}$ is permanent income per capita, and $i$ is an interest rate. Let

$$\log V = \log(Y/PN) - \log(M/PN) \tag{2}$$

Substituting (1) into (2) gives

$$\log V = \log(Y/PN) - A_0 - A_1 \log(Y/PN)^\mathrm{p} - A_2 i + e \tag{3}$$

or

$$\log V = -A_0 + (1 - A_1)\log(Y/PN)^\mathrm{p} - A_2 i + \log(Y/Y^\mathrm{p}) + e \tag{4}$$

$$\log V = B_0 + B_1 \log(Y/PN)^p + B_2 i + B_3 \log \text{cycle} + e \qquad (4.1)$$

where log stands for natural logarithm; $V = (Y/M)$ is nominal national income divided by the stock of money, where the money stock is defined as $M2$; $(Y/PN)^p$ represents real per capita permanent income; and $i$ is an appropriate rate of interest representing the opportunity cost of holding money balances. Preferably, $i$ should be a short-term interest rate, but for Canada, Norway, and Sweden only the long-term bond yield was available for most of the period examined.[4] Cycle stands for the ratio of measured per capita real income to permanent per capita real income. This variable, which measures the influence of transitory income, should have a coefficient of one in the regression. A coefficient that is positive but less than one would reflect the fact that velocity moves procyclically and would be consistent with Friedman's (1957) permanent income hypothesis. Over the cycle, transitory income would increase the demand for money, since cash balances serve as a buffer stock (Darby (1972); Carr and Darby (1981); Laidler (1984)). Over the long run these transitory balances would then be worked off, returning the coefficient to unity.

In addition, the expected rate of inflation ($p^e$) should be included in the velocity function, at least in periods of rapid changes in the price level. It represents the opportunity cost of holding real cash balances in terms of real goods and should enter the demand-for-money function with a negative sign and hence affect velocity positively. To the extent that the actual rate of inflation equals the ex-

We used the ratio of measured to permanent real per capita income, which we denote log cycle, as a proxy for $\log(Y/Y^p)$. By using this proxy we avoid the problem of calculating permanent prices independently from permanent income over periods when price expectations differed considerably. See Klein (1977). However, this proxy would be biased if $N/N^p$ and $p^p/p$ behave differently from $Y/Y^p$ over the cycle.

[4] Klein (1974) argued that a proper specification of the demand for money should include the own rate of return on money, since including a crossrate such as the long-term bond yield, although not including the own rate, will produce a downward-biased interest elasticity. Following Klein, a specification of the demand for money was tried for the United States and the United Kingdom, the only two countries for which the relevant data are available over the whole period, incorporating in addition to permanent income and the cycle variable Klein's measure of the own rate of return on money ($r_m$); the short-term commercial paper rate ($r_s$) – a measure of the opportunity cost of assets that provide services similar to money; and the long-term bond yield ($r_l$) – a measure of the price of assets that provide services different from money. This specification produced a slightly better fit to regression equation (4.1) for the United States but not for the United Kingdom.

A similar specification for Canada was tried over the period 1934–75 when data are available. Again there was a slight improvement over the benchmark function. See also Chapter 5 for the use of the $r_m$ variable for Sweden for the period 1880–1913.

pected rate, nominal interest rates should fully incorporate the influence of expected inflation. However, if there is considerable government regulation of money and capital markets, then the yield on securities may not be a reliable measure of the opportunity cost of holding money, nor would it fully reflect expected changes in the price level. Also, lags in the adjustment of expected to actual inflation may make the use of the nominal interest rate a misleading proxy for the opportunity cost of holding money. Under these circumstances a measure of expected price change may be an important determinant of the demand for money.

For the United States, Canada, and the United Kingdom, at least until the late 1960s, inflation was relatively mild and interest rates were adjusted freely to market forces – with the exception of the 1939–51 period for the United Kingdom and Canada, and 1941–51 for the United States – so that expected price change should not be an important variable in the demand for money for those countries, nor is there much evidence for its significance before the late 1960s. This, however, is not the case for Sweden and Norway, where government regulations of securities markets have been in effect since World War II. For these countries the measured long-term bond rate would not be a proper measure of the opportunity cost of holding money. Consequently, the expected inflation rate is generated by regressing the annual rate of change in the price level on successive past rates of change, choosing the regression that maximized the adjusted $R^2$. The maximizing of $R^2$ occurred for Sweden and Norway after three years. The predicted change in the price level from this regression was then used as a measure of $p^e$.

To account for the influence of institutional factors, a number of proxy variables were then added to the benchmark equation (4.1). First, we use the share of the labor force in nonagricultural pursuits ($LNA/L$) as a proxy for monetization. This ratio is expected to be positively correlated with the spread of the monetary economy and hence should enter the equation with a negative sign. The demand for money will rise as structural change leads to a relative decline in importance of the primary sector. However, our proxy variable $LNA/L$ will not capture the effect on the demand for money of monetization *within* the primary sector. This influence could, for example, be measured by the ratio of noncash to cash wages in the agricultural sector. Chapter 5 reports regression estimates covering the Swedish process of monetization, where the ratio of cash payments to total wages of farmhands is included as a variable explanatory of the fall in velocity. This measure is significant and enters with the correct (negative) sign. (See Table 5.4.)

As a proxy for the spread of commercial banking we use the currency–money ratio ($C/M$). We would expect this variable to be negatively correlated with the spread of the money economy and to enter the velocity function with a positive sign.

Our proxy for financial development – the ratio of total nonbank financial assets to total financial assets ($TNBFA/TFA$) – is expected to enter the velocity function with a positive sign.[5] This should also be the case for the ratio of total private nonbank financial assets to total private financial assets ($TPNBFA/TPFA$) that we used for the United States.[6]

Finally, a six-year moving standard deviation of the annual percent change in real income per head ($s_{\hat{y}}$), representing the influence of economic stability, should be negatively correlated with velocity. A decline in the certainty about the future, reflected by an increase in $s_{\hat{y}}$, should raise the precautionary demand for money and hence should lower velocity.

The expanded velocity function is expressed as follows:

$$\log V = B_0 + B_1\log(Y/PN)^{\mathrm{p}} + B_2 i + B_3\log \text{cycle} + B_4\log(LNA/L) \\ + B_5\log(C/M) + B_6\log(TNBFA/TFA) + B_7\log s_{\hat{y}} + e' \qquad (4.2)$$

Table 4.1 presents regressions of equations (4.1) and (4.2) using OLS for the five countries over the entire period. Although data suitable to construct an annual velocity series for each country were available from 1870 to 1975, other data, required to represent the independent variables for the regression tests, were not. Hence the results for the earliest starting date for each country are presented; for the majority of countries this was the period beginning in 1880. The Cochrane–Orcutt iterative procedure was used to correct for severe autocorrelation in the residuals observed in preliminary testing. Moreover, for Sweden the expected rate of inflation ($p^e$) is incorporated into the regression in regression equations (1A) and (2A).[7]

The results in Table 4.1 for regression equation (1), the benchmark

---

[5] Stauffer (1978) used illiteracy rates as a proxy for financial development in his study of the decline in velocity in the United States during the period 1900–20.
[6] We also tried $TPNBFA/TPFA$ for Canada but found that $TNBFA/TFA$ yielded stronger results.
[7] The same procedure was tried for Norway, but the $p^e$ variable was always insignificant.

Table 4.1. Institutional variables in the long-run velocity function: Five countries (Cochrane–Orcutt technique)

Coefficients of independent variables (t-values in parentheses)

| Eq. no. | Constant | $\log\left(\frac{Y}{PN}\right)^{\mathrm{p}}$ | $i$ | log cycle | $\log\left(\frac{LNA}{L}\right)$ | $\log\left(\frac{C}{M}\right)$ | $\log\left(\frac{TNBFA}{TFA}\right)$ | $\log s_y$ | $p^e$ | $(\bar{R}^2)^b$ | SEE | DW | $\rho$ | $F^x$ |
|---|---|---|---|---|---|---|---|---|---|---|---|---|---|---|
| **A. U.S., 1880–1982** | | | | | | | | | | | | | | |
| (1) | .390 (.576) | .011 (.105) | 2.050 (5.018)* | .840 (11.089)* | | | | | | .984 | .038 | 1.696 | .943 | |
| (2) | -1.019 (-.982) | .219 (1.460) | 2.100 (4.921)* | .785ᵃ (9.324)* | -1.896 (-3.044)* | -.028 (-.466) | .490 (2.566)* | .003 (.361) | | .984 | .038 | 1.729 | .904 | 1.562 |
| (3) | .693 (2.877)* | | | .839ᵃ (8.917)* | -.177 (-.268)* | .001 (.006) | .334 (1.591) | -.014 (-.777) | | .980 | .043 | 1.865 | .952 | |
| (4) | .500 (2.542)* | | 2.198 (5.318)* | .789 (9.402)* | -.869 (-2.130)* | -.046 (-.750) | .362 (2.004)* | .002 (.134) | | .984 | .038 | 1.750 | .926 | |
| **B. Canada, 1900–75** | | | | | | | | | | | | | | |
| (1) | -.530 (-.823) | .202 (2.065)* | 3.616 (2.306)* | .951ᵃ (6.373)* | | | | | | .888 | .052 | 1.766 | .868 | |
| (2) | -2.899 (-2.097)* | .639 (3.549)* | 2.679 (2.097)* | .660 (5.107)* | -2.788 (-4.159)* | .433 (5.384)* | .567 (4.923)* | -.013 (-1.027) | | .932 | .041 | 1.424 | .863 | 12.182* |
| (3) | 2.433 (9.650)* | | | .764ᵃ (5.617)* | -.110 (-.153) | .509 (5.686)* | .497 (3.924)* | -.004 (-.351) | | .911 | .046 | 1.312 | .952 | |
| (4) | 1.984 (8.881)* | | 4.484 (3.517)* | .804ᵃ (6.089)* | -.673 (-1.723)# | .477 (5.539)* | .490 (3.999)* | -.004 (-.287) | | .920 | .044 | 1.338 | .886 | |
| **C. U.K., 1876–1974** | | | | | | | | | | | | | | |
| (1) | .094 (.095) | .065 (.419) | 1.651 (3.352)* | .650ᵃ (3.287)* | | | | | | .907 | .050 | 1.790 | .939 | |
| (2) | -.395 (-.344) | .197 (1.240) | 2.497 (5.014)* | .797ᵃ (4.588)* | -6.271 (-2.313)* | .211 (2.167)* | .746 (3.107)* | -.034 (-2.059)* | | .931 | .043 | 2.081 | .925 | 9.375* |

| Eq. | (1) | (2) | (3) | (4) | (5) | (6) | (7) | (8) | $R^2$ | S.E. | D.W. | $\bar{R}^2$[b] | F[c] |
|---|---|---|---|---|---|---|---|---|---|---|---|---|---|
| (3) | 1.388 (4.324)* | | | .767[a] (3.957)* | .797 (.264) | .370 (3.547)* | .209 (.846) | −.026 (−1.377) | .913 | .049 | 1.875 | .953 | |
| (4) | 1.007 (3.835)* | | 2.490 (4.989)* | .795[a] (4.565)# | −4.183 (−1.867)# | .225 (2.315)* | .729 (3.024)* | .031 (−1.865)# | .931 | .043 | 2.110 | .929 | |

**D. Sweden, 1880–1974**

| Eq. | (1) | (2) | (3) | (4) | (5) | (6) | (7) | (8) | $R^2$ | S.E. | D.W. | $\bar{R}^2$[b] | F[c] |
|---|---|---|---|---|---|---|---|---|---|---|---|---|---|
| (1) | −.484 (−.780) | .256 (2.609)* | −4.715 (−1.375) | 1.155[a] (8.313)* | −1.281 (−3.280)* | .523 (5.670)* | .497 (1.658)# | .003 (.224) | .950 | .049 | 1.224 | .942 | |
| (1A) | −.063 (−.106) | .189 (2.088)* | −4.414 (−1.376) | 1.115[a] (8.492)* | .371 (3.619)* | | | | .956 | .046 | 1.548 | .937 | |
| (2) | .113 (.121) | .237 (1.892)# | 3.938 (1.328) | 1.143[a] (9.542)* | −.916 (−2.263)* | .475 (5.376)* | .567 (1.869)# | .007 (.581) | .966 | .040 | 1.352 | .875 | 12.064* |
| (2A) | 1.058 (1.129) | .111 (.887) | 3.452 (1.211) | 1.123[a] (10.005)* | .305 (3.383)* | | | | .970 | .038 | 1.575 | .899 | 11.402* |
| (3) | 2.122 (11.374)* | | | 1.171[a] (9.841)* | −.376 (−1.048) | .481 (5.585)* | .520 (1.465) | .009 (.664) | .964 | .041 | 1.351 | .936 | |
| (4) | 1.878 (10.380)* | | 5.768 (2.069)* | 1.156[a] (9.633)* | −.649 (−2.336)* | .551 (5.989)* | .491 (1.521) | .005 (.377) | .965 | .041 | 1.366 | .896 | |

**E. Norway, 1880–1974 (excluding 1939–45)**

| Eq. | (1) | (2) | (3) | (4) | (5) | (6) | (7) | (8) | $R^2$ | S.E. | D.W. | $\bar{R}^2$[b] | F[c] |
|---|---|---|---|---|---|---|---|---|---|---|---|---|---|
| (1) | −.192 (−.277) | .116 (1.078) | 3.574 (2.258)* | 1.544 (5.891)* | −.259 (−.527) | .522 (4.639)* | .379 (1.303) | −.018 (−1.073) | .942 | .063 | 1.410 | .932 | |
| (2) | 1.996 (1.942)# | −.028 (−.223) | 3.874 (2.661)* | 1.449 (6.525)* | | | | | .963 | .051 | 1.757 | .951 | 13.402* |
| (3) | 1.969 (7.043)* | | | 1.494 (6.435)* | −.004 (−.009) | .626 (5.647)* | −.045 (−.177) | −.010 (−.557) | .960 | .053 | 1.769 | .913 | |
| (4) | 1.780 (5.026)* | | 3.787 (2.717)* | 1.449 (6.567)* | −.303 (−.678) | .520 (4.667)* | .365 (1.292) | −.018 (−1.080) | .964 | .051 | 1.754 | .951 | |

*Statistically significant at the 5% level.

#Statistically significant at the 10% level.

[a] Not significantly different from one at the 5% level.

[b] Denotes $R^2$ adjusted for degrees of freedom.

[c] Sequential F-test: equation (2) vs. equation (1).

velocity function, reveal the permanent income elasticity of velocity to be positive and significant at the 5% level for the three European countries and positive and significant at the 10% level for Canada. This finding implies permanent income elasticities of the demand for money considerably less than one, in agreement with other studies[8] as well as with the view that there are economies of scale in cash management.[9] The coefficient for permanent income for the United States is negative but not significantly different from zero. This result differs from the significantly negative coefficient suggested by the luxury good hypothesis. The difference between the result here and the frequently cited permanent income elasticity of velocity of $-.8$ found in Friedman's (1959) pioneering study can be explained by several factors: (1) The earlier study did not correct for autocorrelation as is done here; (2) Friedman's estimate was for the period 1870–1954; and (3) his data were expressed in cyclical units.[10]

In addition, the interest rate variable is positive and significant in every country except Sweden, and the implied negative interest elasticity of the demand for money agrees with traditional monetary theory. The negative and nonsignificant coefficient for Sweden suggests that the long-term bond rate may not be the appropriate opportunity cost variable. However, introducing the expected rate of inflation into the Swedish regression turns the coefficient positive and significant as theory postulates, and significantly improves the regression.[11]

For every country except Norway, the cycle variable in the benchmark regression is not significantly different from one. The high level of significance attached to this variable, especially for the United States, suggests that the extreme cyclical behavior over the 1929–46 period may be a key determinant of the U-shaped pattern of velocity for that country.[12]

---

[8] See Goldfeld (1973) and Laidler (1985).

[9] See Baumol (1952) and Tobin (1956).

[10] Indeed the U.S. benchmark regression for 1880–1972 using OLS without the Cochrane–Orcutt adjustment is ($t$-statistics in parentheses)

$$\log V = 3.08 - .41 \log(Y/PN)^P + 6.94i + 1.47 \log \text{cycle}$$
$$(17.8)^* \ (-16.1)^* \qquad (11.5)^* \quad (10.2)^*$$
$$\bar{R}^2 = .89 \qquad DW = .48 \qquad SEE = .106$$

with a negative and significant permanent income elasticity of velocity.

[11] See Lybeck (1975), who concluded that $p^e$ is a significant variable in the long-run demand-for-money function in Sweden. For Norway, Isakson (1976) established a significant effect for $p^e$ for the postwar period. So did Klovland (1983), who found a significant effect for the gold standard period prior to World War I and for the interwar years.

[12] Indeed a benchmark regression for the United States for 1880–1972 omitting the cycle variable had a considerably higher standard error of estimate than the regression reported in Table 4.1, i.e. ($t$-statistics in parentheses),

Inclusion of the four institutional variables in regression equation (2) (as well as in (2A) for Sweden) significantly improves the regression for every country, except the United States, where the improvement is not even marginal. This significant improvement can be observed in the significant sequential $F$-statistics reported following regression equation (2) as well as in a higher adjusted $R^2$.

Moreover, introduction of these variables raises the income elasticity of velocity and hence lowers the income elasticity of the demand for money for three of the five countries.[13] One explanation for these results is that two of these variables, $LNA/L$ and $TNBFA/TFA$, are highly correlated with permanent income,[14] and running the regression with income alone, omitting these variables, yields downward-biased income elasticities of velocity (upward-biased income elasticities of the demand for money) to the extent that the omitted variables represent a true influence on velocity. Alternatively, since income itself is a vector of characteristics of economic development, including the institutional variables, introducing the institutional variables explicitly into the regression would per se reduce the influence of income on velocity. It is not possible to separate the specification bias from the simultaneous equation bias.

Examining each of the institutional coefficients in regression equation (2) in turn, we observe first that $LNA/L$ has the correct negative

$$\log V = .648 - .028 \log(Y/PN)^P + 2.413i$$
$$\phantom{\log V = }(.77) \quad (-.22) \qquad\qquad (3.9)*$$
$$\overline{R}^2 = .963 \qquad DW = 1.74 \qquad SEE = .0589 \qquad \rho = .918$$

and did not predict the U-shaped pattern nearly as well. This phenomenon was observed for the other countries but to a lesser degree.

[13] This effect is consistent with Graves (1978), who found that introducing demographic variables into the demand for money, using both long-run U.S. time series data and post–World War II cross-section data for a number of countries, lowers the income elasticity of money demand. Graves argued that these demographic variables, e.g., urbanization, age, education, income equality, and household size, are highly correlated with real income, and that regressions using real income (permanent and measured) excluding these omitted variables tend to be biased upward.

Negative correlation between age and velocity may also explain downward bias in the income elasticity of velocity. Mayor and Pearl (1984) found evidence, based on a cross-section time series study of counties in the United States for 1950, 1960, and 1970, that life cycle factors proxied by median population age represent a significant determinant of velocity.

[14] The correlation coefficients with $\log(Y/PN)^P$ by country for each of $\log(LNA/L)$ and $\log(TNBFA/TFA)$ are:

|  | $\log(LNA/L)$ | $\log(TNBFA/TFA)$ |
|---|---|---|
| 1. U.S. | .980 | .772 |
| 2. Canada | .977 | .767 |
| 3. U.K. | .921 | .861 |
| 4. Sweden | .990 | .954 |
| 5. Norway | .951 | .961 |

sign for all countries and is significant for all except Norway. Second, $C/M$, our proxy for the spread of commercial banking, is significant, with the correct positive sign, at the 5% level in all countries except the United States, where it is not at all significant.[15] Third, the measure of financial development, $TNBFA/TFA$, is significant, with the correct positive sign, at the 5% level in the United States, Canada, and the United Kingdom. In Sweden it is significant at the 10% level. Finally, the proxy for economic stability, $s_{\dot{y}}$, is significant in only one country – the United Kingdom.

As an alternative to the traditional velocity function, a "pure institutional" function that omits the interest rate and permanent income variables is presented in regression equation (3). This specification should give us an indication of the importance of the institutional variables taken in isolation. Except for the United States, the pure institutional hypothesis, represented by regression equation (3), explains more of the movement of velocity (has a higher $\bar{R}^2$) than does regression equation (1), the benchmark velocity function.

In addition, regressions including the interest rate but excluding permanent income – regression equation (4) in Table 4.1 – explain marginally more of the variation in velocity than regression equation (3), confirming earlier evidence that the interest rate is a key determinant of the demand for money.[16] Comparing regression equations (4) and (2) indicates that except for Canada the exclusion of permanent income leads to a slight or no reduction in $\bar{R}^2$. This result suggests that except for Canada, where the reduction in $\bar{R}^2$ is marked, permanent income captures trend effects similar to those attributable to the institutional proxies, and that permanent income may not play as important a role as has been claimed in the earlier literature.[17]

Finally, our theory predicts that the influence of monetization and the spread of commercial banking dominate the other institutional variables in the trend period of declining velocity, whereas in the trend period of rising velocity financial development and improved economic stability would be predominant.

Table A.1 (see Appendix A at the end of the chapter) presents in panel A regressions for periods of falling velocity and in panel B regressions for periods of rising velocity similar to those reported in

[15] Klovland (1983) reported for Norway a significant effect of the currency–money ratio on the long-run demand for money, associating this variable with the Norwegian monetization process.

[16] Again, see Laidler (1985).

[17] Again, this confirms the conclusions reached by Graves (1978) and by Mayor and Pearl (1984).

Table 4.1. In general, these regressions reveal, in the majority of countries for the period of declining velocity, in support of our hypothesis, that the monetization variables were significant and had the correct sign, whereas the other institutional variables tended to be nonsignificant or had a perverse sign; with the opposite tendency prevailing in the trend period of rising velocity. Moreover, Chow tests (F-tests) for the two periods (Table A.2) rejected the null hypothesis for similarity of the coefficients in the majority of cases in the regressions containing institutional variables.

In sum, except for the measure of economic stability, the suggested institutional variables represent important determinants of the long-run velocity function for the majority of the countries examined.

*An alternative measure of economic stability:* We noted earlier the limited significance of our proxy measure of economic stability as an explanatory variable. An alternative measure of growing economic stability is the government's share in national income. We use two variants of this measure: total government expenditure less interest payments on the national debt, and total government expenditure less interest payments and defense expenditures. The former measure is a comprehensive measure of stability. In the absence of defense expenditures, national income might be considerably lower. The latter measure includes many government-provided services and transfers that may contribute to economic stability and security. We would expect that if this variable captures growing economic stability and security, it would reduce the demand for money and raise velocity. We report in Appendix B at the end of the chapter the results of regressions using these two measures of government's share in national income. (For the data sources see Appendix 1C.)

In Appendix B, Table B.1 presents the results for the five countries for the comprehensive measure; Table B.2 for three countries for which the data are available, for the narrow measure. The results are striking. For the United States and Canada the government share variable is insignificant for both definitions. For the three European countries the comprehensive measure is significant but enters with an incorrect (negative) sign, as does the narrow measure for the United Kingdom. To test for the possibility that the massive increase in government's share in both world wars might explain these results – wartime threats to national security explain both a rise in government's share and a rise in the precautionary demand for money – we calculated the regressions excluding the war years. We report these results in Table B.3. As before, the government share variable is insignificant and/or has the wrong sign.

One possible explanation for the negative coefficient of government expenditures as a share of national income is that this share generally moves countercyclically, reflecting the automatic stabilizing role of many government expenditures, whereas velocity generally moves procyclically. Thus, ceteris paribus, a negative coefficient reflecting the cyclical effect would result. We attempted to account for the cycle by including in the regression the ratio of measured to permanent income. However, inclusion of this variable may capture only part of the cyclical variation in velocity and in the share of government expenditure. To deal with this possible cyclical effect, we included in the regressions up to three lagged values of the government share variable as well as two-, three-, four-, and five-year moving averages. The government share variable still turns out to be negative, however.

Thus our results suggest that financial sophistication is a stronger explanation of the rise in velocity than economic stability as measured in our tests.

## 4.3.    The evidence from pooled time series regressions

This section provides further evidence on the institutional approach to velocity by pooling all of the time series data for the five countries and then running regressions similar to those reported in the previous section. Pooling treats the five countries as part of one entity and assumes that the common behavior of velocity is explained by common economic determinants.

In a similar vein, Friedman and Schwartz (1982) estimated a long-run demand-for-money (velocity) function for the United States and United Kingdom combined for the period 1870–1975. They justified such an aggregation on the grounds that both velocity and its key determinants (except real per capita income) displayed very similar movements in the two countries. The explanation they give for the similar behavior of both velocity and its determinants "is that the two countries were part of a single economic entity. National boundaries may have great political importance and economic significance in other respects, yet be consistent with a financial system that is unified over a much larger area. The international community presumably included (and includes) not only the United States and the United Kingdom but other countries as well." (p. 305)[18]

---

[18] Friedman and Schwartz then estimated long-run demand-for-money (velocity) functions for the United States and the United Kingdom using cyclical phase averaged data over the period 1875–1975. They explained virtually all of the variation in real

We test for similarities and differences of both the underlying benchmark determinants of velocity and our institutional variables by including individual country dummy variables for the intercept and each of the independent variables.

According to the institutional hypothesis, we expect different institutional variables to exhibit different degrees of influence in periods of falling velocity than in periods of rising velocity. We expect monetization and the spread of commercial banking to dominate in periods of falling velocity, and growing financial sophistication and improved economic stability to dominate in periods of rising velocity. We test this hypothesis by running the pooled regression over periods of both declining and rising velocity.

Finally, we examine whether velocity behavior differs under different monetary standards. In the first part of the period – until 1914 – all five countries were linked together under the fixed exchange rate that followed from adherence to the classical gold standard. On those grounds we would expect tight linkages between the five growth rates of the national money supplies, price levels, and interest rates. By contrast, the rest of the period was characterized by various forms of "managed money" – a combination (for all countries and periods) of pure flexible exchange rates, managed floating, and adjustable fixed exchange rates. Under such a set of standards one would expect to see less covariation among monetary variables between countries. According to our hypothesis, if institutional variables represent important determinants of the trend behavior of common velocity, then the influence of such variables on common velocity should be independent of the monetary standard.

## 4.3.1.  Results for the full period

Table 4.2 presents pooled regressions for the five countries over the entire period. In the pooling, corrections for autocorrelation (found

per capita balances by (a) changing financial sophistication for the United States; (b) real per capita income (obtaining an income elasticity slightly above one for the United States and slightly below one for the United Kingdom); (c) the difference between Klein's own-rate of return on money and the rate of return on short-term securities as a proxy for the differential return on nominal assets sacrificed by holding money; (d) the short-term interest rate as a measure of the nominal return on nominal assets; (e) the rate of change of nominal income as a proxy for the rate of return on physical assets; and (f) two dummies to account for observed shifts in the demand function after the two world wars and during the interwar period. Their finding of a remarkably close similarity in the behavior of velocity and of its determinants in each country led them to estimate a combined demand-for-money function. That function had even greater explanatory power than the functions for each country taken separately.

in earlier testing) were made separately for all the independent variables of each country.[19] For the pooling, the real per capita permanent income series for each country was converted to U.S. dollars using the U.S. base period. (For the exchange rates used see Appendix 1D.)

The regressions presented in Table 4.2 are the same as those shown in Table 4.1 for the five individual countries. Regression equation (1) is the benchmark equation. Regression equation (2) adds the four institutional variables to equation (1). Regression equation (3) examines the influence of the institutional variables (plus the cycle variable) alone. Regression equation (4) omits the behavior of permanent income from equation (2).

The results of Table 4.2 are generally stronger than those reported for the individual countries in Table 4.1. In regression equation (2) all the independent variables are significant and of the proper sign (except for $s_{\hat{y}}$). In regression equation (3), however, $TNBFA/TFA$ is insignificant and, judging from the $\bar{R}^2$, this equation performs slightly worse than equation (1). Similar to the individual country results, introducing the institutional variables lowers the income elasticity of the demand for money (regression equation (2) compared to regression equation (1)). However, the omission of permanent income (in regression equation (4)) does reduce the explanatory power of the regression compared to regression equation (2).

Table 4.3 presents the results of $t$-tests on dummy variables for each independent variable for each of the four equations for the five countries. Such tests may shed light on whether similar influences of each independent variable on velocity existed between the different countries.

Examining each regression in turn, we find the following:

1.  For the benchmark equation, judging from the prevalence of insignificant $t$-statistics, both the interest rate and the cycle variable are similar across the five countries (except for the interest rate for Norway). Such similarities likely reflect close linkages of the international business cycle, and international capital mobility.[20] Considerable differences exist between the intercept and per capita permanent income between countries.

2.  Introducing the four institutional variables shows that there

[19] We corrected for serial correlation in pooled time series data according to the approach suggested by Kmenta (1971, pp. 512–14).
[20] See Nurkse (1944), Friedman and Schwartz (1982), Easton (1984), and Huffman and Lothian (1984).

Table 4.2. *Results of pooled regressions (Cochrane–Orcutt technique)*

| | Coefficients of independent variables (*t*-values in parentheses) | | | | | | | | | | | |
|---|---|---|---|---|---|---|---|---|---|---|---|---|
| Eq. no. | Constant | $\log\left(\frac{Y}{PN}\right)^P$ | $i$ | log cycle | $\log\left(\frac{LNA}{L}\right)$ | $\log\left(\frac{C}{M}\right)$ | $\log\left(\frac{TNBFA}{TFA}\right)$ | $\log s_9$ | $\bar{R}^2$ | SEE | DW | $\rho$ |
| (1) | .001 | .087 | 2.778 | .884 | | | | | .379 | .057 | 1.572 | .213 |
| | (.181) | (6.971)* | (7.405)* | (12.427)* | | | | | | | | |
| (2) | .009 | .193 | 2.106 | 1.003 | −1.268 | .361 | .478 | −.009 | .638 | .047 | 1.532 | .231 |
| | (2.102)# | (15.286)* | (6.850)* | (16.934)* | (−11.205)* | (11.223)* | (7.307)* | (−1.355) | | | | |
| (3) | .044 | | | .959 | −1.017 | .154 | .070 | −.034 | .359 | .055 | 1.389 | .299 |
| | (9.573)* | | | (13.793)* | (−5.385)* | (4.355)* | (.959)* | (−4.536)* | | | | |
| (4) | .022 | | 2.865 | .977 | −1.068 | .012 | .005 | −.036 | .528 | .058 | 1.316 | .341 |
| | (4.938)* | | (7.553)* | (13.218)* | (−7.591)* | (.439) | (.074) | (−4.685)* | | | | |

*Entire Sample*: U.S., 1880–1972; Canada, 1900–75; UK, 1876–1974; Sweden, 1880–1974; Norway, 1880–1974.
* Statistically significant at the 1% level.
# Statistically significant at the 10% level.

Table 4.3. t-Tests for intercept and independent-variable dummies: All combinations of five countries (Cochrane–Orcutt technique)

| Eq. no by country / Indepen. var. by country | Constant | | | | $\log(V/PN)^P$ | | | | $i$ | | | | log cycle | | | |
|---|---|---|---|---|---|---|---|---|---|---|---|---|---|---|---|---|
| | U.S. | Canada | UK | Sweden | U.S. | Canada | UK | Sweden | U.S. | Canada | UK | Sweden | U.S. | Canada | UK | Sweden |
| **(1)** | | | | | | | | | | | | | | | | |
| Norway | 1.93† | −1.57 | −.57 | −1.26 | −.64 | 2.02# | .91 | 2.10# | −5.75* | −2.88* | −6.40* | −3.50* | −.77 | −.36 | −1.30 | .52 |
| U.S. | | 2.62# | 2.22# | 2.51# | | 2.67* | −1.39 | −2.83* | | −.70 | .87 | 1.75† | | −.46 | .85 | −1.67† |
| Canada | | | −1.38 | −.75 | | | .72 | .10 | | | 1.08 | 1.91† | | | 1.10 | −1.05 |
| UK | | | | .97 | | | | −.67 | | | | 1.58 | | | | −2.0† |
| **(2)** | | | | | | | | | | | | | | | | |
| Norway | −4.44* | −6.83* | −4.10* | −1.52 | | | | | | | | | −2.74* | −2.84* | −2.52* | −1.21 |
| U.S. | | 1.93† | −.81 | −3.93* | | | | | | | | | | .40 | .33 | −1.96† |
| Canada | | | −3.34* | −7.69* | | | | | | | | | | | .01 | −2.10# |
| UK | | | | −3.55* | | | | | | | | | | | | −1.74† |
| **(3)** | | | | | | | | | | | | | | | | |
| Norway | −.37 | −4.19* | −3.05* | 1.77† | | | | | −1.13 | .004 | −1.28 | .43 | −2.87* | −2.68* | −2.51* | −1.18 |
| U.S. | | 1.86† | 1.40 | −1.51 | | | | | | −.87 | .26 | −.86 | | .007 | .18 | −2.14# |
| Canada | | | −1.01 | −6.79* | | | | | | | .99 | −.41 | | | .16 | −1.91† |
| UK | | | | −5.25* | | | | | | | | −.92 | | | | −1.75† |
| **(4)** | | | | | | | | | | | | | | | | |
| Norway | −2.09# | −2.72* | −1.72† | −.88 | 1.76 | 2.83 | 1.17 | 1.52 | −1.52 | −.82 | −1.31 | −.10 | −3.07* | −3.30* | −2.57* | −1.29 |
| U.S. | | −1.19 | −1.36 | −1.36 | | −1.25 | .49 | .34 | | −.19 | −.33 | −.43 | | .68 | .04 | −2.23# |
| Canada | | | −.62 | −.62 | | | 1.67† | 1.60 | | | .04 | −.32 | | | −.47 | −2.54# |
| UK | | | | −.25 | | | | −.19 | | | | −.36 | | | | −1.70 |

*Entire sample:* U.S., 1880–1972; Canada, 1900–75; UK, 1876–1974; Sweden, 1880–1974; Norway, 1880–1974.

*Statistically significant at the 1% level.
#Statistically significant at the 5% level.
†Statistically significant at the 10% level.

| | log(LNA/L) | | | | log(C/M) | | | | log(TNBFA/TFA) | | | | log $s_y$ | | | |
|---|---|---|---|---|---|---|---|---|---|---|---|---|---|---|---|---|
| Indepen. var. by country → Eq. no. by country | U.S. | Canada | UK | Sweden | U.S. | Canada | UK | Sweden | U.S. | Canada | UK | Sweden | U.S. | Canada | UK | Sweden |
| **(1)** | | | | | | | | | | | | | | | | |
| Norway | | | | | | | | | | | | | | | | |
| U.S. | | | | | | | | | | | | | | | | |
| Canada | | | | | | | | | | | | | | | | |
| UK | | | | | | | | | | | | | | | | |
| **(2)** | | | | | | | | | | | | | | | | |
| Norway | -.34 | .71 | .52 | .53 | -4.39* | .45 | -.76 | .13 | -.13 | .69 | -.61 | .34 | .37 | 1.22 | .04 | 1.67† |
| U.S. | | -.80 | -.58 | -.80 | | -4.45* | -2.93* | -3.89* | | -.63 | .41 | -.38 | | -.58 | .31 | -1.03 |
| Canada | | | -.11 | -.51 | | | 1.10* | .27 | | | 1.09 | -.04 | | | 1.02 | -.65 |
| UK | | | | .41 | | | | -.79 | | | | -.66 | | | | -1.46 |
| **(3)** | | | | | | | | | | | | | | | | |
| Norway | -3.20* | .76 | -.79 | -.28 | -5.51* | -.18 | -2.27# | .31 | .90 | 1.01 | 1.68† | .49 | .35 | 1.29 | -.19 | 1.42 |
| U.S. | | -1.68† | .42 | -2.62 | | -4.85* | -2.02# | -4.80* | | .009 | -1.01 | -.004 | | -.63 | .48 | -.80 |
| Canada | | | 1.03 | .85 | | | 2.01* | -.45 | | | -1.07 | -.008 | | | 1.32 | -.29 |
| UK | | | | -.75 | | | | -2.27# | | | | .67 | | | | -1.45 |
| **(4)** | | | | | | | | | | | | | | | | |
| Norway | -3.16# | -1.11 | -1.48 | -1.49 | -5.47* | -.66 | -2.44* | .05 | 1.02 | 1.05 | 1.60 | .45 | 1.02 | .92 | -.43 | 1.29 |
| U.S. | | -.34 | .81 | -1.77 | | -4.35* | -1.97† | -4.56* | | .19 | -.72 | .19 | | .38 | 1.30 | -.01 |
| Canada | | | .90 | -.52 | | | 1.75† | -.61 | | | -.96 | -.09 | | | 1.25 | -.50 |
| UK | | | | -1.21 | | | | -2.19# | | | | .70 | | | | -1.57 |

are no significant differences between the institutional variables between the five countries except for the currency–money ratio, where the United States and United Kingdom differ from the three other countries. This result may in part be explained by the U.S. experience in the Great Depression.[21] In addition, the fact that the per capita income variable becomes similar across countries when we introduce the institutional variables strengthens our conclusion in the previous section that permanent income is a proxy for these variables. The $t$-values in Table 4.3 for regression equations (3) and (4) do not differ greatly from those for regression equation (2).

We draw the following conclusions from the results of the pooled regressions for the entire period: (1) Pooling provides evidence additional to that of the individual countries in Table 4.1 in favor of the institutional approach; (2) except for the $C/M$ variable, the influence of institutional variables on velocity is similar in all five countries, suggesting that common forces underlying these institutional proxies explain the common behavior of velocity.

### 4.3.2.   A comparison between periods of rising and falling velocity

In Appendix C, Table C.1 (at the end of the chapter), we present pooled regressions of the four specifications of the velocity function for two time periods: the period of falling velocity (panel A) and the period of rising velocity (panel B). As in the case of the full period, the pooled regressions generally perform better than the individual country regressions. Comparing the benchmark equation (1) between the periods of falling and rising velocity, we find that all the independent variables are significant and exhibit the correct sign in both periods, with the exception of the cycle variable, which is insignificant in the period of rising velocity. Perhaps this result may be explained by the fact that for most of the countries, the period of falling velocity coincided with a fixed exchange rate standard and the absence of countercyclical stabilization policy, explaining a common covariation of the business cycle. The period of rising velocity, however, coincided with the Bretton Woods managed exchange rate system and "active" fiscal and monetary policy, which may have led to differences in the cyclical timing for the individual countries.

---

[21] See Jonung (1978b) for a comparison of the behavior of the currency–money ratio in the United States and Sweden during the depression of the 1930s.

Next, examining the full equation (2), according to our hypothesis we expect the influence of the separate institutional variables to differ between periods of falling and rising velocity – that monetization and the spread of commercial banking would dominate in the period of falling velocity, and financial development and economic stability in the period of rising velocity. In regression equation (2) we find limited evidence for this differential impact. The coefficient of $TNBFA/TFA$ goes from barely significant, at the 10% level, in the period of falling velocity to highly significant, at the 1% level, in the period of rising velocity.

The results in regression equations (3) and (4) lend further support to our prior expectations, because in the period of declining velocity, in regression equation (3) only $LNA/L$ and $C/M$ are significant, whereas in the period of rising velocity, only $s_{\hat{y}}$ is significant; in regression equation (4) in the period of falling velocity, $LNA/L$ is significant with the correct sign, and $TNBFA/TFA$ is significant but of the wrong sign. In the period of rising velocity both $TNBFA/TFA$ and $s_{\hat{y}}$ become significant and of the correct sign.

Finally, in Table C.2 we conduct Chow tests ($F$-tests) between the periods of falling and rising velocity. The $F$-values reject the null hypothesis of similarity between the coefficients in every case, which is consistent with our approach.

Table C.3 presents the results of $t$-tests between the coefficients of each independent variable for each of the four regression equations for the five countries. Panel A presents the results for periods of falling velocity, panel B for periods of rising velocity. Examining first the benchmark equation, we observe that the United States differs from the rest in both intercept and permanent income variables in the period of falling velocity but not in the period of rising velocity. Also, Sweden differs from the rest in the interest rate variable in the period of falling velocity, whereas Norway differs in the period of rising velocity. Finally, Norway differs from the rest in the cycle variable in both periods.

When institutional variables are introduced in Table C.3, we observe two phenomena. First, the differences observed between the United States and all other countries in per capita permanent income in the period of falling velocity virtually disappear. This result is consistent with our earlier findings that the permanent income variable is likely serving as a proxy for institutional factors, which exhibited more dramatic behavior in the United States than in other countries. This can be observed in a higher income elasticity of the demand for money in the benchmark equation for the United States than for other countries in the period of declining velocity.[22]

Second, considerable differences exist between countries in all of the institutional variables during the period of falling velocity, but virtually none in the period of rising velocity. This result suggests that the countries have converged in both growth rates and trends of economic and financial development. The results of regression equations (3) and (4) in general add support to the conclusions derived from regression equation (2). The institutional variables differed among countries more in the period of falling velocity than of rising velocity.[23]

### 4.3.3. A comparison of the gold standard and managed money periods

Table C.4 (Appendix C) presents pooled regressions of the four specifications of the velocity function for the pre–World War I gold standard period (panel A) and the subsequent period of managed money (panel B). As in the case of the full period, the pooled regressions generally perform better than the individual country regressions.

Comparing first the benchmark period between the two periods, we find all the coefficients to be significant and correctly signed, with the exception of the cycle variable, which is significantly less than one in the gold standard period. However, an important difference between the two periods is that the $\bar{R}^2$ is considerably lower in the period of managed money than under the gold standard. When we turn to the full equation (2), including the institutional variables, we observe a significant improvement in the regression in both periods. However, the increase in $\bar{R}^2$ is considerably greater in the period of managed money than in the gold standard period. Furthermore, in both periods all the variables are significant and of the correct sign

---

[22] We observe an income elasticity of 1.6 for the United States in the benchmark equation, whereas other countries range from .4 to .8 in this period. See Appendix A, Table A.1. Also see Friedman and Schwartz (1982), who found a similar difference between the United States and the United Kingdom. They also attributed the difference to financial sophistication, which they incorporated in their analysis by a technique different from ours.

[23] As mentioned in Section 4.3.1, one dramatic difference (seen in regression equations (2) through (4) in Table C.1) is the behavior of the currency–money ratio, which for the United States differs from all other countries in the period of falling velocity but not in the period of rising velocity. This result likely reflects the considerable difference in monetary experiences among the countries, in particular during the Great Depression of the 1930s. Bank failures in the United States led to a rise in $C/M$, reversing its generally downward trend. Such behavior did not occur to the same extent elsewhere. See Friedman and Schwartz (1963) and Jonung (1978b).

(with the exception of $s_{\hat{p}}$ in the gold standard period). Finally, in regression equations (3) and (4) we observe that in the period of the gold standard, only the cycle and *LNA/L* variables are significant, whereas in the period of managed money, all variables become significant except *TNBFA/TFA*.

In Chow tests of the gold standard and managed money periods, the *F*-values reject the null hypothesis of similarity between the coefficients in every case. We report these results in Table C.2.

Table C.5 presents the results of *t*-tests between the coefficients of each independent variable for each of the four equations for the five countries. Panel A presents the results for the gold standard period, panel B for the period of managed money. Examining first the benchmark equation, we observe considerable differences among many of the countries in all of the variables in the gold standard period but virtually none in the period of managed money.

When we introduce the institutional variables, we observe, as we did in the period of declining velocity, more uniformity in the influence of the benchmark independent variables on velocity, especially of permanent income across the countries in the gold standard period. With the principal exception of the currency–money ratio, which for the United States differed considerably from that of the other countries, the institutional variables have a similar influence on velocity in the different countries in the period of managed money in contrast to the experience of the gold standard. Similar conclusions can be drawn from regression equations (3) and (4) in Table C.5. We interpret these results as reflecting common movements in the institutional measures producing over time a similar behavior of velocity. This process occurred independent of the monetary standard.

### 4.3.4. Conclusions

Several conclusions emerge from the pooled time series regressions presented in this section. First, pooling the data for the five countries over the whole period 1880–1975 produces results similar to the individual country regressions reported in Section 4.2. The introduction of institutional variables adds considerably to the explanation of long-term velocity behavior and reduces the income elasticity of the demand for money.

Second, we provide some evidence distinguishing between the influence of different institutional variables in periods of falling compared to periods of rising velocity. Monetization and the spread of commercial banking predominate in periods of falling velocity, financial sophistication and growing economic stability in periods of rising velocity.

The introduction of institutional variables underscores similarities and differences in economic and financial developments among the five countries. When our period is decomposed into the earlier period of falling velocity and the subsequent period of rising velocity, greater similarities become evident in the latter period. This finding suggests that the institutional framework was converging over time in the five countries.

Third, our comparison of velocity behavior between the gold standard and the managed money periods reveals a growing similarity in the behavior of the institutional variables that seems to have operated independent of the monetary standard.

# APPENDIX A

Table A.1. *Institutional variables in the long-run velocity function: Five countries (Cochrane–Orcutt technique)*

| Eq. no. | Constant | $\log\left(\frac{Y}{PN}\right)^P$ | $i$ | log cycle | $\log\left(\frac{LNA}{L}\right)$ | $\log\left(\frac{C}{M}\right)$ | $\log\left(\frac{TNBFA}{TFA}\right)$ | $\log s_9$ | $\bar{R}^2$ | SEE | DW | $\rho$ |
|---|---|---|---|---|---|---|---|---|---|---|---|---|
| **A. Falling velocity** | | | | | | | | | | | | |
| *U.S., 1880–1945* | | | | | | | | | | | | |
| (1) | .831 | −.073 | 2.119 | .856 | | | | | .982 | .0427 | 1.703 | .952 |
| | (.84) | (.49) | (4.12)* | (9.07)* | | | | | | | | |
| (2) | .565 | .085 | 2.236 | .789 | −2.321 | −.039 | .210 | .009 | .984 | .0413 | 1.648 | .784 |
| | (−.45) | (.46) | (4.17)* | (7.28)* | (−3.92)* | (−.66) | (1.04) | (.44) | | | | |
| (3) | −.077 | | | .824 | −2.252 | −.036 | .093 | −.012 | .980 | .0468 | 1.798 | .792 |
| | (−.31) | | | (6.83)* | (−7.96)* | (−.53) | (.47) | (−.54) | | | | |
| (4) | .007 | | 2.275 | .797 | −2.075 | −.038 | .161 | .007 | .984 | .0410 | 1.656 | .780 |
| | (.03) | | (4.31)* | (7.51)* | (−8.50)* | (−.66) | (.95) | (.33) | | | | |
| *Canada, 1900–46* | | | | | | | | | | | | |
| (1) | −2.066 | .382 | 5.580 | .896 | | | | | .840 | .0547 | 1.655 | .933 |
| | (−1.29) | (1.71)# | (1.86)# | (5.42)* | | | | | | | | |
| (2) | −4.922 | .751 | 8.201 | .874 | −3.641 | .173 | .598 | .007 | .915 | .0400 | 1.727 | .445 |
| | (−3.62)* | (4.44)* | (5.55)* | (6.82)* | (−7.30)* | (2.226)* | (5.92)* | (.33) | | | | |
| (3) | 1.211 | | | .696 | −3.313 | .489 | .485 | −.011 | .887 | .0460 | 1.409 | .867 |
| | (3.81)* | | | (4.70)* | (−4.36)* | (4.34) | (3.03)* | (−.77) | | | | |
| (4) | 1.285 | | 6.221 | .791 | −2.150 | .432 | .554 | −.012 | .955 | .0448 | 1.551 | .748 |
| | (5.07)* | | (2.81)* | (5.27)* | (−4.79)* | (4.18)* | (3.66)* | (−.71) | | | | |
| *UK, 1876–1946* | | | | | | | | | | | | |
| (1) | −3.479 | .533 | 2.760 | .597 | | | | | .878 | .0452 | 2.214 | .989 |
| | (−1.73) | (1.84)# | (4.54)* | (3.03)* | | | | | | | | |

|  | | | | | | | | | | | |
|---|---|---|---|---|---|---|---|---|---|---|---|
| (2) | .050 (.03) | .075 (.29) | 2.810 (4.42)* | .887 (4.38)* | −16.82 (−2.39)* | .106 (.87) | 1.812 (1.79)* | −.032 (−1.49) | .891 | .0450 | 1.941 | .902 |
| (3) | .748 (1.58) | | | .874 (3.98)* | −16.95 (−2.14)* | .235 (1.83)* | 1.766 (1.56) | −.038 (−1.61) | .846 | .0508 | 1.784 | .915 |
| (4) | .565 (1.41) | | 2.817 (4.47)* | .902 (4.66)* | −16.60 (−2.39)* | .117 (1.02) | 1.848 (1.86)* | −.031 (−1.47) | .881 | .0447 | 1.933 | .902 |

*Sweden, 1880–1922*

|  | | | | | | | | | | | |
|---|---|---|---|---|---|---|---|---|---|---|---|
| (1) | −1.410 (−.49) | .347 (.79) | −8.256 (−1.02) | 1.179 (6.06)* | | | | | .975 | .0436 | .939 | .960 |
| (2) | −5.501 (−1.21) | .777 (1.36) | 1.597 (.18) | 1.122 (5.67)* | −2.697 (−2.32)* | .375 (2.67)* | −.435 (−.71) | .031 (1.22) | .983 | .0362 | 1.397 | .839 |
| (3) | .758 (1.23) | | | 1.304 (9.26)* | −1.124 (−3.70)* | .445 (3.48)* | −.563 (−1.11) | .036 (1.49) | .983 | .0362 | 1.288 | .847 |
| (4) | .545 (.56) | | 2.755 (.31) | 1.309 (9.12)* | −1.188 (−3.47)* | .451 (3.46)* | −.638 (−1.06) | .034 (1.33) | .982 | .0366 | 1.318 | .840 |

*Norway, 1880–1922*

|  | | | | | | | | | | | |
|---|---|---|---|---|---|---|---|---|---|---|---|
| (1) | −13.167 (−2.23)* | 1.456 (2.11)* | 6.758 (3.23)* | 1.265 (4.33)* | | | | | .964 | .0510 | 1.381 | .979 |
| (2) | −32.285 (−4.72)* | 2.853 (4.45)* | 7.385 (4.79)* | .863 (3.83)* | .469 (.93) | .310 (2.56)* | −6.597 (−5.84)* | −.018 (−1.03) | .983 | .0354 | 1.814 | .908 |
| (3) | .168 (.20) | | | 1.673 (5.56)* | .220 (.48) | .533 (3.36)* | −1.161 (−3.52)* | −.023 (−1.02) | .962 | .0529 | 1.492 | .651 |
| (4) | −1.461 (−1.81)# | | 8.274 (4.24)* | 1.375 (5.46)* | −.044 (−.09) | .402 (2.84)* | −1.597 (−4.71)* | −.043 (−2.02)* | .974 | .0437 | 1.623 | .741 |

Table A.1. (*cont.*)

| Eq. no. | Constant | $\log\left(\frac{Y}{PN}\right)^P$ | $i$ | log cycle | $\log\left(\frac{LNA}{L}\right)$ | $\log\left(\frac{C}{M}\right)$ | $\log\left(\frac{TNBFA}{TFA}\right)$ | $\log s_y$ | $\bar{R}^2$ | SEE | DW | $\rho$ |
|---|---|---|---|---|---|---|---|---|---|---|---|---|
| **B. Rising velocity** | | | | | | | | | | | | |
| *U.S., 1946–72* | | | | | | | | | | | | |
| (1) | −.718 (1.17) | .170 (1.95)# | 1.487 (3.19)* | .726 (4.45)* | | | | | .972 | .0184 | 2.013 | .760 |
| (2) | −.969 (−.68) | .498 (2.07)# | .612 (1.13) | .794 (4.07)* | .766 (.56) | .749 (2.92)* | .814 (2.93)* | .003 (.12) | .976 | .0171 | 1.647 | .604 |
| (3) | 2.059 (3.63)* | | | .525 (3.20)* | 3.836 (4.04)* | .554 (2.62)* | .276 (1.13) | −.018 (−.62) | .968 | .0196 | 1.867 | .674 |
| (4) | 1.507 (2.65)* | | 1.112 (2.18)* | .563 (3.70)* | 2.513 (2.39)* | .351 (1.66) | .219 (.87) | −.007 (−.27) | .973 | .0180 | 1.783 | .719 |
| *Canada, 1947–75* | | | | | | | | | | | | |
| (1) | 2.348 (1.29) | −.180 (−.72) | 4.277 (1.91)# | 1.352 (2.84)* | | | | | .855 | .0446 | 2.195 | .731 |
| (2) | 1.435 (.63) | .205 (.70) | 1.675 (1.43) | 1.153 (4.97)* | .258 (.19) | .805 (9.49)* | .315 (2.50)* | .029 (1.43) | .973 | .0195 | 2.564 | .625 |
| (3) | 3.468 (17.73)* | | | 1.345 (5.35)* | 2.503 (8.76)* | .869 (9.31)* | .236 (3.13)* | .039 (1.92)# | .968 | .0210 | 2.558 | .384 |
| (4) | 3.012 (14.22)* | | 2.316 (2.71)* | 1.75 (5.34)* | 1.078 (2.04)# | .807 (9.70)* | .244 (2.75)* | .027 (1.35) | .973 | .0192 | 2.526 | .636 |
| *UK, 1947–74* | | | | | | | | | | | | |
| (1) | 3.217 (1.24) | −.381 (−.95) | .090 (.12) | −.710 (−1.15) | | | | | .951 | .0438 | 1.697 | .876 |

| | | | | | | | | | | | | | |
|---|---|---|---|---|---|---|---|---|---|---|---|---|---|
| (2) | -.573 | .465 | .094 | .437 | 5.252 | .784 | .267 | .012 | .992 | .0182 | 2.496 | .305 |
| | (-.34) | (1.90)# | (.15) | (1.41) | (1.30) | (6.22)* | (1.35) | (.98) | | | | |
| (3) | 2.703 | | | .444 | 12.892 | .778 | .206 | .010 | .991 | .0188 | 2.784 | .236 |
| | (21.24)* | | | (1.48) | (18.85)* | (9.65)* | (1.84)# | (.84) | | | | |
| (4) | 2.571 | | .367 | .424 | 11.717 | .720 | .307 | .007 | .991 | .0192 | 2.809 | .229 |
| | (9.58)* | | (.56) | (1.37) | (5.32)* | (5.46)* | (1.44) | (.53) | | | | |

*Sweden, 1923–74*

| | | | | | | | | | | | | | |
|---|---|---|---|---|---|---|---|---|---|---|---|---|---|
| (1) | -.777 | .256 | -2.941 | .619 | | | | | .902 | .0463 | 1.238 | .576 |
| | (-3.04)* | (7.32)* | (-1.96)* | (2.50)* | | | | | | | | |
| (2) | -4.186 | .716 | 5.747 | .518 | -2.764 | .524 | .481 | .018 | .939 | .0366 | 1.330 | .618 |
| | (-1.96)* | (2.76)* | (1.95)# | (2.58)* | (-2.81)* | (4.21)* | (1.19) | (1.14) | | | | |
| (3) | 1.839 | | | .751 | .036 | .146 | .800 | .032 | .917 | .0427 | 1.160 | .698 |
| | (9.46)* | | | (3.29)* | (.10) | (1.80)# | (1.62) | (1.76)# | | | | |
| (4) | 1.739 | | 9.262 | .676 | -.401 | .492 | .576 | .023 | .931 | .0389 | 1.215 | .703 |
| | (9.59)* | | (3.20)* | (3.23)* | (1.08) | (3.76)* | (1.26) | (1.38) | | | | |

*Norway, 1923–74*

| | | | | | | | | | | | | | |
|---|---|---|---|---|---|---|---|---|---|---|---|---|---|
| (1) | -2.044 | .293 | 1.693 | 1.211 | | | | | .949 | .0574 | 1.385 | .843 |
| | (-1.98)* | (2.63)* | (1.09) | (2.44)* | | | | | | | | |
| (2) | 4.815 | -.289 | 2.153 | 1.251 | 1.451 | .386 | .441 | -.008 | .964 | .0485 | 1.190 | .458 |
| | (1.19) | (-.77) | (1.27) | (2.51)* | (1.09) | (3.35)* | (3.53)* | (-.35) | | | | |
| (3) | 1.722 | | | 1.076 | .552 | .268 | .432 | -.015 | .964 | .0484 | 1.114 | .531 |
| | (8.65)* | | | (2.27)* | (2.03)# | (4.41)* | (3.45)* | (-.67) | | | | |
| (4) | 1.701 | | 1.971 | 1.188 | .431 | .320 | .409 | -.010 | .964 | .0481 | 1.154 | .517 |
| | (8.66)* | | (1.19) | (2.46)* | (1.50) | (4.30)* | (3.29)* | (-.43) | | | | |

*Statistically significant at the 5% level.
#Statistically significant at the 10% level.

Table A.2. *Chow tests (F-tests) for the equality of coefficients between periods of falling and rising velocity*

| Eq. no. | F-value | Eq. no. | F-value |
|---------|---------|---------|---------|
| *U.S.* | | *Sweden* | |
| (1) | .39 | (1) | 3.01* |
| | (4.83) | | (4.85) |
| (2) | 1.73 | (2) | 3.29 |
| | (8.75) | | (8.77) |
| (3) | 6.69* | (3) | 50.5* |
| | (6.79) | | (6.81) |
| (4) | 5.59* | (4) | 35.31* |
| | (7.77) | | (7.79) |
| | | | |
| *Canada* | | *Norway* | |
| (1) | 1.05 | (1) | 3.19* |
| | (4.66) | | (4.73) |
| (2) | 5.89* | (2) | 5.37 |
| | (6.79) | | (8.65) |
| (3) | 37.68* | (3) | 17.64* |
| | (6.62) | | (6.69) |
| (4) | 23.98* | (4) | 20.19* |
| | (7.60) | | (7.57) |
| | | | |
| *UK* | | | |
| (1) | 5.46* | | |
| | (4.89) | | |
| (2) | 3.39 | | |
| | (8.81) | | |
| (3) | 28.41* | | |
| | (6.85) | | |
| (4) | 10.88* | | |
| | (7.83) | | |

*Note:* Degrees of freedom in parentheses.
*Statistically significant at the 5% level.

# APPENDIX B

Table B.1. *Institutional variables in the long-run velocity function: Five countries (including government's share in national income as an independent variable) (Cochrane–Orcutt technique)*

| Eq. no. | Constant | $\log\left(\frac{Y}{PN}\right)^{P}$ | $i$ | log cycle | $\log\left(\frac{LNA}{L}\right)$ | $\log\left(\frac{C}{M}\right)$ | $\log\left(\frac{TNBFA}{TFA}\right)$ | log $TG^{a}$ | $\bar{R}^2$ | SEE | DW | $\rho$ |
|---|---|---|---|---|---|---|---|---|---|---|---|---|
| | | | | Coefficients of independent variables (*t*-values in parentheses) | | | | | | | | |
| *U.S., 1880–1972* | | | | | | | | | | | | |
| (2) | -.937 | .204 | 2.087 | .792 | -1.897 | -.033 | .489 | .004 | .984 | .0380 | 1.764 | .903 |
| | (.91) | (1.37) | (4.93)* | (8.78)* | (-3.06)* | (-.52) | (.257)* | (.24) | | | | |
| (3) | .739 | | | .846 | -.161 | -.002 | .334 | .002 | .980 | .0435 | 1.827 | .952 |
| | (3.17)* | | | (8.38)* | (-.24) | (-.02) | (1.57) | (.12) | | | | |
| (4) | .490 | | 2.195 | .802 | -.927 | -.053 | .374 | .006 | .985 | .0380 | 1.790 | .926 |
| | (2.57)* | | (5.43)* | (8.95)* | (-2.15)* | (-.84) | (2.04)* | (.41) | | | | |
| *Canada, 1900–75* | | | | | | | | | | | | |
| (2) | -2.196 | .529 | 3.414 | .675 | 2.327 | .478 | .584 | -.037 | .928 | .0416 | 1.427 | .874 |
| | (-1.31) | (2.54)* | (2.66)* | (5.04)* | (-3.10)* | (4.90)* | (4.81)* | (-1.33) | | | | |
| (3) | 2.487 | | | .737 | -.090 | .555 | .497 | -.027 | .911 | .0461 | 1.326 | .950 |
| | (9.95)* | | | (5.30)* | (-.13) | (5.38)* | (3.94)* | (-.90) | | | | |
| (4) | 2.031 | | 4.712 | .764 | -.634 | .538 | .493 | -.038 | .922 | .0433 | 1.372 | .866 |
| | (9.34)* | | (3.85)* | (5.70)* | (-1.85)# | (5.47)* | (4.10)* | (1.34) | | | | |
| *UK, 1876–1974* | | | | | | | | | | | | |
| (2) | -1.045 | .339 | 2.299 | .779 | -6.424 | .240 | .879 | -.041 | .931 | .0434 | 2.002 | .931 |
| | (-.68) | (1.53) | (4.53)* | (-4.33)* | (-2.19)* | (2.40)* | (3.83)* | (-1.85)# | | | | |
| (3) | 1.653 | | | .798 | 1.861 | .404 | .347 | -.029 | .913 | .0485 | 1.804 | .960 |
| | (5.70)* | | | (4.04)* | (.56) | (3.81)* | (1.53) | (-1.31) | | | | |
| (4) | 1.366 | | 2.382 | .806 | -2.556 | .260 | .895 | -.025 | .921 | .0437 | 2.054 | .955 |
| | (5.27)* | | (4.77)* | (4.53)* | (-.88) | (2.60)* | (3.81)* | (1.22) | | | | |

*Sweden, 1880–1974*

| | | | | | | | | | | | | |
|---|---|---|---|---|---|---|---|---|---|---|---|---|
| (2) | -5.128 | .811 | 5.451 | .479 | -2.382 | .560 | .654 | -.295 | .976 | .0339 | 1.327 | .760 |
| | (-4.75)* | (6.29)* | (2.43)* | (3.08)* | (-7.56)* | (7.28)* | (3.35)* | (-4.68)* | | | | |
| (3) | 1.987 | | | .696 | .324 | .554 | .608 | -.281 | .962 | .0380 | 1.233 | .963 |
| | (9.73)* | | | (4.48)* | (.72) | (6.99)* | (1.81)# | (-4.09)* | | | | |
| (4) | 1.743 | | 5.647 | .668 | .078 | .611 | .570 | -.292 | .971 | .0374 | 1.282 | .955 |
| | (7.81)* | | (2.05)* | (4.34)* | (.19) | (7.33)* | (1.73)# | (-4.29)* | | | | |

*Norway, 1880–1974*

| | | | | | | | | | | | | |
|---|---|---|---|---|---|---|---|---|---|---|---|---|
| (2) | -5.392 | .646 | 2.503 | .627 | -.222 | .378 | .059 | -.509 | .976 | .0409 | 1.737 | .953 |
| | (-2.60)* | (3.35)* | (2.57)* | (2.83)* | (-.50) | (4.45)* | (.40) | (-6.52)* | | | | |
| (3) | 1.625 | | | .923 | .815 | .522 | .261 | -.429 | .971 | .0450 | 1.699 | .961 |
| | (5.24)* | | | (4.19)* | (2.19)* | (6.76)* | (1.60) | (-5.71)* | | | | |
| (4) | 1.473 | | 2.516 | .941 | .744 | .537 | .177 | -.388 | .973 | .0436 | 1.807 | .959 |
| | (4.87)* | | (2.43)* | (4.41)* | (2.06)* | (7.17)* | (1.10) | (-5.21)* | | | | |

*Statistically significant at the 5% level.
#Statistically significant at the 10% level.
aTG stands for log (total government expenditure less interest payments/national income).

Table B.2. Institutional variables in the long-run velocity function: Three countries (including government's share in national income less defense expenditures) (Cochrane–Orcutt technique)

| Eq. no. | Constant | $\log\left(\frac{Y}{PN}\right)^P$ | $i$ | log cycle | $\log\left(\frac{LNA}{L}\right)$ | $\log\left(\frac{C}{M}\right)$ | $\log\left(\frac{TNBFA}{TFA}\right)$ | log TGDEF[a] | $\bar{R}^2$ | SEE | DW | $\rho$ |
|---|---|---|---|---|---|---|---|---|---|---|---|---|
| | | | | Coefficients of independent variables (t-values in parentheses) | | | | | | | | |
| **U.S., 1880–1972** | | | | | | | | | | | | |
| (2) | −1.008 | .214 | 2.074 | .808 | −1.955 | −.036 | .472 | .012 | .985 | .0379 | 1.788 | .903 |
| | (−.99) | (1.47) | (4.93)* | (8.90)* | (−3.15)* | (−.58) | (2.48)* | (.70) | | | | |
| (3) | .756 | | | .867 | .053 | −.007 | .313 | .012 | .980 | .0433 | 1.856 | .957 |
| | (3.18)* | | | (8.55)* | (.07) | (−.10) | (1.48) | (.65) | | | | |
| (4) | .493 | | 2.183 | .811 | −.906 | −.053 | .347 | .011 | .985 | .0380 | 1.795 | .927 |
| | (2.58)* | | (5.42)* | (8.96)* | (−2.18)* | (−.85) | (1.90)# | (.65) | | | | |
| **Canada, 1900–75** | | | | | | | | | | | | |
| (2) | −2.366 | .543 | 3.299 | .704 | −2.381 | .420 | .584 | −.009 | .926 | .0421 | 1.412 | .887 |
| | (−1.37) | (2.54)* | (2.51)* | (5.20)* | (−3.04)* | (4.89)* | (4.73)* | (−.39) | | | | |
| (3) | 2.461 | | | .771 | −.026 | .509 | .496 | −.00005 | .959 | .0464 | 1.323 | .955 |
| | (9.64)* | | | (5.55)* | (−.03) | (5.67)* | (3.91)* | (−.002) | | | | |
| (4) | 1.992 | | 4.486 | .803 | −.630 | .477 | .487 | −.005 | .920 | .0438 | 1.349 | .889 |
| | (8.81)* | | (3.52)* | (5.96)* | (−1.61) | (5.53)* | (3.99)* | (−.18) | | | | |
| **UK, 1876–1974** | | | | | | | | | | | | |
| (2) | .206 | .158 | 2.408 | .584 | −.788 | .180 | .956 | −.075 | .936 | .0418 | 2.280 | .969 |
| | (.14) | (.73) | (5.01)* | (3.28)* | (−.24) | (1.85)# | (4.20)* | (−3.05)* | | | | |
| (3) | 1.497 | | | .618 | 3.240 | .345 | .345 | −.073 | .918 | .0472 | 1.973 | .962 |
| | (5.23)* | | | (3.19)* | (.99) | (3.39)* | (1.57) | (−2.66)* | | | | |
| (4) | 1.222 | | 2.463 | .623 | −.741 | .197 | .921 | −.078 | .936 | .0417 | 2.239 | .960 |
| | (4.74)* | | (5.17)* | (3.63)* | (−.25) | (2.08)* | (4.11)* | (−3.19)* | | | | |

*Statistically significant at the 5% level.    #Statistically significant at the 10% level.

[a]TGDEF stands for log (total government expenditure less interest payments/national income).

Table B.3. *Institutional variables in the long-run velocity function: Five countries (including government's share in national income, excluding war years) (Cochrane–Orcutt technique)*

| Eq. no. | Constant | $\log\left(\frac{Y}{PN}\right)^{\mathrm{P}}$ | $i$ | log cycle | $\log\left(\frac{LNA}{L}\right)$ | $\log\left(\frac{C}{M}\right)$ | $\log\left(\frac{TNBFA}{TFA}\right)$ | log TG | $\bar{R}^2$ | SEE | DW | $\rho$ |
|---|---|---|---|---|---|---|---|---|---|---|---|---|
| | | | | | Coefficients of independent variables (*t*-values in parentheses) | | | | | | | |
| *U.S., 1880–1913, 1919–38, 1946–72* | | | | | | | | | | | | |
| (2) | -2.567 | .488 | 1.119 | .875 | -2.094 | .243 | .288 | -.058 | .989 | .0305 | 1.713 | .808 |
| | (-3.23)* | (4.26)* | (2.83)* | (9.73)* | (-4.88)* | (3.79)* | (1.36) | (-2.75)* | | | | |
| (3) | .867 | | | .940 | .625 | .206 | -.218 | -.058 | .986 | .0350 | 1.650 | 9.22 |
| | (4.29)* | | | (9.01)* | (1.12) | (2.65)* | (-.76) | (-2.93)* | | | | |
| (4) | .637 | | 1.544 | .870 | -.021 | .112 | -.065 | -.040 | .988 | .0318 | 1.711 | .909 |
| | (3.44)* | | (4.08)* | (9.00)* | (-.05) | (1.50) | (-.24) | (-2.13)* | | | | |
| *Canada, 1900–13, 1919–38, 1946–75* | | | | | | | | | | | | |
| (2) | -3.618 | .766 | .482 | .551 | -2.786 | .578 | .595 | -.026 | .947 | .0349 | 1.756 | .798 |
| | (-2.36)* | (3.94)* | (.37) | (4.04)* | (-4.22)* | (6.38)* | (4.15)* | (-.73) | | | | |
| (3) | 2.717 | | | .652 | -.076 | .699 | .398 | -.034 | .924 | .0419 | 1.489 | .852 |
| | (10.79)* | | | (4.32)* | (-.22) | (6.22)* | (2.58)* | (-.84) | | | | |
| (4) | 2.317 | | 3.935 | .731 | -.417 | .650 | .347 | -.023 | .933 | .0393 | 1.435 | .769 |
| | (10.36)* | | (3.60)* | (5.00)* | (-1.49) | (6.82)* | (2.42)* | (-.58) | | | | |
| *UK, 1876–1913, 1919–38, 1946–74* | | | | | | | | | | | | |
| (2) | -4.44 | .829 | 1.493 | .370 | -9.148 | .243 | .746 | -.120 | .946 | .0368 | 2.290 | .843 |
| | (-3.17)* | (4.14)* | (2.92)* | (1.77)# | (-3.63)* | (2.62)* | (3.72)* | (-2.54)* | | | | |
| (3) | 1.722 | | | .575 | 1.906 | .528 | .150 | -.068 | .927 | .0428 | 1.803 | .909 |
| | (7.66)* | | | (2.53)* | (.94) | (5.16)* | (.78) | (-1.51) | | | | |
| (4) | 1.392 | | 1.926 | .616 | -2.540 | .345 | .638 | -.031 | .936 | .0398 | 2.059 | .897 |
| | (6.32)* | | (3.61)* | (2.89)* | (-1.15) | (3.25)* | (2.85)* | (-.70) | | | | |

Table B.3. (cont.)

Coefficients of independent variables ($t$-values in parentheses)

| Eq. no. | Constant | $\log\left(\frac{Y}{PN}\right)^P$ | $i$ | log cycle | $\log\left(\frac{LNA}{L}\right)$ | $\log\left(\frac{C}{M}\right)$ | $\log\left(\frac{TNBFA}{TFA}\right)$ | $\log TG$ | $\bar{R}^2$ | SEE | DW | $\rho$ |
|---|---|---|---|---|---|---|---|---|---|---|---|---|
| *Sweden, 1880–1913, 1919–38, 1946–74* | | | | | | | | | | | | |
| (2) | -5.205 | .812 | 4.415 | .283 | -1.973 | .567 | .667 | -.473 | | | | |
| | (-4.34)* | (5.75)* | (1.93)# | (1.90)# | (-5.29)* | (7.15)* | (3.05)* | (-6.78)* | .986 | .0273 | 1.405 | .868 |
| (3) | 2.012 | | | .455 | .903 | .566 | .684 | -.482 | | | | |
| | (10.26)* | | | (3.05)* | (2.37)* | (6.58)* | (2.33)* | (-6.31)* | .982 | .0303 | 1.155 | .962 |
| (4) | 1.769 | | 5.056 | .392 | .618 | .609 | .712 | -.502 | | | | |
| | (7.84)* | | (1.94)# | (2.60)* | (1.59) | (6.98)* | (2.48)* | (-6.61)* | .983 | .0297 | 1.243 | .961 |
| *Norway, 1880–1913, 1919–38, 1946–74* | | | | | | | | | | | | |
| (2) | -4.907 | .606 | 2.642 | .475 | -.103 | .453 | .073 | -.568 | | | | |
| | (-1.78)# | (2.31) | (1.70)# | (1.66) | (-.23) | (3.93)* | (.24) | (-4.68)* | .976 | .0415 | 1.682 | .952 |
| (3) | 2.466 | | | .588 | .632 | .511 | .261 | -.607 | | | | |
| | (.87) | | | (2.13)* | (1.61) | (4.444)* | (.77) | (-4.97)* | .972 | .0446 | 1.464 | .998 |
| (4) | 1.401 | | 4.047 | .771 | .459 | .493 | .475 | -.444 | | | | |
| | (4.10)* | | (2.81)* | (2.95) | (1.16) | (4.24)* | (1.70)# | (-4.01)* | .975 | .0423 | 1.734 | .962 |

*Statistically significant at the 5% level.
#Statistically significant at the 10% level.

# APPENDIX C

Table C.1. *Results of pooled regressions (Cochrane–Orcutt technique)*

|  | | Coefficients of independent variables (t-values in parentheses) | | | | | | | | | | |
|---|---|---|---|---|---|---|---|---|---|---|---|---|
| Eq. no. | Constant | $\log\left(\frac{Y}{PN}\right)^{\mathrm{p}}$ | $i$ | log cycle | $\log\left(\frac{LNA}{L}\right)$ | $\log\left(\frac{C}{M}\right)$ | $\log\left(\frac{TNBFA}{TFA}\right)$ | $\log s_{\dot{y}}$ | $\bar{R}^2$ | SEE | DW | $\rho$ |
| **A. Falling velocity** | | | | | | | | | | | | |
| (1) | −.014 | .102 | 3.724 | 1.040 | | | | | .707 | .056 | 1.376 | .308 |
|  | (−3.239)* | (15.386)* | (7.784)* | (13.265)* | | | | | | | | |
| (2) | −.006 | .124 | 3.137 | 1.040 | −1.207 | .202 | .198 | −.007 | .770 | .051 | 1.465 | .253 |
|  | (−1.306) | (5.673)* | (7.027)* | (14.335)* | (−7.127)* | (4.736)* | (1.680)† | (−.807) | | | | |
| (3) | .001 | | | 1.013 | −1.130 | .192 | .092 | −.006 | .440 | .053 | 1.583 | .184 |
|  | (.330) | | | (13.832)* | (−3.279)* | (4.100)* | (.719) | (−.440) | | | | |
| (4) | −.002 | | 3.156 | .990 | −1.268 | .038 | −.227 | −.015 | .754 | .053 | 1.434 | .268 |
|  | (−.422) | | (6.679)* | (13.002)* | (−7.178)* | (1.163) | (−2.382)# | (−1.619) | | | | |
| **B. Rising velocity** | | | | | | | | | | | | |
| (1) | −.038 | .143 | 1.456 | .081 | | | | | .781 | .064 | 1.488 | .256 |
|  | (−4.168)* | (16.513)* | (2.414)# | (.407) | | | | | | | | |
| (2) | .019 | .227 | 2.017 | .617 | −.950 | .448 | .489 | −.001 | .906 | .039 | 1.279 | .359 |
|  | (2.526)* | (21.532)* | (5.415)* | (4.509)* | (−9.045)* | (15.692)* | (8.476)* | (−1.059) | | | | |
| (3) | .081 | | | −.178 | −.196 | .045 | .123 | −.130 | .408 | .080 | 1.096 | .448 |
|  | (6.327)* | | | (−.711) | (−.858) | (.882) | (1.129) | (−8.735)* | | | | |
| (4) | .073 | | 2.416 | −.401 | −.503 | .094 | .279 | −.143 | .495 | .084 | 1.099 | .449 |
|  | (5.233)* | | (2.754)* | (−1.517) | (−2.095)# | (1.529) | (2.515)* | (−9.451)* | | | | |

*Falling velocity*: U.S., 1880–1945; Canada, 1900–46; UK, 1876–1946; Sweden, 1880–1922; Norway, 1880–1922.
*Rising velocity*: U.S., 1946–72; Canada, 1947–75; UK, 1947–74; Sweden, 1923–74; Norway, 1923–74.
*Statistically significant at the 1% level.
†Statistically significant at the 10% level.
#Statistically significant at the 5% level.

Table C.2. *Chow tests (F-tests) for the equality of coefficients between falling vs. rising velocity and gold standard vs. managed money periods*

| Eq. no. | Falling vs. rising velocity | Gold standard vs. managed money |
|---------|-----------------------------|----------------------------------|
| (1)     | 13.58*                      | 2.71*                            |
|         | (4.434)                     | (4.434)                          |
| (2)     | 8.15*                       | 8.17*                            |
|         | (8.420)                     | (8.420)                          |
| (3)     | 40.12*                      | 8.82*                            |
|         | (6.424)                     | (6.424)                          |
| (4)     | 28.07*                      | 11.12*                           |
|         | (7.422)                     | (7.422)                          |

*Note:* Degrees of freedom in parentheses.
*Statistically significant at the 5% level.

Table C.3. t-Tests for intercept and independent-variable dummies: All combinations of five countries (Cochrane–Orcutt technique)

| Eq. no. by country / Indepen. var. by country | Constant | | | | $\log(Y/PN)^p$ | | | | i | | | | log cycle | | | |
|---|---|---|---|---|---|---|---|---|---|---|---|---|---|---|---|---|
| | U.S. | Canada | UK | Sweden | U.S. | Canada | UK | Sweden | U.S. | Canada | UK | Sweden | U.S. | Canada | UK | Sweden |
| **A. Falling velocity** | | | | | | | | | | | | | | | | |
| **(1)** | | | | | | | | | | | | | | | | |
| Norway | 7.97* | -1.21 | -.49 | -.77 | -3.75* | 2.19# | .93 | 1.74† | -2.0# | -.49 | -1.91* | -2.67* | -2.56# | -2.65* | -2.74* | -1.29 |
| U.S. | | 8.57* | 7.52* | 7.71* | | -4.91* | -4.04* | -4.15* | | -.96 | -.17 | 2.30# | | .37 | .78 | -1.36 |
| Canada | | | -.45 | -.18 | | | 1.25 | .24 | | | .89 | 2.48# | | | .45 | -1.53 |
| UK | | | | .23 | | | | -.91 | | | | 2.31# | | | | -1.73† |
| **(2)** | | | | | | | | | | | | | | | | |
| Norway | 1.15 | 1.90† | 1.59 | 1.57 | | | | | | | | | -3.12* | -3.64* | -3.20* | -1.51 |
| U.S. | | -2.34# | -1.46 | -1.26 | | | | | | | | | | 1.05 | .75 | -1.81† |
| Canada | | | 1.74† | 1.36 | | | | | | | | | | | -.10 | -2.51# |
| UK | | | | .04 | | | | | | | | | | | | -2.07# |
| **(3)** | | | | | | | | | | | | | | | | |
| Norway | 1.43 | 2.41# | 2.40# | 1.84† | | | | | -2.98* | -1.40 | -2.69* | -.71 | -2.38* | -2.44* | -1.70† | -.41 |
| U.S. | | -.67 | -.81 | -.02 | | | | | | -.34 | -.61 | .17 | | .28 | -.47 | -2.52# |
| Canada | | | -.38 | 1.49 | | | | | | | .16 | .26 | | | -.65 | -2.54# |
| UK | | | | 1.24 | | | | | | | | .22 | | | | -1.58 |
| **(4)** | | | | | | | | | | | | | | | | |
| Norway | -1.61 | -1.80† | -.76 | .80 | .40 | 3.90* | 1.63 | 1.84† | -2.96* | -1.61 | -2.63* | -1.54 | -2.45# | 3.35# | -1.83† | -.63 |
| U.S. | | .58 | .37 | -.22 | | -3.47* | -1.20 | -1.46 | | -.20 | -.78 | 1.02 | | 1.55 | -.39 | -2.30# |
| Canada | | | -.31 | -2.94* | | | 2.30# | 1.86† | | | -.03 | 1.04 | | | -1.57 | -3.37* |
| UK | | | | -1.19 | | | | -.34 | | | | 1.08 | | | | -1.48 |

B. Rising velocity

| | | | | | | | | | | | | | | | | |
|---|---|---|---|---|---|---|---|---|---|---|---|---|---|---|---|---|
| **(1)** | | | | | | | | | | | | | | | | |
| Norway | .39 | -.18 | 1.17 | 1.24 | -.28 | .35 | -.93 | -.50 | -2.52* | -2.08# | -3.72* | 1.48 | 1.22 | 1.85† | -.80 | 1.65 |
| U.S. | | .35 | -.49 | -.14 | | -.45 | .38 | -.04 | | .32 | .98 | .27 | | -.71 | 1.59 | -.06 |
| Canada | | | -.67 | -.47 | | | 1.02 | .67 | | | .24 | .05 | | | 2.05# | .78 |
| UK | | | | .55 | | | | -.60 | | | | -.09 | | | | -1.80† |
| **(2)** | | | | | | | | | | | | | | | | |
| Norway | -.17 | | -4.16* | -2.93* | | | | | | | | | -1.15 | -.13 | -1.19 | -.72 |
| U.S. | | -9.72* | 1.74† | .93 | | | | | | | | | | -1.00 | .42 | -.68 |
| Canada | | | -4.07* | -9.00* | | | | | | | | | | | 1.09 | .55 |
| UK | | | | -1.93† | | | | | | | | | | | | -.85 |
| **(3)** | | | | | | | | | | | | | | | | |
| Norway | -1.35 | .83 | -6.73* | -2.63* | | | | | .49 | -.17 | -.95 | 2.47# | -1.29 | -.34 | -1.30 | -1.25 |
| U.S. | | -8.94* | .60 | -.59 | | | | | | -.24 | .50 | -2.81* | | -.90 | .40 | -.27 |
| Canada | | | -1.16 | -7.46* | | | | | | | .62 | -2.46# | | | 1.03 | .80 |
| UK | | | | -4.81* | | | | | | | | -3.09* | | | | -.60 |
| **(4)** | | | | | | | | | | | | | | | | |
| Norway | -.17 | | -.04 | .40 | -.02 | -.32 | .39 | -1.00 | -.36 | -.003 | -.74 | 2.48# | -.65 | -.22 | -.94 | -.85 |
| U.S. | | -.21 | -.12 | -.91 | | .19 | -.21 | .37 | | -.28 | .42 | -2.76* | | -.44 | .47 | .03 |
| Canada | | | -.005 | -1.00 | | | -.54 | .21 | | | .57 | -2.28# | | | .79 | .59 |
| UK | | | | -.44 | | | | 1.14 | | | | -2.98* | | | | -.50 |

*Falling velocity*: U.S., 1880–1945; Canada, 1900–46; UK, 1876–1946; Sweden, 1880–1922; Norway, 1880–1922.

*Rising velocity*: U.S., 1946–72; Canada, 1947–75; UK, 1947–74; Norway, 1923–74.

*Statistically significant at the 1% level.

#Statistically significant at the 5% level.

†Statistically significant at the 10% level.

Table C.3. (cont.)

| Indepen. var. by country / Eq. no. by country | log(LNA/L) | | | | log(C/M) | | | | log(TNBFA/TFA) | | | | log $s_9$ | | | |
|---|---|---|---|---|---|---|---|---|---|---|---|---|---|---|---|---|
| | U.S. | Canada | UK | Sweden | U.S. | Canada | UK | Sweden | U.S. | Canada | UK | Sweden | U.S. | Canada | UK | Sweden |
| A. Falling velocity | | | | | | | | | | | | | | | | |
| (1) | | | | | | | | | | | | | | | | |
| Norway | | | | | | | | | | | | | | | | |
| U.S. | | | | | | | | | | | | | | | | |
| Canada | | | | | | | | | | | | | | | | |
| UK | | | | | | | | | | | | | | | | |
| (2) | | | | | | | | | | | | | | | | |
| Norway | -.12 | -2.61* | -.90 | -.29 | -2.66* | -.50 | -1.07 | -.38 | 2.29* | 2.34# | 2.93* | 1.76† | -.41 | .02 | -.94 | .84 |
| U.S. | | 1.62 | .81 | .04 | | -2.71* | -1.72† | -2.07# | | -.24 | -1.80† | 1.00 | | -.54 | .54 | -1.20 |
| Canada | | | .14 | -2.13# | | | .70 | -.05 | | | -1.76† | 1.14 | | | 1.19 | -.94 |
| UK | | | | -.83 | | | | -.61 | | | | 2.13# | | | | -1.64 |
| (3) | | | | | | | | | | | | | | | | |
| Norway | -4.42* | -2.22# | 2.51# | -.08 | 3.42* | -.22 | -2.03# | -.17 | 2.16# | 2.25# | 2.66# | 1.72† | .82 | .95 | -.40 | 1.52 |
| U.S. | | .87 | 2.15* | -1.96† | | -4.10* | -1.20 | -3.03* | | -.89 | -1.71† | 1.00 | | .07 | 1.24 | -.83 |
| Canada | | | 1.86† | -1.85† | | | 2.16# | -.02 | | | -1.50 | 1.25 | | | 1.50 | -1.01 |
| UK | | | | -2.47* | | | | -1.77† | | | | 2.00# | | | | -1.89† |
| (4) | | | | | | | | | | | | | | | | |
| Norway | -3.61* | -4.09* | -2.88* | -.14 | -3.40* | -.71 | -2.39# | -.59 | 2.31* | 2.44# | 2.65 | 1.83† | .89 | .62 | -.40 | 1.65† |
| U.S. | | 2.62* | 2.45# | -2.06# | | -3.55* | -.71 | -2.60# | | -1.12 | -1.27 | 1.03 | | .49 | 1.33 | -.88 |
| Canada | | | 1.62 | -3.54* | | | 2.09# | -.02 | | | -1.0 | 1.39 | | | 1.17 | -1.42 |
| UK | | | | -2.82* | | | | -1.72† | | | | 1.67† | | | | -2.0# |

## B. Rising velocity

|  | 1 | 2 | 3 | 4 | 5 | 6 | 7 | 8 | 9 | 10 | 11 | 12 | 13 | 14 | 15 |
|---|---|---|---|---|---|---|---|---|---|---|---|---|---|---|---|
| **(1)** Norway | 1.80† | | | | | | | | | | | | | | |
| U.S. | | | | | | | | | | | | | | | |
| Canada | | | | | | | | | | | | | | | |
| UK | | | | | | | | | | | | | | | |
| **(2)** Norway | .83 | .43 | -1.50 | .66 | 3.43* | 1.77† | -1.00 | -.37 | -.43 | -1.08 | .99 | -.04 | -.36 | .72 | 1.82† |
| U.S. | .36 | .39 | 2.12# | | -.59 | -.12 | .89 | | -.17 | .23 | -.97 | | .18 | -.44 | -.82 |
| Canada | | .11 | 1.06 | | | .88 | 3.77* | | | .64 | -1.13 | | | -.86 | -1.57 |
| UK | | | .59 | | | | 2.18# | | | | -1.47 | | | | -.60 |
| **(3)** Norway | .56 | -.80 | -1.97† | .03 | 2.94* | 1.10 | 1.24 | -.46 | -.51 | -.49 | .39 | .05 | -.36 | .46 | 1.41 |
| U.S. | .10 | 1.11 | 1.34 | | -.98 | -.47 | -.35 | | -.25 | -.15 | -.62 | | .26 | -.22 | -.56 |
| Canada | | .97 | .83 | | | .89 | 1.52 | | | .14 | -.60 | | | -.67 | -1.30 |
| UK | | | -.64 | | | | .27 | | | | -.63 | | | | -.54 |
| **(4)** Norway | -.13 | 1.03 | -.33 | .34 | 3.02* | 1.74† | 1.36 | -.11 | -.59 | -.36 | .66 | .002 | -.27 | .16 | 1.12 |
| U.S. | .55 | -.63 | .74 | | .49 | -.35 | -.02 | | .04 | .02 | -.38 | | .19 | -.10 | -.51 |
| Canada | | -.98 | -.03 | | | .28 | 1.56 | | | -.04 | -.89 | | | -.36 | -.89 |
| UK | | | 1.08 | | | | .88 | | | | -.76 | | | | -.63 |

Table C.4. *Results of pooled regressions (Cochrane–Orcutt technique)*

| Eq. no. | Constant | $\log\left(\frac{Y}{PN}\right)^\rho$ | $i$ | log cycle | $\log\left(\frac{LNA}{A}\right)$ | $\log\left(\frac{C}{M}\right)$ | $\log\left(\frac{TNBFA}{TFA}\right)$ | $\log s_\varphi$ | $\bar{R}^2$ | SEE | DW | $\rho$ |
|---|---|---|---|---|---|---|---|---|---|---|---|---|
| | | | | Coefficients of independent variables (*t*-values in parentheses) | | | | | | | | |
| A. Gold standard | | | | | | | | | | | | |
| (1) | −.016 | .146 | 2.006 | .702 | | | | | .904 | .049 | .818 | .580 |
| | (−3.271)* | (21.021)* | (3.031)* | (4.808)* | | | | | | | | |
| (2) | .009 | .230 | 1.118 | .630 | −.933 | .458 | .154 | .007 | .959 | .032 | 1.522 | .236 |
| | (2.007)* | (14.532)* | (2.479)* | (6.378)* | (−7.458)* | (10.047)* | (1.908)† | (.898) | | | | |
| (3) | .002 | | | .977 | −1.920 | −.020 | .092 | .003 | .760 | .050 | .890 | .553 |
| | (.266) | | | (6.581)* | (−9.022)* | (−.305) | (.623) | (.229) | | | | |
| (4) | −.006 | | 3.086 | .888 | −1.869 | .018 | .042 | .009 | .883 | .049 | .855 | .570 |
| | (−.909) | | (4.792)* | (6.023)* | (−9.969)* | (.311) | (.289) | (.764) | | | | |

### B. Managed money

| | | | | | | | | | | | | |
|---|---|---|---|---|---|---|---|---|---|---|---|---|
| (1) | -.058 (-3.788)* | .192 (7.659)* | 2.903 (5.721)* | .949 (10.294)* | | | | | .412 | .065 | 1.527 | .236 |
| (2) | .006 (.741) | .219 (12.989)* | 2.532 (6.578)* | 1.068 (14.925)* | -1.045 (-5.705)* | .399 (10.715)* | .567 (7.591)* | -.017 (-1.896)† | .654 | .049 | 1.641 | .178 |
| (3) | .044 (6.676)* | | | .917 (9.197)* | -.868 (-2.898)* | .129 (2.634)* | -.022 (-.237) | -.087 (-7.940)* | .377 | .070 | 1.318 | .334 |
| (4) | .045 (7.237)* | | 3.008 (6.182)* | 1.001 (11.183)* | -.716 (-2.603)* | .129 (3.187)* | .036 (.412) | -.069 (-6.886)* | .439 | .062 | 1.427 | .283 |

*Gold standard:* U.S., 1880–1913; Canada, 1900–13; UK, 1876–1913; Sweden, 1880–1913; Norway, 1880–1913.

*Managed money:* U.S., 1914–72; Canada, 1914–75; UK, 1914–74; Sweden, 1914–74; Norway, 1914–74.

*Statistically significant at the 1% level.

#Statistically significant at the 5% level.

†Statistically significant at the 10% level.

Table C.5. t-Tests for intercept and independent-variable dummies: All combinations of five countries (Cochrane–Orcutt technique)

| Indepen. var. by country / Eq. no. by country | Constant | | | | log(Y/PN)^p | | | | i | | | | log cycle | | | |
|---|---|---|---|---|---|---|---|---|---|---|---|---|---|---|---|---|
| | U.S. | Canada | UK | Sweden | U.S. | Canada | UK | Sweden | U.S. | Canada | UK | Sweden | U.S. | Canada | UK | Sweden |
| **A. Gold standard** | | | | | | | | | | | | | | | | |
| **(1)** | | | | | | | | | | | | | | | | |
| Norway | 11.88* | -2.11# | .09 | .99 | 3.09* | 2.32# | .22 | -.05 | -2.92* | -.91 | -2.84* | -4.10* | 1.00 | 3.15* | -2.20# | -.75 |
| U.S. | | 11.70* | 10.44* | 10.42* | | -4.04* | -3.55* | -2.77* | | -.52 | -.21 | 3.24* | | 3.97# | 2.32# | -.54 |
| Canada | | | -1.74† | -2.52# | | | 2.22# | 2.31# | | | .48 | 2.92* | | | -1.40 | -4.20* |
| UK | | | | -.66 | | | | .26 | | | | 3.26* | | | | -2.62# |
| **(2)** | | | | | | | | | | | | | | | | |
| Norway | .26 | .11 | .55 | .39 | | | | | | | | | .48 | -1.93† | -.82 | .33 |
| U.S. | | .25 | .19 | .09 | | | | | | | | | | 4.36* | 2.69* | .38 |
| Canada | | | -.58 | -.36 | | | | | | | | | | | -1.87† | -4.13* |
| UK | | | | -.24 | | | | | | | | | | | | -2.41# |
| **(3)** | | | | | | | | | | | | | | | | |
| Norway | .10 | 1.35 | 1.16 | 1.16 | | | | | -3.07* | -1.13 | 2.65# | -3.77* | -.11 | -2.47# | -1.56 | .008 |
| U.S. | | -.04 | -.02 | -.33 | | | | | | .007 | -1.33 | 2.85* | | 4.19* | 2.95* | -.29 |
| Canada | | | .39 | -.81 | | | | | | | -.16 | 2.04# | | | -1.56 | -4.46* |
| UK | | | | -.87 | | | | | | | | 2.99* | | | | -3.26* |
| **(4)** | | | | | | | | | | | | | | | | |
| Norway | .51 | 1.14 | 1.59 | 1.75† | -.72 | .73 | -.77 | -.71 | -1.76† | -.49 | -1.42 | -3.15* | .01 | -2.03# | -1.34 | .17 |
| U.S. | | .20 | .09 | -.25 | | -1.11 | .09 | -.0003 | | -.27 | -1.32 | 2.65* | | 3.50* | 2.67* | -.35 |
| Canada | | | -.75 | -1.20 | | | 1.14 | 1.10 | | | .12 | 2.11# | | | -1.22 | -3.79* |
| UK | | | | -.92 | | | | -.09 | | | | 2.79* | | | | -3.04 |

## B. Managed money

| | | | | | | | | | | | | | | | | |
|---|---|---|---|---|---|---|---|---|---|---|---|---|---|---|---|---|
| **(1)** | | | | | | | | | | | | | | | | |
| Norway | −.24 | −.64 | −.55 | −.54 | .39 | 1.09 | .73 | 1.31 | −4.15* | −2.21* | −5.22* | −2.86* | −.46 | .36 | −.71 | .64 |
| U.S. | | .37 | .32 | .22 | | −.45 | −.31 | −.67 | | −.77 | .81 | 1.39 | | −1.02 | .42 | −1.33 |
| Canada | | | −.01 | −.19 | | | .06 | −.32 | | | 1.28 | 1.65 | | | 1.11 | −.33 |
| UK | | | | −.16 | | | | −.29 | | | | 1.19 | | | | −1.35 |
| **(2)** | | | | | | | | | | | | | | | | | |
| Norway | −6.30* | −7.19* | −5.16* | −2.99* | | | | | | | | | −2.25# | −1.90† | −1.67† | −.71 |
| U.S. | | .81 | −2.12# | −5.09* | | | | | | | | | | −.32 | −.24 | −1.89† |
| Canada | | | −3.72* | −7.06* | | | | | | | | | | | .01 | −1.44 |
| UK | | | | −3.28* | | | | | | | | | | | | −1.20 |
| **(3)** | | | | | | | | | | | | | | | | | |
| Norway | −5.20* | −5.86* | −5.67* | −3.39* | | | | | −.92 | −.08 | −1.34 | .94 | −2.32* | −1.64 | −1.32 | −.70 |
| U.S. | | −.49 | −.49 | −3.02* | | | | | | −.65 | .52 | −1.31 | | −.76 | −.75 | −1.98† |
| Canada | | | −.05 | −4.13* | | | | | | | .97 | −.94 | | | −.14 | −1.13 |
| UK | | | | −3.71* | | | | | | | | −1.46 | | | | .80 |
| **(4)** | | | | | | | | | | | | | | | | | |
| Norway | −1.36 | −1.51 | −.78 | −.70 | .60 | 1.56 | .45 | .64 | −1.04 | −.54 | −.86 | .67 | −2.31* | −2.07# | −1.30 | −.73 |
| U.S. | | .14 | −.50 | −.77 | | −.80 | .20 | .08 | | −.23 | −.31 | −1.08 | | −.04 | −.71 | −1.91† |
| Canada | | | −.63 | −.94 | | | 1.09 | .99 | | | .06 | −.92 | | | −.62 | −1.63 |
| UK | | | | −.16 | | | | .15 | | | | −1.01 | | | | −.76 |

*Gold standard:* U.S., 1880–1913; Canada, 1900–13; UK, 1876–1913; Sweden, 1880–1913; Norway, 1880–1913.

*Managed money:* U.S., 1914–72; Canada, 1914–75; UK, 1914–74; Sweden, 1914–74; Norway, 1914–74.

\* Statistically significant at the 1% level.

\# Statistically significant at the 5% level.

† Statistically significant at the 10% level.

Table C.5. (cont.)

| Indepen. var. by country / Eq. no. by country | $\log(LNA/L)$ | | | | $\log(C/M)$ | | | | $\log(TNBFA/TFA)$ | | | | $\log s_9$ | | | |
|---|---|---|---|---|---|---|---|---|---|---|---|---|---|---|---|---|
| | U.S. | Canada | UK | Sweden | U.S. | Canada | UK | Sweden | U.S. | Canada | UK | Sweden | U.S. | Canada | UK | Sweden |
| **A. Gold standard** | | | | | | | | | | | | | | | | |
| **(1)** | | | | | | | | | | | | | | | | |
| Norway | | | | | | | | | | | | | | | | |
| U.S. | | | | | | | | | | | | | | | | |
| Canada | | | | | | | | | | | | | | | | |
| UK | | | | | | | | | | | | | | | | |
| **(2)** | | | | | | | | | | | | | | | | |
| Norway | -.04 | -1.97† | .01 | -.33 | 1.82† | 1.79† | -1.73† | .96 | -.008 | 1.55 | .80 | .23 | -1.20 | -1.22 | -3.71* | -.16 |
| U.S. | | 1.89† | -.02 | .28 | | -.04 | 3.46* | .93 | | -.32 | -.35 | -.20 | | -.60 | 1.38 | -1.11 |
| Canada | | | -.90 | -1.80† | | | 3.37* | .93 | | | -.12 | -.03 | | | 3.67* | -1.08 |
| UK | | | | .06 | | | | -2.71* | | | | .001 | | | | -3.68* |
| **(3)** | | | | | | | | | | | | | | | | |
| Norway | -.99 | -1.68† | .37 | .02 | .69 | 1.47 | -3.13* | -.05 | .12 | 2.13# | .45 | .75 | -.54 | -.40 | -2.24# | 1.03 |
| U.S. | | 1.43 | -.49 | -.69 | | -.70 | 3.37* | .72 | | -.42 | -.11 | -.59 | | -.36 | 1.09 | -1.28 |
| Canada | | | -1.14 | -1.64 | | | 4.08* | 1.49 | | | .58 | -.43 | | | 2.48# | -1.76† |
| UK | | | | .36 | | | | -3.01* | | | | -.59 | | | | -3.28* |
| **(4)** | | | | | | | | | | | | | | | | |
| Norway | -.61 | -.35 | .21 | .19 | .86 | 1.73† | -2.76* | .27 | .42 | 2.93* | .55 | 1.12 | -.33 | -.92 | -2.24# | .88 |
| U.S. | | .23 | -.29 | -.58 | | -.79 | 3.26* | .61 | | -.10 | .23 | -.47 | | .18 | 1.18 | -.91 |
| Canada | | | -.37 | -.38 | | | 4.12* | 1.48 | | | .98 | -.57 | | | 1.84† | 2.01# |
| UK | | | | .19 | | | | -2.98* | | | | -.88 | | | | 3.10* |

## B. Managed money

| | 1 | 2 | 3 | 4 | 5 | 6 | 7 | 8 | 9 | 10 | 11 | 12 | 13 | 14 | 15 | 16 |
|---|---|---|---|---|---|---|---|---|---|---|---|---|---|---|---|---|
| **(1)** | | | | | | | | | | | | | | | | |
| Norway | | | | | | | | | | | | | | | | |
| U.S. | | | | | | | | | | | | | | | | |
| Canada | | | | | | | | | | | | | | | | |
| UK | | | | | | | | | | | | | | | | |
| **(2)** | | | | | | | | | | | | | | | | |
| Norway | .62 | .62 | 1.41 | -.26 | -4.13* | .63 | 1.33 | .44 | -.33 | .41 | -.78 | .65 | .64 | -.32 | .48 | 1.38 |
| U.S. | | -.20 | -1.22 | .73 | | -4.20* | -4.41* | -3.75* | | -.63 | .41 | -.77 | | .86 | .14 | -.58 |
| Canada | | | -1.08 | .71 | | | -.72 | .13 | | | 1.04 | -.52 | | | -.71 | -1.51 |
| UK | | | | 1.45 | | | | .80 | | | | -.98 | | | | -.73 |
| **(3)** | | | | | | | | | | | | | | | | |
| Norway | -.41 | .63 | .12 | -.43 | -5.50* | -.61 | -.45 | .76 | -.27 | .59 | .90 | .94 | .94 | -.13 | -.21 | 1.05 |
| U.S. | | -.82 | -.19 | .02 | | 4.34* | -3.73* | -4.95* | | -.74 | -1.00 | -1.03 | | .95 | 1.05 | .05 |
| Canada | | | .04 | .83 | | | -.06 | -1.20 | | | -.54 | -.75 | | | .07 | -1.02 |
| UK | | | | .19 | | | | -1.02 | | | | -.41 | | | | -1.15 |
| **(4)** | | | | | | | | | | | | | | | | |
| Norway | -.20 | -1.06 | -.79 | -.96 | -5.06* | -.90 | -.79 | .58 | .52 | .80 | 1.24 | 1.06 | 1.18 | -.25 | -.38 | 1.01 |
| U.S. | | .58 | .64 | .36 | | -3.64* | -3.04* | -4.41* | | -.02 | -.63 | -.75 | | 1.27 | 1.40 | .32 |
| Canada | | | .35 | -.36 | | | .03 | -1.25 | | | -.75 | -.80 | | | .11 | -1.11 |
| UK | | | | -.51 | | | | -1.14 | | | | -.35 | | | | -1.25 |

# CHAPTER 5

# Monetization and the behavior of velocity in Sweden, 1871–1913

## 5.1. Introduction

This chapter, following the institutional approach of Chapters 3 and 4, examines the causes underlying the rapid decline of income velocity of money in Sweden in the period 1871–1913. Two sets of explanatory factors are discussed and subjected to empirical tests. The first set encompasses a number of measures of the monetization of the Swedish economy. Here the growth of commercial banking and the substitution of money for barter are stressed. The second set consists of the standard explanatory variables in money demand studies, that is, real income and interest rates. This chapter should be regarded as a case study of the determinants of velocity in a country undergoing the process of monetization.

The Swedish prewar period 1871–1913 is interesting to study for a number of reasons. Consistent and accurate monthly data on monetary aggregates and interest rates covering all commercial banks as well as measures of changes in wage and payments arrangements are available from the early 1870s. A sharp drop in velocity took place in the interval of stable monetary and political conditions prior to the outbreak of World War I. Sweden adopted the gold standard in 1873. Domestic money and capital markets were not restricted by any major regulations after the banking reforms of the 1860s. Entry into commercial banking was for all practical purposes free. The years 1871–1913 were also characterized by unprecedented rapid economic growth, when Sweden was transformed from an agricultural society to an industrial nation. In this period the Swedish growth rate was probably the highest among European countries.

This chapter is organized as follows. First, the behavior of velocity is described. Second, an account of the process of monetization is given covering changes in commercial banking, in wage contracts, in payments practices, and in the composition of the population. Third, the influence on velocity of the standard explanatory variables of the demand-for-money is discussed. Fourth, these variables as well as various measures of monetization are included in a number of econometric tests. Finally, the results are summarized.

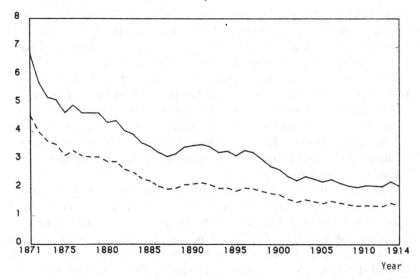

Chart 5.1. Behavior of Velocity in Sweden, 1871–1913. (*V2* solid line, *V3* dashed line). (*Note:* *V2* is calculated as the ratio between nominal income and the money stock defined as the sum of notes and demand and time deposits with the commercial banks (*M2*). *V3* is the ratio between nominal income and *M2* plus deposits with the savings bank system. Nominal income is taken from Johansson (1967), and the money stock from Jonung (1975).)

## 5.2. The behavior of velocity

The income velocity of money, measured by the ratio of nominal income to the money stock (*M2*), declined rapidly in Sweden between 1871 and 1913. The ratio (*V2*) dropped from slightly below 7 in 1871 to about a third of this level in 1913, as shown in Chart 5.1. The decline, which was most pronounced in the early 1870s, took place in two distinct steps; the first one from 1871 to 1887, and the second one from 1896 to 1902. Between 1887 and 1896 and from 1902 until the outbreak of World War I, income velocity remained virtually unchanged.

The negative secular trend in velocity with an *M2* definition of money is not altered by the use of a money stock definition that includes deposits at savings banks, that is, with an *M3* measure. In this case income velocity (*V3*) fell from 4.5 in 1871 to about 1.5 in 1913 (Chart 5.1).

When money is defined as the sum of notes and demand deposits

($M$1) held by the public, the drop in velocity ($V$1) is not as pronounced. In this case velocity ($V$1) fell from a high of 12–14 around
1880 to a level of about 10 in 1913. This fairly constant level compared to the sharp fall in the income velocity of broader money stock
definitions reflects a more rapid growth rate of bank demand and
time deposits than of bank notes in the pre–World War I period.

This chapter focuses on the behavior of the income velocity of money
defined as $V$2 because an $M$2 definition of money is appropriate in
the Swedish context. There was a high degree of substitution between
demand and time deposits, and banking regulations did not distin-
guish one from the other.[1]

The charts in Chapter 2 show that the income velocity of money
also declined in the pre–World War I period in a number of other
countries, including Australia, Canada, Denmark, Finland, France,
Germany, Great Britain, Holland, Italy, Japan, Norway, and the United
States. Consequently, the decline in velocity in Sweden in the latter
half of the nineteenth century and prior to 1914 was part of a common cross-country pattern.

## 5.3.   The process of monetization

Which factors contributed to the secular decline in the income velocity of money in Sweden prior to World War I? The answer given here
emphasizes the role of monetization. Monetization encompassed numerous institutional developments that encouraged the growing use
of money at the expense of existing forms of exchange and wealth
for settling transactions and storing wealth. The rise of a banking
system supplying the public with notes and deposit facilities and the
substitution of bank produced money for barter and payments in kind
were two major components of this process. These changes caused
the money stock in the long run to grow more rapidly than nominal
income, thus reducing velocity. The account of this process in Sweden
given here focuses on three developments: the rise of commercial
banking, changes in wage contracts and in labor markets, and changes
in exchange arrangements in the markets for goods.

### 5.3.1.   The rise of commercial banking

The first Swedish commercial banks were founded in the early 1830s,
but their expansion was rather unimpressive prior to the 1860s. This

---

[1] The empirical definition of the Swedish money stock for the period 1871–1913 is
discussed in detail by Jonung (1975).

slow development was to a considerable extent attributable to the legal ceiling of 6 percent on interest rates on commercial bank loans. This limit restricted commercial banks in the competition for funds. Individuals and firms preferred other financial intermediaries, such as private bankers and merchant houses, that were free to pay a higher return since they were not subject to the interest rate ceiling.[2]

Considerable financial intermediation apparently was arranged through the exchanges *(växelbörserna)* in Stockholm and Gothenburg, where brokers channeled funds from lenders to borrowers.[3] These exchanges were well-functioning markets where interest rates fluctuated freely to equilibrate the demand for and the supply of funds. Commercial banks including the rudimentary central bank of Sweden, the *Riksbank,* actually were guided by the rates registered at the exchanges, losing customers whenever the market rate rose above the legal limit of 6 percent.

Since the ceiling on interest rates prevented the commercial banks from attracting deposits, the main source of funds during the first decades of their existence was bank note issuance.[4] However, when the legal maximum was abolished in 1864, banks were able to attract funds from the public on more competitive terms than before. Deposits started to expand more quickly than the note issue. In the mid-1860s the volume of bank deposits surpassed the amount of commercial bank notes in circulation and continued to grow faster than the volume of notes prior to World War I. Consequently, the currency–money ratio fell from 42 percent in 1871 to 10 percent in 1913 (column (5) in Table 5.1).

The sharp decline in velocity during the period from the early 1870s to the end of the prewar period reflected the growth of the supply of banking facilities. Several indicators in Table 5.1 attest to this development. The number of commercial banks increased from twenty-eight in 1871 to a maximum of eighty-four in 1908, when the bank concentration process started, lowering the number to seventy-five in 1913. The number of commercial bank offices more than quadrupled: from 141 in 1871 to 630 in 1913. The number of bank accounts

---

[2] For an account of the interaction between the incentive structure contained in the legal framework and the growth of commercial banking in Sweden, see Jonung (1978b). Brisman (1931), as well as Sandberg (1978), describes the development of the Swedish banking system in the nineteenth century.

[3] Brisman (1931, pp. 99–100).

[4] Other reasons the first commercial banks relied on the issuance of notes as the main method of financing their activities were the difficulties of attracting deposits from a public unfamiliar with commercial banking and a poorly developed system of communications that limited easy access to bank offices.

Table 5.1. *Selected measures of the growth of commercial banking in Sweden, 1871–1913*

| Year | No. of commercial banks (1) | No. of commercial bank offices (2) | No. of accounts per capita (3) | Volume of deposits (*Kronor* per capita) (4) | Ratio of notes to money stock (%) (5) |
|------|------|------|------|------|------|
| 1871 | 28 | 141 | .01 | 20 | 42.2 |
| 1880 | 44 | 205 | .03 | 53 | 21.1 |
| 1890 | 43 | 190 | .03 | 72 | 19.6 |
| 1900 | 67 | 269 | .09 | 144 | 13.8 |
| 1913 | 75 | 630 | .25 | 296 | 9.9 |

*Sources* (by column): (1) Commercial banks in operation at the end of the year according to the bank reports. (2) Brisman (1934, pp. 219–21). (3) The number of accounts is computed as the sum of the certificates of deposits and the accounts shown in the December bank reports. The number of accounts of the commercial banks that did not issue notes, the *aktiebanker*, was first shown in 1872. The figure for 1871 is estimated using the ratio between the number of accounts with the note-issuing banks and the number of accounts with the *aktiebanker* for 1872. Data on the Swedish population are taken from Table A.4 in *Historical Statistics of Sweden*, Stockholm, 1955. (4) The volume of deposits with the commercial banking system, encompassing demand and time deposits, is computed as the annual average of end-of-month data. (5) The volume of notes includes the notes issued by the *Riksbank* and by the note-issuing commercial banks. The money stock consists of notes and demand and time deposits held by the public. Both are annual averages of end-of-month data.

per capita increased sharply, from one account per hundred inhabitants in 1871 to twenty-five accounts per hundred inhabitants in 1913. The volume of commercial bank deposits per capita grew from 20 *kronor* in 1871 to 296 *kronor* in 1913.

The fall in velocity was most pronounced during two periods, 1871–87 and 1896–1909, which roughly coincide with two intervals of swift expansion of the banking industry,[5] suggesting that the rapid expansion of the commercial banking system in the prewar period contributed substantially to the secular fall in velocity.

This conclusion is supported by the behavior of the deposit turn-

[5] If existing banks gradually began to report their deposits, measured velocity will record a spurious decline. Such a statistical artifact may have occurred during the 1870s when the coverage of the banking statistics expanded to include a few commercial banks not previously counted. For this reason, data on velocity for the first half of the 1870s may slightly overstate the actual decline. This period has been excluded from the regressions presented in Section 5.5.

over rate of the *Stockholms Enskilda Bank,* a major commercial bank. This rate remained practically constant for demand as well as for time deposits between 1871 and 1913.[6] The turnover rate of deposits can be regarded as a crude proxy for the transactions velocity of money, that is, for the total volume of transactions divided by the average money stock per unit of time. A constant turnover rate can be reconciled with a declining income velocity of money in the following way.[7] The spread of the money economy is reflected in an expansion of nominal money holdings relative to the flow of money income, thus reducing the income velocity of money. If the public utilizes the additions as frequently as their initial money holdings to settle transactions, that will account for a constant level of the transactions velocity and for the turnover rate. This interpretation is consistent with the evidence that the Swedish economy was rapidly monetized in the pre–World War I period. Similarly, the turnover rate of deposits at savings banks remained constant during this time span whereas the income velocity of a money stock definition (*M*3) including savings bank deposits declined.[8]

### 5.3.2. Changes in wage contracts and labor markets

In labor markets within agriculture and industry in the prewar period, the use of money grew at the expense of payments in kind. Judging from many accounts, a major share of wages in agriculture – which was the largest sector of the Swedish economy in the nineteenth century – involved payments and benefits in kind. Several forms of wage contracts between farmers and their employees defined varying proportions of cash to benefits in kind.

In their study of wages in Sweden, Bagge, Lundberg, and Svennilson (1935) distinguished six different types of agricultural workers: crofters, cottagers, laborers living in, farm servants, *statare,* and wage earners proper. In addition, a considerable number of sons and

---

[6] Gasslander (1956, pp. 52–7). No data are available covering all commercial banks. The behavior of the turnover rate of the deposits of the *Stockholms Enskilda Bank* is assumed here to be representative of the whole banking system. The constancy of the turnover rate is matched by that of the turnover rate of savings bank deposits in 1871–1913. See note 8.

[7] Selden (1956, pp. 215–19) presents four hypotheses to explain divergent trends in the transactions velocity of money and the income velocity of money. Only one of his four explanations – a growth in the use of money – appears applicable to the Swedish monetary experience of 1871–1913.

[8] See Chart 5.1. The turnover rate of deposits at the savings banks was .25 in 1880 and .20 in 1913 measured as the average ratio of the sum of savings bank deposits and withdrawals during a year to total savings bank deposits at the end of the year.

Table 5.2. *Composition of the Swedish population over fifteen years of age engaged in agriculture, 1870 and 1920*

| Group | 1870 (thousands) | (%) | 1920 (thousands) | (%) |
|---|---|---|---|---|
| *Farm entrepreneurs* | 246.9 | 19.6 | 274.4 | 26.0 |
| *Working members of the family in the above group*[a] | 271.4 | 21.6 | 272.8 | 27.6 |
| *Agricultural workers* | 676.0 | 53.7 | 451.8 | 42.8 |
| Crofters[b] (*jordtorpare*) | 134.2 | 10.7 | 46.5 | 4.4 |
| Cottagers[a] (*backstugesittare*) | 97.8 | 7.8 | 12.7 | 1.2 |
| Laborers living in (*inhysehjon*) | 110.4 | 8.8 | 4.7 | 0.4 |
| Male and female servants (*drängar* and *pigor*) | 240.7 | 19.1 | 116.4 | 11.0 |
| *Statare* | 35.3 | 2.8 | 47.6 | 4.5 |
| Wage earners proper (day-laborers) | 57.6 | 4.6 | 223.9 | 21.2 |
| *Rural laborers (unspecified)* | 65.0 | 5.2 | 37.4 | 3.5 |
| Total labor force engaged in agriculture | 1,259.3 | | 1,055.5 | |
| Total agricultural population | 3,017 | | 2,596 | |
| Total population of Sweden | 4,164 | | 5,876 | |

[a] Over fifteen years old.
[b] Including children over fifteen years old and sons-in-law.
*Source:* Bagge, Lundberg, and Svennilson (1935, Tables 185 and 186). The data are derived from the census returns.

daughters of farmers who were employed at home received little or no monetary payment. The composition of the agricultural labor force according to these categories is displayed in Table 5.2.

The crofters (*jordtorpare*) generally dwelt on small plots of land for which they paid rent by doing a specific number of days of work. The crofter system declined in importance after the 1870s. In some cases the rent was changed to cash. In other cases crofters bought land with the help of government loans, and some became *statare*. Between 1870 and 1920 the share of crofters in the agricultural labor force fell from about 11 percent to 4 percent (Table 5.2).

The cottagers (*backstugesittare*) lived in small cottages on a patch of land. Their economic situation was similar to that of the crofters except that they were not required to do day-work. Instead they accepted agricultural work on a semipermanent basis, being paid in cash and in kind. This group declined sharply in size, from ninety-eight thousand members in 1870 to thirteen thousand in 1920, primarily due to emigration to the United States and to migration to urban areas.

Laborers living in *(inhysehjon)*, generally the poorest group of agricultural workers, were lodged with farmers and crofters as second-class members of the household. They apparently received little if any cash payment. This category, the third largest group of rural workers in the 1870s, had practically disappeared by the second decade of the twentieth century.

Male and female servants boarded by the farmer *(drängar* and *pigor)* constituted the largest group of farm workers – almost 20 percent of the agricultural labor force in 1870. They were hired on a yearly basis and obtained free board and other benefits in kind plus an annual, semiannual, or monthly cash wage. The number of farm servants was almost halved between 1870 and 1920 (see Table 5.2).

In this period from 1870 to 1920 the work performed by crofters and farm servants was partially taken over by a new social group, the *statare*, particularly at large estates in southern and central Sweden. The *statare* were generally paid an annual cash wage and certain benefits in kind, the *stat*, such as free housing and various farm products.

Wage earners proper form a residual group of farm workers who cannot appropriately be classified in any of the other five categories. As a rule they were paid a daily cash wage, sometimes also benefits in kind. This group expanded more rapidly than any other group of agricultural workers in the prewar period.[9]

The changes in the composition of the agricultural labor force contributed to an increased demand for money as the number of wage earners proper – who received a larger money wage share than other groups of agricultural workers – increased at the expense of crofters, cottagers, laborers living in, and farm servants. The decline of the two latter classes is interpreted by Bagge et al. (1935, p. 91) as indicating the diminishing role of payments in kind. Within all agricultural groups there was also a general trend toward a higher fraction of total earnings paid in money. For example, the share of the cash wage to the

[9] A detailed description of the payment practices existing in the agricultural sector is found in Bagge et al. (1935, pp. 92–7 and 183–203). The account here draws on their work, which also includes a brief discussion of the structure of the rural labor market. See also Utterström (1957) and Back (1961) on the economic history of the agricultural workers.

Table 5.3. *Selected measures of the spread of the monetary economy,*
*1860–1910*

| Year | Urban population as a % of total population (1) | Employment in agriculture as a % of total employment (2) | Cash wage per year as a % of total wage of *statare* (3) | Cash wage per year as a % of total wage of blast-furnace workers at Söderfors iron works (4) |
|------|------|------|------|------|
| 1860 | 11.3 | n.a. | 30.8 | 69.2 |
| 1870 | 12.9 | 81.0 | 35.2 | 79.6 |
| 1880 | 15.1 | 77.1 | 34.3 | 89.5 |
| 1890 | 20.1 | 73.0 | 36.7 | 92.3 |
| 1900 | 21.5 | 65.0 | 37.0 | 100.0 |
| 1910 | 24.8 | 59.2 | 45.9 | 100.0 |

*Sources* (by column): (1) Computed from *Historical Statistics of Sweden*, Stockholm, 1955, Table A.4. (2) Calculated from Johansson (1967, Table 58). (3) Computed from data on the volume of the annual cash wages and the total annual earnings of *statare* on selected estates as displayed in Bagge et al. (1935, Table 208). (4) Computed from Bagge, Lundberg, and Svennilson (1933, Table 67). These estimates are biased upward because the value of free housing is not included in the estimates of the benefits in kind. Free housing was abolished in 1908 at the Söderfors iron works.

total wage of *statare* rose from 30 percent in 1860 to 45 percent in 1910[10] (see Table 5.3).

To a large extent, the Swedish industrialization process took place at the manufacturing estates (the *bruk*), rural industries that traditionally relied on a mixture of nonmonetary and monetary wage payments.[11] According to Gårdlund's (1942) detailed description of the barter–credit economy, which prevailed especially at the iron, paper, and glass works in the countryside, workers generally kept pigs and sometimes even cows and often produced grain on their own farmland, which was supplied to the employees as a part of their wages. A truck system existed, the workers obtaining merchandise from the company store (the *bruksaffär*) on credit. Before money wages were paid out, the credit received at the store was deducted. Gårdlund (1942,

[10]  See Bagge et al. (1935, pp. 91–2).
[11]  Swedish industry was located primarily in the countryside during the prewar period. This pattern, markedly different from that of Great Britain and the United States, is explained by the rural location of natural resources such as mines, water power, and forests.

p. 359) classifies this form of economic organization as *brukshushåll-ning*, literally, the manufacturing estate economy.

The share of payment in kind in the total wage bill of industrial workers declined during the prewar period. At the Söderfors iron works, a well-known *bruk* in central Sweden, for the average of all full-time employed workers, it fell from 26 percent of total earnings in 1860 to 10 percent in 1885 and to a level slightly above 1 percent in 1905 [12] (see also Table 5.3). These figures are strongly biased downward, however, because they do not impute the monetary value of free housing.

In Gårdlund's opinion, the decline in the *brukshushållning* in the 1890s was hastened by the advent of the trade unions, a movement that rapidly gained in strength in the first decade after the turn of the century. The unions in central bargaining opposed the system of payments in kind and demanded its replacement by cash wages – except for free medical attention.[13] At the local level, however, the workers were often not opposed to the *brukshushållning*. Indeed, in many instances the employers actively supported its elimination. The complicated bargaining process of converting benefits in kind into monetary values – the *avlösning* – lasted for many years. Most of this process occurred in 1905–10, and probably ended before the outbreak of World War I.[14] Still, substantial nonpecuniary wage elements remained after the war in many industries.[15]

In the middle of the nineteenth century Sweden was a country with a large agricultural sector; in the 1870s approximately 80 percent of the total labor force was employed in agriculture and subsidiary occupations (see Table 5.3). The total number of Swedes within the agricultural sector declined by more than 300,000 persons in this period (see Table 5.2), whereas the urban population roughly doubled its share of the total population between 1870 and 1910 (see Table 5.3). This transformation – the relative decline of the agricultural sector and the rise of industry – contributed to an increased demand for money. Both the production of goods and services for own consump-

---

[12] These numbers are derived from Tables 68 and 69 in Bagge et al. (1933). A description of the various payments in kind and the methods used to estimate their monetary value is given in ibid., pp. 351–63.

[13] Gårdlund (1942, p. 412). The increased time frequency of money wage payments during the first decade of the twentieth century – from once a month to once a week at some factories – is regarded by Gårdlund as an indicator of the decline of the *brukshushållning*.

[14] Bagge et al. (1933, p. 87).

[15] In 1919, for instance, 80 percent of the twenty-six thousand workers at the sawmill industries had free housing (Bagge et al. (1933, p. 156)).

tion and the volume of barter transactions were less prevalent in industry and in urban areas than in agriculture and in the countryside.

### 5.3.3.   Changes in market arrangements

The rising share of cash payments in wages within agriculture and industry was accompanied by a rise in monetary exchanges in the markets for goods. Since at least the Middle Ages, markets had played an important role in the rural economy. Members of farm households traveled to markets held at certain dates to exchange their products for other goods. Markets were generally held in September and October, when the harvest was over, and in April, when preparations were being made for the sowing.[16]

Exchange at rural markets was often based on barter even at the end of the nineteenth century. In earlier times money was not even the unit of account; for example, one *kovärde* was the value of a cow, one *linvärde* the value of one pound of linen, and so on.[17] The old system of barter at regularly recurring markets yielded gradually to more continuous monetary transactions in stores and shops inside as well as outside of towns.

After the liberalization of the laws regulating domestic trade in the middle of the nineteenth century, when the towns lost their ancient privileges of monopoly of certain business activities, small shops were gradually established in the countryside. Eventually they took over several of the functions that the markets and towns had previously served. Initially, the country stores served as a form of trading post, engaging both in barter and in monetary exchange. The local population exchanged its produce at the store for goods that the shopkeeper obtained from his business connections in nearby towns.

Gradually, payments in cash became more and more prevalent, although the barter system remained until World War II, when it was ended by the introduction of the system of commodity rationing.[18] Clearly, the country stores contributed to the spread of the monetary economy in the prewar period, by decreasing transaction costs and by establishing markets for local products and for goods brought in from the outside.

---

[16] According to the *Svenska almanacka* (the Swedish Almanac), on average 25 percent of the markets occurring in 1870, 1880, 1890, 1900, and 1913 took place in April, and 35 percent in September and October. Thus the markets followed closely the activities of the agricultural sector.

[17] See Ejdestam, Hedin, and Nygren (1965, pp. 57–8).

[18] Ibid., p. 58.

This description of the spread of the monetary economy in the Swedish countryside has great similarities with Clower's (1969, pp. 7–15) account of the development of payment arrangements. Clower distinguished four stages of exchange arrangements: (1) isolated barter, (2) "fairground" barter, (3) trading-post barter, and (4) monetary exchange. As an economy develops it moves from the first stage to the fourth stage. In rural Sweden during the nineteenth century, there was a trend away from isolated barter and fairground barter to country-store barter and to exchanges involving the use of money. Despite this trend, all four kinds of payment arrangements existed side by side. (See also Section 2.2.2 in Chapter 2.)

As a part of the monetization process, a national market for goods gradually developed in the nineteenth century. This process was encouraged by rapid growth in the communications system, in particular by the construction of railroads. Ceteris paribus, this growth of the monetary economy should be expected to have reduced the range of variation of prices for identical goods between various regions within Sweden. Basically, the same argument is formally presented in a model by Brunner and Meltzer (1971) that proposes that the mean and variance of the distribution of exchange ratios decline with the development of one or several assets as commonly accepted means of exchange.

There is support for this proposition in Jörberg's (1972, Part 2, pp. 222–9) monumental study of the history of Swedish prices. His coefficients of variation, computed for a collection of regional price indices on a five-year basis, fall for thirty-three out of forty-three indices from 1865–9 to 1910–14, with an average reduction from .21 to .19. There are, however, two major reasons why it is not proper to use all these prices. First, all goods are given the same weight, which introduces a bias since some goods were more frequently exchanged than others, both domestically and internationally. Second, the spread of prices expanded for certain goods, such as bar iron and cows, due to increased regional specialization, which gave rise to differences in the characteristics of the goods in question.

The foodstuff price index alone is likely to be a better indicator for a number of reasons. It includes fairly homogeneous goods. The goods covered were widely exchanged within Sweden and not heavily influenced by foreign developments. The index is also weighted, which probably has the effect that the largest weights are given to foods that were most frequently traded. The range of variations in the prices of such goods should be expected to fall as the barter economy declined in importance. Actually, the coefficient of variation of the foodstuff price index declined from .069 in 1865–9 to .054 in 1910–14, corresponding to twice as large a relative fall shown by the regional price indices.

Thus an expansion of the monetary economy should be expected to have two opposing effects on the distribution of prices: (1) to decrease the variance as argued by Brunner and Meltzer (1971); and (2) to increase the variance as the larger extent of the market, created by the use of money, allows specialization in production and consumption, contributing to a wider range of qualities of the "same" good. Strictly speaking, new sets of goods are obtained. It is difficult, however, to account for this latter effect in the computations covering the price indices just discussed.

To sum up, these computations indicate that the range of the variation of prices fell within Sweden during the pre–World War I period. This decline was partially the result of growth in the monetary economy,[19] but other developments also contributed to the fall. Substantial improvements in communications facilitated trade and exchange by lowering transportation costs, thus increasing trade between regional markets and reducing regional price differences. Thus the expansion of the communications network, by contributing to the extension of the money economy, contributed to the decline in velocity in the prewar period.[20]

## 5.4.    The influence of real income and interest rates

### 5.4.1.    The growth in real income

In their study of the United States, Friedman and Schwartz (1963) argued for the existence of a secular relationship between real income and velocity. As was discussed in Chapter 2, they viewed "the services rendered by money balances as a 'luxury' of which the amount demanded rises more than in proportion to the rise in real income"; that

---

[19] Compare with Jörberg's assertion (1972, p. 28) that the spread of regional prices was generally falling in Sweden during the nineteenth century.

[20] The total length of railway lines expanded from 1,727 kilometers in 1870 to 14,132 kilometers in 1913 (*Historical Statistics of Sweden*, Stockholm, 1960, Table 44). The construction of railroads took place in two periods of rapid growth, the first one during the 1870s and the second one around the turn of the century (see Hedin (1967, pp. 9–10)). It is worth noting that these two intervals coincide with the two periods of rapid fall in velocity (see Chart 5.1). Also, Sommarin (1942, p. 108) noted that the construction of railroads contributed to the development of the savings bank system. New savings banks were founded in many places where railroad stations were built.

is, the real income elasticity of the demand for real money holdings has a value larger than unity.[21] Consequently, the income velocity of money should be expected to fall secularly as real income rises. Friedman and Schwartz based this proposition on the behavior of the U.S. income velocity, which was falling from the early 1880s until the end of World War II.

How well does the luxury good hypothesis explain the secular trend of the income velocity of money in Sweden? A look at the U-shaped behavior of velocity during the period 1871–1971 as displayed in Chart 2.4 in Chapter 2 reveals that after 1922, velocity moved in the same direction as real income. Consequently, the real income effect has been swamped since the early 1920s by other influences, which have given rise to a picture inconsistent with the hypothesis.

For the prewar period 1871–1913, the luxury good hypothesis is at a first glance in agreement with the data. Real income rose at an annual average rate of 3 percent during these years, whereas the corresponding figure is 6 percent for the money stock ($M2$). These numbers indicate that the real income elasticity of demand for real cash balances was about 1.5 – a 1-percent increase in real income per year caused a decline in velocity of half a percentage point.

However, as argued in Chapter 4, the fall in velocity in Sweden during the period 1871–1913 may be explained by developments other than a real income effect, that is, by the monetization process. Thus, if the fall in velocity is simply related to the rise in real income, important explanatory factors that have moved more or less in accord with economic growth may be ignored.

Friedman and Schwartz's (1963) explanation of the fall of U.S. velocity was questioned by Tobin (1965) (see Chapter 2). Tobin suggested that the decline in U.S. velocity during the period 1880–1915 was influenced by the spread of commercial banking in the United States at the expense of savings banks. The ratio of mutual savings deposits to commercial bank deposits fell from 80 percent in 1877 to 25 percent in 1915. The corresponding figures for Sweden are 51 and 55 percent. Thus the decline in the Swedish income velocity of money ($V2$) is considerably more pronounced when the stable ratio of commercial bank deposits to savings bank deposits in the prewar period is taken into account.

---

[21] As pointed out in Chapter 2, Friedman and Schwartz have noted the influence of financial sophistication on the behavior of velocity and in subsequent work have downgraded the role of the luxury good hypothesis. See, e.g., Schwartz (1975) and Friedman and Schwartz (1982).

*5.4.2.   Fluctuations in interest rates*

Movements in interest rates are generally regarded as a central determinant of the demand for money and thus of velocity. The exact theoretical and empirical specification of the relevant interest rates remains an open issue. As a rule, the return on a suitable money substitute
is included in empirical studies to represent the alternative cost of
holding money.

It is difficult, however, to obtain data on the return of any financial
asset in Sweden that was a close substitute for money during the prewar period. Domestic financial markets were not as well developed as
in the United Kingdom and the United States, although Sweden was
closely connected with international capital markets in the pre−World
War I period. Most of the Swedish national debt was held outside the
country prior to 1914. Therefore, since the British capital market influenced Swedish capital and credit markets strongly during the classical gold standard period in Sweden, 1873−1914, the British bond
rate is probably a suitable measure of the alternative cost of holding
money.[22]

Most empirical money demand studies have included only one interest rate to represent the opportunity cost of holding money (see
Chapter 2). Klein (1973, 1974) argued that the demand for money is
also influenced by the pecuniary return to money holdings, and that
the own-price should be included in the specification of the velocity
function, an increase in the own-price increasing the demand for money
and thus reducing velocity, ceteris paribus. In Klein's model, the demand for money is dependent on the pecuniary return to money, the
pecuniary return to a money substitute, and the return to a "bond"
that yields a pecuniary return but, unlike money and the money substitute, yields no monetary services. Owing to lack of data on three
financial assets that would correspond to these concepts, Klein's model
cannot be fully tested for Sweden. Some elements of his approach,
however, can be used, specifically the role of the pecuniary return on
money. This return is derived in Table 5.4 as a weighted average of
the rates paid on the components of the Swedish money stock; that is,
on note issues of the *Riksbank* and the commercial banks, and on demand and time deposits of the commercial banks.

These two rates − the yield on British government bonds and the
pecuniary return to the Swedish money stock − are shown in Table
5.4. Although the trend of the yield on bonds was negative for most

---

[22] On this point see Jonung (1984).

Table 5.4. *Yield on British consols and the pecuniary return on the Swedish money stock, selected years, 1871–1910 (%)*

| Year | Yield on British consols | Pecuniary return on Swedish money stock |
|------|--------------------------|------------------------------------------|
| 1871 | 3.23 | 2.17 |
| 1880 | 3.05 | 3.25 |
| 1890 | 2.85 | 3.27 |
| 1900 | 2.76 | 3.99 |
| 1910 | 3.08 | 3.82 |

*Notes:* The pecuniary return on the money stock, $r_m$, is computed as the weighted average of the rates paid on demand and time deposits in the following way:

$$r_m = (C/M)r_c + (DD/M)r_d + (TD/M)r_t$$

where $r_c$, $r_d$, and $r_t$ represent the interest rates paid on notes, $C$, demand deposits, $DD$, and time deposits, $TD$, respectively; see Klein (1973, 1974). $r_c$ is equal to zero, $r_d$ is set equal to the rate paid on *upp- och avskrivningsräkning*, and $r_t$ to the rate paid on six-month certificates of deposits.

of the period, the decline was fairly limited. This near-constancy suggests that movements in the bond rate were not, per se, a main causal factor behind the fall in Swedish velocity in the pre-1914 period. However, the decline in the British bond rate, as a measure of the opportunity cost of holding money, is consistent with the fall in velocity.

The pecuniary return to the money stock exhibits larger changes than the bond rate. It rose significantly prior to World War I, most noticeably in the 1870s and 1890s. In these two decades the composition of the Swedish money stock changed substantially: In both decades the share held by notes declined markedly, primarily as the outcome of monetization. Legislative changes also contributed to this fall in the share of notes to deposits, in particular the abolition in the 1870s of the one-*krona* note of the *Riksbank* and of the five-*kronor* notes of the private commercial banks, and the grant of the *Riksbank's* monopoly on the issuance of notes at the end of the 1890s. These legislative steps led to the substitution of deposits for bank notes on a significant scale. The relative increase of deposits at the expense of notes was the main reason for the rise in the pecuniary return on the money stock, since interest rates on demand and time deposits remained fairly constant in the prewar period.

The rise in the pecuniary return to money is consistent with the fall in velocity. However, movements in this return as well as in the bond rate were fairly small in the prewar period. Interest rate developments, per se, thus appear not to have been a prime determinant of the fall in velocity.[23]

Price expectations, generally introduced into econometric work as a function of past movements in the general price level, are commonly regarded as a determinant of the demand for money, notably in periods of rapid changes in prices. The Swedish price level, however, did not exhibit any sharp swings in the pre-1914 period. It followed the worldwide pattern of a secular decline between the early 1870s and mid-1890s, and a secular rise from then until the outbreak of war in 1914. Movements in prices were so moderate that price expectations may safely be excluded as an important determinant of velocity prior to 1914.

## 5.5.    Empirical results

As argued previously, changes in commercial banking, in wage contracts, in labor markets, in the markets for goods, and in payment arrangements exerted an important influence on velocity in Sweden in the pre-1914 period. Empirical tests of the impact of monetization require a proper measure of these developments. It is difficult to find an all-inclusive indicator of this process. (See also the discussion in Chapter 4 on measures of institutional changes.)

In the absence of an obvious single measure, several proxy variables were adopted in the regression estimates. These are grouped under two headings in Table 5.5: measures of the growth of commercial banking, and measures of the expansion of monetary payments. The first group includes the number of commercial bank accounts per capita, the number of commercial bank offices, and the currency–money ratio as measured by the ratio of *Riksbank* and private bank notes to the total volume of notes and commercial bank deposits. The growth of monetary payments is measured by the ratio of cash payments to total wages of farmhands, the share of the labor force engaged in agriculture, and the ratio of the urban population to the total population. None of the six measures adopted should be expected to give a complete representation of the monetization process.

---

[23] Klein's (1973) measure of the pecuniary return of the money stock may also be regarded as reflecting changes in the composition of the U.S. money stock. His results may thus be interpreted as indirect support for the view that the spread of money use contributed to the fall in U.S. velocity.

Table 5.5. *Influence on velocity of the monetization process, 1875–1913 (two-stage Cochrane–Orcutt technique)*

| Independent variables | Regression coefficient[a] | $t$-value | $R^2$ | SEE | DW | $\rho$ |
|---|---|---|---|---|---|---|
| *Growth of commercial banking* | | | | | | |
| (1) Number of commercial bank accounts per capita | −.220 (.051) | −4.28 | .337 | .045 | 1.974 | .013 |
| (2) Number of commercial bank offices | −.117 (.117) | −1.00 | .027 | .051 | 1.840 | .080 |
| (3) Currency–money ratio | .849 (.081) | 10.52 | .754 | .043 | 1.642 | .179 |
| *Growth of monetary payments* | | | | | | |
| (4) Ratio of cash payments to total wages of farmhands | −.831 (.324) | −2.57 | .155 | .068 | .956 | .522 |
| (5) Share of labor force engaged in agriculture | 2.024 (.348) | 5.81 | .484 | .053 | 1.661 | .170 |
| (6) Ratio of urban population to total population | −1.323 (.184) | −7.19 | .589 | .051 | 1.708 | .146 |
| *Growth of real income* | | | | | | |
| (7) Real income per capita | −.645 (.085) | −7.56 | .614 | .070 | 1.836 | .082 |

[a] Standard error in parentheses.
*Sources:* See Tables 5.1 through 5.3.

Rather, each stands for one aspect of this process; together they form a vector that accounts for the growth of the money economy.

Table 5.5 summarizes a number of regressions exploring the hypothesis that the monetization of the Swedish economy contributed to the decline in velocity in 1871–1913. Each of the six proxies for the spread of the money economy is regressed separately on the income velocity of money ($V2$), using the following regression equation:

$$\log V2 = a + b \log \text{mon} \tag{5.1}$$

where log stands for the natural logarithm, and mon for the monetization variable.

All the regression coefficients for the six monetization variables in Table 5.5 are significant – except for the number of commercial bank offices (regression (2)) – and have the expected sign. The number of commercial bank accounts per capita (regression (1)), the number of commercial bank offices (regression (2)), the ratio of cash payments to total wages for farmhands (regression (4)), and the ratio of the urban population to the total population (regression (6)) are negatively associated with velocity, whereas the currency–money ratio (regression (3)) and the share of the labor force engaged in agriculture (regression (5)) are positively related. (The Cochrane–Orcutt method was used to correct for autocorrelation.) The currency–money ratio, the ratio of the urban population to the total population, and the share of the labor force engaged in agriculture, in that order, have the strongest influence on velocity as measured by the $t$-value of the regression coefficients and by the $R^2$. The ratio of cash payments, although statistically significant, has little explanatory power, judging from the value of its $R^2$.

Real income per capita is also regressed on velocity in Table 5.5 as a simple test of the luxury good hypothesis. The regression coefficient is highly significant, with the expected negative sign, and supports the luxury good hypothesis. To sum up, the tests in Table 5.5 are consistent with the view that the monetization process, as well as real income growth, influenced velocity in a significant way.

Table 5.6 reports the results of regressions on velocity of measures of monetization, interest rates, and real income to assess the simultaneous influence of these variables on velocity. All estimates in the table are based on the second stage of the two-stage Cochrane–Orcutt method, that is, on the transformed variables. In regression equation (1) the currency–money ratio ($C/M$) and the rate on British consols ($r_b$) are regressed on velocity. Both explanatory variables are significant and have the correct sign. A considerable improvement of the $R^2$ results with the addition of the interest rate variable ($r_b$) to regression (3) for the currency–money ratio alone in Table 5.5.

The addition of the pecuniary return on the money stock ($r_m$) to regression equation (2) in Table 5.6 makes a marginal improvement over regression equation (1), judging from the $R^2$ and the standard error of estimate. As argued in the previous section, the pecuniary return to money is primarily determined by the behavior of the currency–money ratio. This variable ($r_m$) may actually represent the monetization process in much the same way as the currency–money ratio does, rather than the pecuniary return to money. This interpretation is consistent with the positive sign of both the $C/M$ variable and the $r_m$ variable in regression equation (2).[24]

Regression equation (3) in Table 5.6, with real income per capita ($y_n$) and the bond rate ($r_b$) as explanatory variables, shows a significant

---

[24] See also note 23.

Table 5.6. *Velocity (V2) regressed on monetization variables, interest rates, and real income, 1875–1913 (two-stage Cochrane–Orcutt technique)*

| Regression estimate[a] | $(\bar{R}^2)$[b] | SEE | DW | $\rho$ |
|---|---|---|---|---|
| (1) $\log V2 = -.888 + .952(C/M) + .621r_b$ <br> $\qquad\qquad\;(18.26)\qquad\;(3.73)$ | .902 | .037 | 1.952 | .024 |
| (2) $\log V2 = -1.051 + .985(C/M) + .541r_b + .116r_m$ <br> $\qquad\qquad\quad(18.57)\qquad\;(3.27)\quad(1.97)$ | .909 | .035 | 2.074 | −.037 |
| (3) $\log V2 = 2.480 - .787y_n - .087r_b$ <br> $\qquad\qquad(-7.01)\;(-.26)$ | .569 | .077 | 1.818 | .091 |
| (4) $\log V2 = -.282 + .771(C/M) - .300(\text{urb}) + .461r_b$ <br> $\qquad\qquad\;(7.11)\qquad\;(-1.74)\qquad(2.71)$ | .931 | .035 | 2.040 | −.020 |
| (5) $\log V2 = -.776 + .828(C/M) - 1.039(\text{urb}) + .568y_n + .369r_b$ <br> $\qquad\qquad\;(9.89)\qquad\;(-5.86)\qquad\;(5.87)\quad(2.76)$ | .952 | .025 | 1.924 | .038 |

[a] $t$-values in parentheses.
[b] Given in terms of changes.
*Sources:* See Tables 5.1 through 5.5.

and correctly signed regression coefficient for the real income variable, but not for the bond rate. Adding the bond rate does not improve the result obtained for the real income variable alone in regression (7) in Table 5.5. In regression equation (4) the ratio of the urban population to the total population (urb) is added to regression equation (1). All explanatory variables have correct and significant coefficients. There is, however, only a marginal improvement in the fit of the regression.

Other experiments with the inclusion of various combinations of monetization variables – not reported here – generally reveal a similar outcome. When the real income variable is added to regression equation (4) in regression equation (5) in Table 5.6, it enters with an incorrect positive sign although the regression coefficient is statistically significant. There is only a marginal improvement in the fit of the regression equation. The real income variable thus does not add to the explanation given by the monetization variables.

To sum up, the fall in the income velocity of money in Sweden in the pre–World War I period is explained as the outcome of the monetization process. The results for Sweden in this chapter are consistent with the econometric tests in Chapter 4 covering the pre-1914 period in the United States, Canada, the United Kingdom, Norway, as well as Sweden.

# CHAPTER 6

# The global evidence since the 1950s

## 6.1.  Introduction

According to the evidence presented in Chapter 2, the income velocity of money displays a U-shaped curve over the last century. This is the case for a number of countries for which data on velocity exist for long periods of time. However, for most countries such long-run data are not available, precluding econometric tests of the kind presented in Chapters 4 and 5. Nevertheless, it is possible to adapt our approach to the global behavior of velocity in the post–World War II period since statistics are available for this period or parts of it for practically all countries with the exception of the East European economies. The purpose of this chapter is to examine our approach using data for about eighty countries from the early 1950s to the early 1980s.

Our explanation suggests that the income velocity of money should behave differently across countries depending on the stage of financial development. Industrialized countries with well-developed financial systems should generally display a rising trend in velocity, whereas poor countries at an earlier stage of economic growth should, as a rule, have falling trends. Velocity in economies "in between" should exhibit a fairly flat pattern with a weak positive or negative trend. Consequently, we expect to be able to construct a global U-shaped velocity curve where the falling section represents financially less developed economies, the turnaround section middle-income economies, and the rising section rich, highly industrialized countries. To the extent such a curve is found, our approach is supported.

Data from *International Financial Statistics* are used to calculate two measures of velocity, one for a narrow measure of money and one for a broad measure (quasi-money).[1] These two velocity measures (here termed $V1$ and $V2$, respectively) do not correspond exactly to the measures used in previous chapters. In particular, the broad measure apparently includes components excluded from our definition and is closer to $M3$ or $M4$ definitions of money for many countries.

To limit the number of countries studied, those with a population

---

[1] The numerator of the velocity ratio is gross domestic product (GDP) for most countries, but for countries for which GDP is unavailable we used national income.

under 2.5 million in 1975 have been excluded. In addition, countries for which fewer than nine consecutive observations of velocity exist are not included in the sample. Accordingly, velocity, both $V1$ and $V2$, in a total of eighty-four countries is examined here. We are well aware that the IFS data may in many cases be of dubious quality. No reason exists, however, for a systematic bias in the data. We are thus of the opinion that this evidence can throw light on the influence of institutional factors on velocity.

## 6.2.  Patterns expected

The institutional approach suggests that this cross-section data base should give rise to a U-shaped pattern when countries are ordered by stage of economic and financial development. An early stage would represent the monetization process and the rise of the monetary economy at the expense of barter. A later stage would stand for financial sophistication, when money substitutes are developed and economic stability is improved. Because it is difficult to construct a few simple measures of these institutional developments for all countries studied, we have chosen real income per capita as a crude proxy measure of the stage of financial development.

We follow the grouping of the world economies suggested by the World Bank in the *World Development Report 1983*. The following four major groups of countries are isolated: (1) industrial-market economies, with an average GNP per capita of $11,120 in 1981; (2) upper middle-income economies, with an average GNP per capita of $2,490; (3) lower middle-income economies, with an average GNP per capita of $850; and (4) low-income economies, with an average GNP per capita of $270. The individual countries included in these four groups are displayed in Table 6.1. The four groups are of roughly equal size – nineteen industrialized countries, nineteen upper middle-income economies, twenty-seven lower middle-income economies, and nineteen low-income countries – altogether eighty-four countries.

The World Bank grouping also includes East European nonmarket economies (eight countries) and high-income oil exporters (four countries). These countries are excluded as separate entities. Except for Roumania for a few years, no velocity series are available from the East European countries. Of the oil-exporting countries only Libya and Saudi Arabia fulfill the restrictions placed on the selection of countries. We include these two economies among upper middle-income countries, although their per capita real income levels are high enough to classify them in the group of rich countries.

Table 6.1. *Country groupings by level of economic development*

| Group | Countries |
|-------|-----------|
| Industrial-market (rich) economies ($11,120 p.c.) | Switzerland, Sweden, Norway, Germany, Denmark, United States, France, Belgium, Netherlands, Canada, Australia, Finland, Austria, Japan, United Kingdom, New Zealand, Italy, Spain, Ireland |
| Upper middle-income economies ($2,490 p.c.) | Saudi Arabia, Libya, Singapore, Israel, Greece, Venezuela, Uruguay, Yugoslavia, South Africa, Chile, Argentina, Portugal, Mexico, Brazil, Algeria, Malaysia, Iraq, Iran, Korea |
| Lower middle-income economies ($850 p.c.) | Paraguay, Jordan, Syrian Arab Republic, Turkey, Costa Rica, Tunisia, Colombia, Dominican Republic, Ivory Coast, Jamaica, Ecuador, Peru, Guatemala, Nigeria, Nicaragua, Morocco, Philippines, Thailand, El Salvador, Egypt, Zambia, Honduras, Bolivia, Indonesia, Yemen Arab Republic, Senegal, Kenya |
| Low-income economies ($270 p.c.) | Ghana, Togo, Sudan, Pakistan, Madagascar, Sierra Leone, Sri Lanka, Haiti, Tanzania, India, Upper Volta, Burundi, Uganda, Zaire, Malawi, Burma, Nepal, Ethiopia, Bangladesh |

*Notes:* Within each group, countries are ranked according to real per capita income in 1981 U.S. dollars starting with the country with the highest income.
The GNP per capita estimates refer to all countries within each group, respectively. They are not representative for the countries shown in the table since lack of data reduces the selection of economies. However, the GNP per capita estimates give a rough indication of the global spread of incomes.
*Source: World Development Report 1983*, Washington, D.C., 1983, Table 1.

Our institutional approach (see Chapter 3) suggests long-run velocity patterns as depicted in Chart 6.1. This chart gives a schematic illustration of the behavior of velocity for the narrow and the broad definition of the money stock. Both $V1$ and $V2$ display a U-shaped pattern, but the $V1$ curve has an earlier turning point than the $V2$ curve. This relationship reflects, among other things, substitution of interest-bearing time deposits for demand deposits with financial development, and the channeling of savings into commercial banks. Three phases may be distinguished in the stylized chart: phase 1, when both $V1$ and $V2$ are falling; phase 2, when $V1$ is rising and $V2$ continues to fall; and phase 3, when both velocity curves are rising. We would expect to find for the countries of Table 6.1 a picture similar to that in Chart 6.1.

The secular picture is also examined using simple regression estimates of the following form:

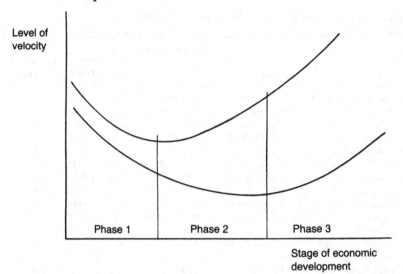

Chart 6.1. Stylized long-run patterns of $V1$ and $V2$ ($V1$ upper solid line, $V2$ lower solid line).

$$V = a + bt \qquad (6.1)$$

where $t$ stands for time. Velocity is thus regressed on time as the independent variable. In this way the time trend of velocity, that is, the $b$ coefficient, is calculated. We expect $b$ to be negative for low-income countries and positive for high-income countries and to be close to zero for middle-income economies, or at least of smaller absolute magnitude than for the richest and poorest economies. We also expect the $b$ coefficient to be different for $V1$ and $V2$, as shown in Chart 6.1. Next, we examine how well the data fit the patterns suggested by our approach.

## 6.3. Empirical results

To examine the aggregate behavior of velocity, Table 6.2 shows regression equations for the four groupings of countries. (The aggregate velocity curve is calculated as the average of individual country curves; see the notes to Table 6.2.) There the coefficient $b$ for $V1$ is positive for the rich and the upper middle-income economies and negative for the poor economies and the lower middle-income countries – a result in line with our approach. The regressions for $V2$ –

Table 6.2. *Velocity behavior for country groupings*

| Group | Period | Regression estimates $b^a$ | $R^2$ | DW | Growth of velocity (%) |
|---|---|---|---|---|---|
| 1. Industrial-market | V1: 1952–82 | .067 (21.7) | .940 | .871 | 1.4 |
| (rich) economies | V2: 1952–82 | −.009 (−13.2) | .853 | 1.305 | −.5 |
| 2. Upper middle- | V1: 1953–82 | .068 (6.4) | .575 | .487 | .8 |
| income economies | V2: 1953–82 | −.068 (−16.1) | .900 | .894 | −2.6 |
| 3. Lower middle- | V1: 1952–82 | −.034 (−5.2) | .462 | .863 | .0 |
| income economies | V2: 1952–82 | −.118 (−26.0) | .957 | 1.270 | −2.2 |
| 4. Low-income | V1: 1962–82 | −.125 (−10.2) | .840 | 1.091 | −1.6 |
| economies | V2: 1962–82 | −.176 (−21.8) | .960 | 1.178 | −3.3 |
| 5. Germany, Italy, | V1: 1952–82 | −.031 (−10.9) | .797 | 1.100 | −.6 |
| Japan | V2: 1952–82 | −.040 (−12.9) | .847 | .328 | −2.6 |
| 6. Industrial- | V1: 1952–82 | .086 (26.2) | .958 | .854 | 1.7 |
| market economies excl. group 5 | V2: 1952–82 | −.004 (−4.0) | .341 | .857 | −.2 |
| 7. High-inflation | V1: 1952–82 | .273 (10.2) | .774 | .317 | 3.8 |
| economies | V2: 1952–82 | .032 (3.7) | .301 | .740 | .2 |
| 8. Upper middle-in- | V1: 1953–81 | −.022 (−4.6) | .413 | 1.146 | −.5 |
| come economies excl. group 7 | V2: 1953–81 | −.104 (−20.2) | .936 | .760 | −3.2 |

*Notes:* The group-specific velocity curve used for calculating the table is derived in the following way. The mean level of velocity is calculated for the first year when data on velocity is available for every country within the group (that is the base year). For the other years the arithmetic means of the annual first differences are calculated. Going forward from the base year, these values are successively added to the mean level of the base year. Going backward from the base year, the values are successively subtracted. In this manner we construct the common velocity curve for the whole period. The procedure is halted when more than one-third of the countries have dropped out of the sample (this occurs in 1962 for the low-income countries).
Regression equation: $V = a + bt$, where $t$ stands for time.
$^a$ *t*-statistics in parentheses.

see also Table 6.2 – reveal that the *b* coefficient is negative for all groups of countries. The coefficient becomes gradually smaller in absolute value as real income increases. A comparison with the stylized curves in Chart 6.1 suggests that the V1 and V2 curves have passed through the first and second phase but not yet reached the third phase, when both curves display an upward trend.

The trends calculated in Table 6.2 for the four country groups are displayed in Charts 6.2 through 6.5 together with the actual behavior of velocity. These charts reveal that a linear trend follows actual velocity fairly closely. Experiments with nonlinear trends did not offer

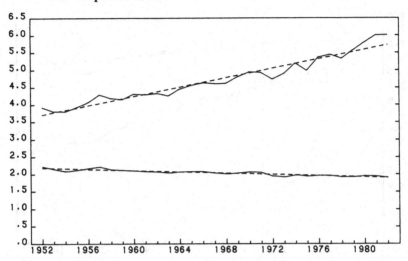

Chart 6.2. Income velocity of money of industrial-market economies
(V1 upper solid line, V2 lower solid line; trend values dashed line).
(*Notes:* See Table 6.1 for the countries covered. See Table 6.2 for the
trend of velocity.)

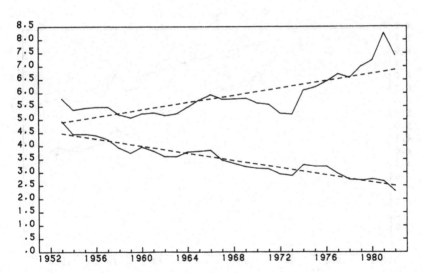

Chart 6.3. Income velocity of money of upper middle-income economies (V1 upper solid line, V2 lower solid line; trend values dashed
line). (*Notes:* See Table 6.1 for the countries covered. See Table 6.2
for the trend of velocity.)

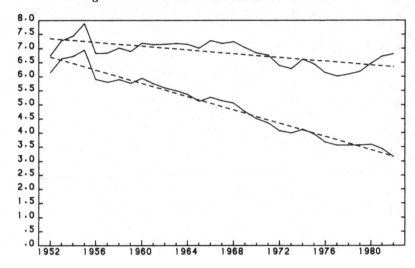

Chart 6.4. Income velocity of money of lower middle-income economies (*V*1 upper solid line, *V*2 lower solid line; trend values dashed
line). (*Notes:* See Table 6.1 for the countries covered. See Table 6.2
for the trend of velocity.)

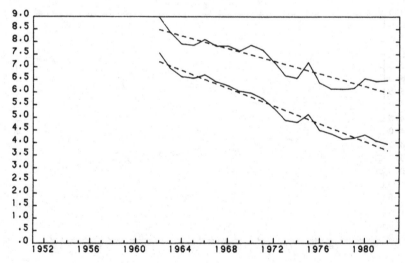

Chart 6.5. Income velocity of money of low-income economies (*V*1
upper solid line, *V*2 lower solid line; trend values dashed line). (*Notes:*
See Table 6.1 for the countries covered. See Table 6.2 for the trend
of velocity.)

any advantages. The velocity curve for the poor countries in Chart 6.5 does not start until 1962 since most poor countries did not achieve nation status until the 1960s.

Charts 6.2 through 6.5 are combined, using a common scale for velocity, in Chart 6.6 to construct the global curve. Here a global velocity curve can clearly be discerned with a U-shaped pattern for the $V1$ curve. However, the velocity curve for the broader money stock measure continues to be downward-sloping for all four groups of economies, albeit at a "slower" rate. Chart 6.6 also shows that the level of velocity curves for the rich and the upper middle-income groups is lower than for the other two groups.

So far, the aggregate behavior of velocity has been considered. Calculation of velocity trends for each individual country reveals a number of interesting features. Table 6.3 displays regressions for $V1$ and $V2$ on time for all eighty-four countries as well as the average growth rate for $V1$ and $V2$ calculated as cumulative annual changes from the starting year to the terminal year. See also Appendix A at the end of the chapter, which displays in charts the velocity curves for each of the eighty-four countries in our sample.

Two groups of countries do not fit into our classification scheme by level of per capita income: within the rich group, Germany, Italy, and Japan; and within the upper middle-income group five high-inflation countries.

Among the group of nineteen rich economies underlying Chart 6.2, velocity $V1$ grows secularly in all except Germany, Italy, and Japan, which display falling trends (see regressions 4, 14, and 17 in Table 6.3 as well as Appendix A to this chapter). The common trend behavior for these countries is estimated in regression 5 in Table 6.2. This pattern is also shown by the common velocity curves calculated for these three countries in Chart 6.7.

We do not have a simple explanation of this trend for Germany, Italy, and Japan. One possible explanation (or part of it) would emphasize the financial effects on these countries of having been "losers" in World War II. The war could have temporarily set the financial system "backward" compared to the situation in the rest of the rich countries, as exemplified by the destruction of the national currencies and/or national debt in each of these countries, and the decartelization of the banking system in Germany and Japan. Thus we would expect velocity to start rising in the future, following the standard pattern of the rich countries. Also, the commercial banking system in these three countries has played a more important role in financing industry and government than in many other countries. Thus the

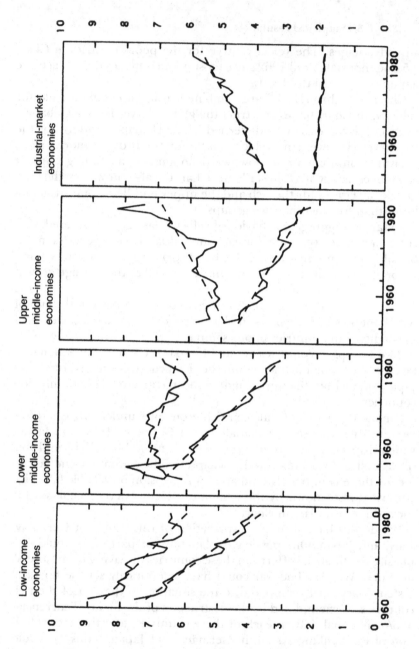

Chart 6.6. Global velocity curve: Eighty-four countries (*V*1 upper
solid line, *V*2 lower solid line; trend values dashed line). (*Notes:* See
Table 6.1 for the countries covered. See Table 6.2 for the trend of
velocity.)

Table 6.3. *Global trend behavior of velocity: Eighty-four countries*

| Country (GNP p.c. 1981 U.S. $) | Period | Regression estimates | | | Growth of velocity (%) |
|---|---|---|---|---|---|
| | | $b^a$ | $R^2$ | DW | |
| *Industrial-market (rich) economies* | | | | | |
| 1. Switzerland | V1: 1952–82 | .026 (7.22) | .643 | .920 | 1.5 |
| ($17,340) | V2: 1952–82 | .001 (.42) | .006 | .810 | −.2 |
| 2. Sweden | V1: 1952–82 | .068 (8.13) | .695 | .869 | .1 |
| ($14,870) | V2: 1952–82 | .004 (2.42) | .168 | 1.000 | −.2 |
| 3. Norway | V1: 1952–82 | .060 (7.33) | .650 | .455 | 1.8 |
| ($14,060) | V2: 1952–82 | −.001 (−.43) | .006 | .432 | .3 |
| 4. Germany | V1: 1952–82 | −.005 (−.94) | .030 | 1.680 | −.2 |
| ($13,450) | V2: 1952–82 | −.052 (−12.21) | .837 | .322 | −2.7 |
| 5. Denmark | V1: 1952–82 | .024 (6.04) | .557 | 1.187 | .5 |
| ($13,120) | V2: 1952–82 | .009 (6.16) | .566 | 1.151 | .4 |
| 6. United States | V1: 1952–82 | .126 (29.24) | .967 | .339 | 2.9 |
| ($12,820) | V2: 1952–82 | .024 (12.03) | .817 | .808 | 1.0 |
| 7. France | V1: 1952–82 | .028 (4.36) | .413 | .301 | .6 |
| ($12,190) | V2: 1952–82 | −.047 (−14.87) | .891 | .598 | −1.8 |
| 8. Belgium | V1: 1952–82 | .074 (17.00) | .909 | .435 | 2.2 |
| ($11,920) | V2: 1952–82 | .001 (1.00) | .033 | 1.323 | .1 |
| 9. Netherlands | V1: 1952–82 | .073 (19.40) | .929 | 1.595 | 1.9 |
| ($11,790) | V2: 1952–82 | −.019 (−9.24) | .746 | .641 | −.8 |
| 10. Canada | V1: 1952–82 | .082 (4.18) | .376 | .346 | 1.8 |
| ($11,400) | V2: 1952–82 | −.030 (−9.80) | .768 | .562 | −1.1 |
| 11. Australia | V1: 1952–82 | .188 (35.23) | .977 | 1.543 | 3.9 |
| ($11,080) | V2: 1952–82 | .025 (17.50) | .913 | .946 | 1.6 |
| 12. Finland | V1: 1952–82 | .100 (5.33) | .495 | .655 | .7 |
| ($10,680) | V2: 1952–82 | −.013 (−4.93) | .456 | .705 | −1.1 |
| 13. Austria | V1: 1952–82 | .076 (9.34) | .757 | .897 | 1.5 |
| ($10,210) | V2: 1952–82 | −.062 (−19.30) | .930 | .495 | −3.3 |
| 14. Japan | V1: 1952–82 | −.026 (−5.41) | .510 | .768 | −.4 |
| ($10,080) | V2: 1952–82 | −.020 (−9.88) | .777 | 1.569 | −1.8 |
| 15. United Kingdom | V1: 1952–82 | .135 (31.17) | .971 | 1.709 | 2.9 |
| ($9,110) | V2: 1952–82 | .023 (4.59) | .421 | .424 | 1.0 |
| 16. New Zealand | V1: 1952–82 | .209 (18.54) | .925 | .593 | 3.9 |
| ($7,700) | V2: 1952–82 | .044 (3.95) | .358 | .227 | 1.5 |
| 17. Italy | V1: 1952–82 | −.064 (−12.27) | .843 | .259 | −1.5 |
| ($6,960) | V2: 1952–82 | −.041 (−13.99) | .875 | .229 | −2.1 |
| 18. Spain | V1: 1952–82 | .016 (3.79) | .347 | .384 | .6 |
| ($5,640) | V2: 1952–82 | −.029 (−12.66) | .856 | .298 | −1.8 |
| 19. Ireland | V1: 1952–82 | .080 (7.89) | .682 | .247 | 1.9 |
| ($5,230) | V2: 1952–82 | .013 (8.46) | .711 | .896 | .7 |
| *Upper middle-income economies* | | | | | |
| 20. Saudi Arabia | V1: 1952–82 | .058 (.88) | .043 | 1.195 | .9 |
| ($12,600) | V2: 1952–82 | .022 (.46) | .012 | 1.099 | −.4 |
| 21. Libya | V1: 1960–78 | −.206 (−5.20) | .614 | .572 | −3.2 |
| ($8,450) | V2: 1960–78 | −.164 (−5.66) | .653 | .572 | −3.5 |
| 22. Singapore | V1: 1968–81 | −.007 (−.45) | .016 | 1.694 | −.1 |
| ($5,240) | V2: 1968–81 | −.010 (−1.60) | .175 | .844 | −1.3 |

Table 6.3. *(cont.)*

| Country (GNP p.c. 1981 U.S. $) | Period | $b^a$ | $R^2$ | DW | Growth of velocity (%) |
|---|---|---|---|---|---|
| *Upper middle-income economies* | | | | | |
| 23. Israel | V1: 1952–82 | .311 (5.16) | .478 | .161 | 5.3 |
| ($5,160) | V2: 1952–82 | −.108 (23.94) | .952 | .691 | −4.0 |
| 24. Greece | V1: 1952–82 | −.145 (−7.11) | .643 | .160 | −2.4 |
| ($4,420) | V2: 1952–82 | −.174 (−8.83) | .736 | .121 | −5.9 |
| 25. Venezuela | V1: 1952–82 | −.057 (−3.16) | .256 | .369 | −.9 |
| ($4,220) | V2: 1952–82 | −.091 (−9.64) | .762 | .670 | −2.7 |
| 26. Uruguay | V1: 1955–82 | .194 (7.36) | .676 | 1.147 | 2.0 |
| ($2,820) | V2: 1955–82 | −.000 (−.01) | .000 | .470 | −3.2 |
| 27. Yugoslavia | V1: 1960–81 | −.001 (−0.5) | .000 | .494 | .3 |
| ($2,790) | V2: 1960–81 | −.033 (−7.59) | .743 | 1.148 | −1.9 |
| 28. South Africa | V1: 1952–82 | .110 (11.85) | .829 | .528 | 2.0 |
| ($2,770) | V2: 1952–82 | −.015 (−4.37) | .397 | .622 | −.1 |
| 29. Chile | V1: 1964–82 | .496 (3.95) | .479 | .702 | 5.7 |
| ($2,560) | V2: 1964–82 | −.067 (−1.09) | .065 | .782 | −.8 |
| 30. Argentina | V1: 1965–81 | .366 (3.59) | .518 | 1.016 | 6.7 |
| ($2,560) | V2: 1965–81 | −.023 (−.68) | .037 | 1.664 | −.9 |
| 31. Portugal | V1: 1952–80 | .021 (5.45) | .534 | .554 | 1.1 |
| ($2,520) | V2: 1953–80 | −.024 (−11.66) | .840 | .406 | −1.7 |
| 32. Mexico | V1: 1952–81 | .014 (1.50) | .075 | .849 | .4 |
| ($2,250) | V2: 1952–81 | −.090 (−4.87) | .459 | .325 | −2.7 |
| 33. Brazil | V1: 1952–81 | .181 (10.27) | .790 | .442 | 3.5 |
| ($2,220) | V2: 1952–81 | .153 (12.37) | .845 | .772 | 3.4 |
| 34. Algeria | V1: 1964–81 | −.057 (−3.89) | .486 | .472 | −2.6 |
| ($2,140) | V2: 1964–81 | −.060 (−4.02) | .503 | .415 | −3.1 |
| 35. Malaysia | V1: 1955–82 | .020 (1.33) | .064 | .422 | .8 |
| ($1,840) | V2: 1955–82 | −.073 (−8.38) | .730 | .385 | −2.4 |
| 36. Iraq | V1: 1953–76 | .033 (2.15) | .173 | 1.242 | .5 |
| | V2: 1953–76 | −.008 (−.69) | .021 | 1.119 | −.3 |
| 37. Iran | V1: 1959–80 | −.092 (−2.09) | .195 | .847 | −4.4 |
| | V2: 1959–80 | −.151 (−7.71) | .768 | .830 | −6.1 |
| 38. Korea | V1: 1953–82 | −.159 (−4.53) | .423 | .869 | −2.3 |
| ($1,700) | V2: 1953–82 | −.366 (11.37) | .822 | .636 | −6.0 |
| *Lower middle-income economies* | | | | | |
| 39. Paraguay | V1: 1952–82 | −.018 (−.60) | .012 | .695 | 1.6 |
| ($1,630) | V2: 1952–82 | −.217 (−8.35) | .706 | .415 | −1.5 |
| 40. Jordan | V1: 1959–82 | −.106 (−5.81) | .605 | .341 | −2.7 |
| ($1,620) | V2: 1959–82 | −.104 (−8.95) | .784 | .372 | −4.5 |
| 41. Syrian A.R. | V1: 1963–81 | −.086 (−10.10) | .857 | 1.497 | −2.3 |
| ($1,570) | V2: 1963–81 | −.086 (−11.43) | .885 | 1.640 | −2.5 |
| 42. Turkey | V1: 1952–82 | .013 (.92) | .028 | .336 | .5 |
| ($1,540) | V2: 1952–82 | −.035 (−3.70) | .321 | .595 | −1.4 |
| 43. Costa Rica | V1: 1952–80 | −.034 (−3.93) | .364 | 1.263 | −.3 |
| ($1,430) | V2: 1952–80 | −.104 (−10.29) | .797 | .628 | −2.9 |
| 44. Tunisia | V1: 1960–78 | −.001 (−.12) | .001 | 1.683 | −.4 |
| ($1,420) | V2: 1960–78 | −.057 (−9.41) | .839 | .973 | −2.5 |

108

| Country (GNP p.c. 1981 U.S. $) | Period | Regression estimates $b^a$ | $R^2$ | DW | Growth of velocity (%) |
|---|---|---|---|---|---|
| 45. Colombia | V1: 1952–81 | .009 (.77) | .021 | .414 | .3 |
| ($1,380) | V2: 1952–81 | −.026 (−3.60) | .316 | 1.225 | −1.1 |
| 46. Dominican Rep. | V1: 1952–80 | .084 (4.80) | .461 | 1.767 | 1.1 |
| ($1,260) | V2: 1952–80 | −.064 (−3.85) | .354 | 1.246 | −.7 |
| 47. Ivory Coast | V1: 1962–78 | −.111 (−12.40) | .911 | 1.362 | −1.8 |
| ($1,200) | V2: 1962–78 | −.147 (−19.80) | .963 | 2.025 | −3.4 |
| 48. Jamaica | V1: 1953–82 | −.082 (−4.78) | .450 | 1.041 | −.7 |
| ($1,180) | V2: 1953–82 | −.089 (−10.11) | .785 | .772 | −2.8 |
| 49. Ecuador | V1: 1952–82 | −.133 (−14.87) | .884 | .824 | −1.5 |
| ($1,180) | V2: 1952–82 | −.105 (−14.35) | .876 | .647 | −1.8 |
| 50. Peru | V1: 1952–82 | −.064 (−2.78) | .210 | .328 | .6 |
| ($1,170) | V2: 1952–82 | −.027 (−4.49) | .411 | .821 | −.9 |
| 51. Guatemala | V1: 1952–81 | .015 (.97) | .033 | .802 | .1 |
| ($1,140) | V2: 1952–81 | −.181 (−16.30) | .905 | .605 | −2.7 |
| 52. Nigeria | V1: 1952–81 | −.110 (−3.73) | .332 | .431 | −2.1 |
| ($870) | V2: 1952–81 | −.167 (−11.18) | .817 | .775 | −3.4 |
| 53. Nicaragua | V1: 1960–78 | .004 (.11) | .001 | .925 | .2 |
| ($860) | V2: 1960–78 | −.157 (−5.48) | .639 | .859 | −2.1 |
| 54. Morocco | V1: 1958–82 | −.039 (−8.74) | .769 | .795 | −1.2 |
| ($860) | V2: 1958–82 | −.049 (−9.54) | .799 | .551 | −1.8 |
| 55. Philippines | V1: 1952–82 | .171 (11.06) | .808 | .786 | 2.2 |
| ($790) | V2: 1952–82 | −.030 (−3.00) | .237 | .428 | −1.1 |
| 56. Thailand | V1: 1952–82 | .151 (11.50) | .820 | .424 | 1.8 |
| ($790) | V2: 1952–82 | −.102 (−24.79) | .955 | .529 | −3.0 |
| 57. El Salvador | V1: 1952–82 | −.014 (−.75) | .019 | .301 | −.5 |
| ($650) | V2: 1952–82 | −.111 (−21.83) | .943 | .951 | −2.7 |
| 58. Egypt | V1: 1952–82 | .004 (.65) | .014 | .615 | .5 |
| ($650) | V2: 1952–82 | −.027 (−4.55) | .417 | .327 | −1.7 |
| 59. Zambia | V1: 1965–82 | −.156 (−5.10) | .619 | 1.623 | −3.5 |
| ($600) | V2: 1965–82 | −.158 (−6.60) | .731 | .945 | −5.3 |
| 60. Honduras | V1: 1952–82 | −.068 (−3.63) | .312 | .531 | −.7 |
| ($600) | V2: 1952–82 | −.166 (−12.56) | .845 | .552 | −2.7 |
| 61. Bolivia | V1: 1952–79 | −.365 (−3.96) | .376 | .707 | −1.2 |
| ($600) | V2: 1952–79 | −.461 (−5.61) | .548 | .809 | −2.6 |
| 62. Indonesia | V1: 1965–82 | −.411 (−4.15) | .519 | .804 | −.6 |
| ($530) | V2: 1965–82 | −.562 (−5.37) | .643 | .772 | −3.6 |
| 63. Yemen A.R. | V1: 1973–82 | −.250 (−2.89) | .510 | .514 | −8.6 |
| ($460) | V2: 1973–82 | −.211 (−2.93) | .518 | .508 | −8.8 |
| 64. Senegal | V1: 1962–81 | −.141 (−3.39) | .389 | .355 | −.7 |
| ($430) | V2: 1962–81 | −.193 (−4.58) | .539 | .321 | −2.0 |
| 65. Kenya | V1: 1966–82 | −.063 (−2.40) | .278 | .749 | −1.3 |
| ($420) | V2: 1966–82 | −.071 (−5.04) | .629 | .806 | −2.1 |
| *Low-income economies* | | | | | |
| 66. Ghana | V1: 1955–78 | −.083 (−3.87) | .405 | .860 | −1.1 |
| ($400) | V2: 1955–78 | −.115 (−9.13) | .791 | 1.079 | −1.6 |
| 67. Togo | V1: 1962–81 | −.312 (−11.56) | .881 | 1.603 | −5.3 |
| ($380) | V2: 1962–81 | −.358 (−16.27) | .936 | 1.603 | −6.5 |

109

Table 6.3. *(cont.)*

| Country (GNP p.c. 1981 U.S. $) | Period | Regression estimates $b^a$ | $R^2$ | DW | Growth of velocity (%) |
|---|---|---|---|---|---|
| *Low-income economies* | | | | | |
| 68. Sudan | V1: 1956–78 | −.271 (−14.35) | .907 | .720 | −3.6 |
| ($380) | V2: 1956–78 | −.289 (−11.91) | .871 | .679 | −4.2 |
| 69. Pakistan | V1: 1960–82 | −.118 (−4.85) | .528 | .774 | −1.3 |
| ($350) | V2: 1960–82 | −.119 (−6.83) | .690 | .691 | −2.4 |
| 70. Madagascar | V1: 1962–79 | −.052 (−3.20) | .405 | 1.006 | −1.5 |
| ($330) | V2: 1962–79 | −.099 (−8.80) | .838 | 1.151 | −2.7 |
| 71. Sierra Leone | V1: 1964–81 | −.223 (−5.30) | .637 | 1.658 | −1.0 |
| ($320) | V2: 1964–81 | −.223 (−9.17) | .840 | 1.740 | −2.7 |
| 72. Sri Lanka | V1: 1952–82 | .087 (6.53) | .595 | .724 | 1.6 |
| ($300) | V2: 1952–82 | .032 (−3.99) | .354 | .738 | −1.2 |
| 73. Haiti | V1: 1966–82 | −.447 (−8.60) | .831 | 1.472 | −4.6 |
| ($300) | V2: 1966–82 | −.502 (−12.14) | .908 | .616 | −7.3 |
| 74. Tanzania | V1: 1966–81 | −.174 (−5.69) | .698 | 1.101 | −5.2 |
| ($280) | V2: 1966–81 | −.164 (−7.20) | .787 | .957 | −5.9 |
| 75. India | V1: 1952–81 | .021 (2.94) | .236 | 1.245 | .4 |
| ($260) | V2: 1952–81 | −.061 (−7.84) | .687 | .450 | −2.2 |
| 76. Upper Volta | V1: 1965–79 | −.294 (−4.2) | .598 | 1.148 | −1.6 |
| ($240) | V2: 1965–79 | −.382 (−5.83) | .739 | 1.060 | −3.5 |
| 77. Burundi | V1: 1964–82 | −.165 (−3.84) | .464 | 1.678 | −.9 |
| ($230) | V2: 1964–82 | −.167 (−4.18) | .507 | 1.743 | −1.2 |
| 78. Uganda | V1: 1966–78 | −.001 (−.01) | .000 | .975 | 2.4 |
| ($220) | V2: 1966–78 | .062 (.90) | .068 | 1.006 | 3.4 |
| 79. Zaire | V1: 1963–82 | .025 (.72) | .028 | 1.382 | −.3 |
| ($210) | V2: 1963–82 | −.006 (−.22) | .003 | 1.221 | −.9 |
| 80. Malawi | V1: 1965–82 | .046 (.90) | .049 | .612 | .8 |
| ($200) | V2: 1965–82 | −.124 (−4.88) | .598 | .676 | −2.0 |
| 81. Burma | V1: 1952–82 | −.033 (−1.61) | .082 | .370 | −1.8 |
| ($190) | V2: 1952–82 | −.053 (−3.07) | .245 | .396 | −2.7 |
| 82. Nepal | V1: 1958–82 | −.652 (−6.96) | .678 | .428 | −5.1 |
| ($150) | V2: 1958–82 | −.757 (10.39) | .824 | .417 | −7.8 |
| 83. Ethiopia | V1: 1961–82 | −.295 (−9.45) | .817 | .553 | −3.8 |
| ($140) | V2: 1961–82 | −.280 (−19.77) | .951 | .889 | −4.5 |
| 84. Bangladesh | V1: 1974–82 | −.437 (−1.59) | .265 | 2.121 | .3 |
| ($140) | V2: 1974–82 | −.364 (−2.56) | .483 | 2.315 | −3.0 |

*Notes:* Regression equation: $V = a + bt$, where $t$ stands for time; $t = 0$ for 1950. Annual average growth in velocity is calculated as the compound growth rate.
$^a$ $t$-statistics in parentheses.
*Source:* Velocity is calculated from data in *International Financial Statistics*. Grouping of countries and per capita income is from *World Development Report 1983*, Washington, D.C., Table 1.

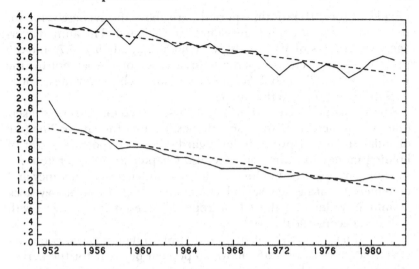

Chart 6.7. Income velocity of money of Germany, Italy, and Japan (*V*1 upper solid line, *V*2 lower solid line; trend values dashed line). (*Note:* See Table 6.2 for the trend of velocity.)

supply of money substitutes in the form of bonds and stocks has been comparatively limited in these countries, which would help to explain why velocity there has not exhibited the rising trend of other advanced countries. However, the velocity curve *V*1 in Germany is almost horizontal, and *V*2 is falling, which may indicate that *V*1 will start rising in the near future in that country.

When Germany, Italy, and Japan are separated from the rest of the set of rich, industrialized economies, a more pronounced upward trend appears in *V*1 as well as a flat *V*2 curve, thus moving this group of countries closer to phase 3 of Chart 6.1. See also regressions 5 and 6 in Table 6.2.

The behavior of *V*2 across the nineteen individual rich countries in Table 6.3 is divergent, four countries displaying a rising tend ($b > .02$), nine countries a flat trend ($-.02 < b < .02$), and six countries a falling trend ($b < -.02$). Thus a few countries, namely the United States, Australia, the United Kingdom, and New Zealand, have actually reached phase 3 of Chart 6.1.

Turning to the upper middle-income group, the individual regressions for *V*1 show that Israel, Uruguay, Chile, Argentina, and Brazil display very high growth rates for this velocity concept. The *b* coefficients are .311, .194, .496, .366, and .181, respectively. These values, calculated for different time periods, are above the average value for the group, as seen from regression 2 in Table 6.2. The annual average growth rates of $V1$ are also very high: 5.3, 2.0, 5.7, 6.7, and 3.5 percent, respectively, compared to an average of 1.0 percent for the whole group in Table 6.2. See also the velocity charts for these countries in Appendix A to this chapter.

The strong positive trend of $V1$ for these five countries is most likely due to extremely high and rising domestic rates of inflation. The rate of inflation should properly be regarded as an opportunity cost of holding money (on this point see also Chapter 2). As the rate rises, the public reduces its holding of money – in particular currency and non-interest-bearing deposits, which dominate the narrow money stock definition underlying the $V1$ concept. This result is consistent with prevailing economic theory.[2]

To highlight the role of high and rising inflation rates, countries with average inflation rates above 20 percent per year for the period are singled out; the group comprises the five countries just mentioned: Israel, Uruguay, Chile, Argentina, and Brazil.[3] The average velocity curve as well as its time trend is calculated for them. See regression 7 in Table 6.2 and Chart 6.8. The chart shows that $V1$ has a sharp upward trend, rising for the group from a level of 4 to a level of 13 from 1952 to 1982. $V2$, however, remains fairly flat. This result likely reflects interest payments on time deposits, which partially compensate for high rates of inflation. The effect is to raise the demand for interest-bearing time deposits relative to non-interest-bearing demand deposits.

Because the high-inflation economies display a specific pattern, they are excluded from the sample of upper middle-income countries used to calculate the global velocity curve displayed in Chart 6.9. This arrangement gives rise to a sharp difference in the behavior of $V1$ as compared to Chart 6.6. Here, when the high-inflation countries are excluded, the trend of $V1$ for upper middle-income countries falls instead of rises as in Chart 6.6. The trend of $V2$, however, is not affected much. The turnaround point of the global $V1$ curve is thus "pushed forward" to occur "between" upper middle-income and rich, industrialized economies. Judging from Chart 6.9, the velocity curves

---

[2] Laidler (1985) summarizes evidence for money demand studies for high-inflation countries. These studies show a strong influence of inflation (expected inflation) on the demand for money and thus on velocity in the manner shown by Chart 6.8 and Table 6.2.

[3] An inspection of the velocity curves of individual countries reveals that periods of high and rising inflation rates tend to be associated with rising velocity ($V1$).

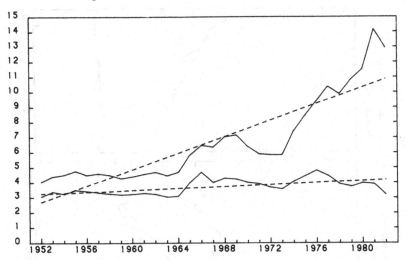

Chart 6.8. Income velocity of money of high-inflation economies (Israel, Uruguay, Chile, Argentina, and Brazil) (*V*1 upper solid line, *V*2 lower solid line; trend values dashed line). (*Note:* See Table 6.2 for the trend of velocity.)

of lower middle-income and upper middle-income countries are now quite similar.

Individual country behavior among upper middle-income countries is more divergent than is the case among rich countries (see Appendix A). Excluding high-inflation countries, *V*1 rises only in Saudi Arabia, South Africa, Mexico, Portugal, Malaysia, and Iraq. Actually, the patterns of South Africa and Portugal are close to those of the industrialized market economies. *V*2 falls or is flat except for Saudi Arabia and Brazil. The observed pattern of *V*2 behavior fits nicely into our approach.

The pattern for individual countries in the lower middle-income group is well in accord with our approach. *V*1 has an upward trend in three out of twenty-seven economies (Dominican Republic, Philippines, and Thailand), a flat trend in eight cases, and a downward trend in the remaining countries. *V*2 is flat or falling in all instances. To sum up, as seen from Charts 6.6 and 6.9 as well as in the charts in Appendix A, the lower middle-income countries behave in roughly the same mode as the upper middle-income countries, ignoring high-inflation economies.

For most of the low-income countries in Table 6.3, *V*1 and *V*2 fall

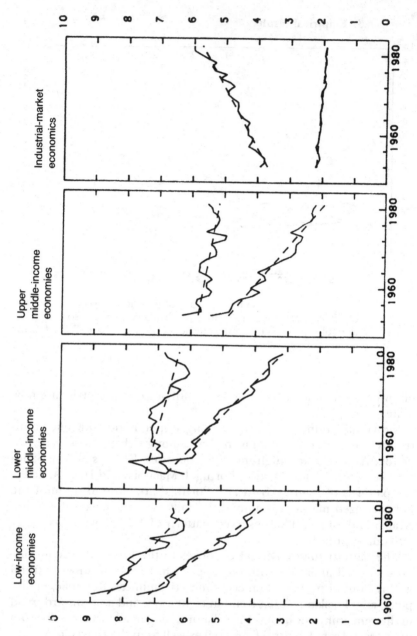

Chart 6.9. Global velocity curve excluding high-inflation economies (Israel, Uruguay, Chile, Argentina, and Brazil) (*V*1 upper solid line, *V*2 lower solid line; trend values dashed line). (*Notes:* See Table 6.1 for the countries covered. See Table 6.2 for the trend of velocity.)

fairly sharply, in particular for African states such as Togo, Sudan, Tanzania, Upper Volta, and Ethiopia. Only four countries actually display an upward trend in $V1$, namely Sri Lanka, India, Zaire, and Malawi. All other countries have a downward or flat trend in both $V1$ and $V2$, confirming our approach on a global level. It is also worth pointing out that velocity falls more sharply in the least developed (poorest) countries than in richer countries. See also the charts in Appendix A to this chapter.

To summarize the evidence for the individual countries in Table 6.3, Table 6.4 classifies all countries used to construct the global velocity curve by phase of secular velocity behavior. According to our hypothesis, as illustrated in Chart 6.1, $V1$ and $V2$ should each pass through three phases: phase 1, when both $V1$ and $V2$ are falling; phase 2, when $V1$ is rising and $V2$ continues to fall; and phase 3, when both velocity curves are rising. In Table 6.4, the eighty-four countries in our sample are grouped into three phases based on the signs of the regression coefficient $b$ calculated in Table 6.3. In accordance with our hypothesis, low-income and lower middle-income countries dominate the first phase, middle-income countries dominate the second phase, and rich countries dominate the third phase.

An alternative piece of evidence derives from running a pooled cross-section time series regression similar to the approach taken in Chapter 4. However, unlike in Chapter 4 we do not have consistent measures of our institutional variables for all countries in our global sample. As a substitute for these proxies we adopt real per capita income as a very rough measure of financial development. We run the regression of the form shown in equation (6.2). This equation is expressed as a quadratic function to capture the postulated U-shaped velocity curve. A log-linear form is adopted to avoid problems of heteroscedasticity and to make the results consistent with the econometric work in chapters 4 and 5.

$$\log V_{it} = b_0 + b_1 \log\left(\frac{Y}{N}\right)_{it} + b_2 \left[\log\left(\frac{Y}{N}\right)_{it}\right]^2 + b_3 \hat{P}_{it} + \sum_{i=2}^{I} b_{4i} D_i + u_{it} \quad (6.2)$$

$$t = 1, \ldots, N \qquad i = 1, \ldots, I$$

where $V_{it}$ is velocity for country $i$ in year $t$, $(Y/N)_{it}$ is per capita real income for country $i$ in year $t$ measured in U.S. dollars, $\hat{P}_{it}$ is the rate of inflation for country $i$ in year $t$ defined as the first difference of the log of the price level, and $D_i$ is a one-zero dummy for country $i$. Ac-

Table 6.4. *Countries grouped by phase of secular behavior of velocity*

| Phase | Countries |
|---|---|
| **Phase 1** (both $V1$ and $V2$ falling) | |
| Rich | Germany, Japan, Italy |
| Upper middle-income | Libya, Singapore, Greece, Venezuela, Yugoslavia, Algeria, Iran, Korea |
| Lower middle-income | Paraguay, Jordan, Syria, Costa Rica, Tunisia, Ivory Coast, Jamaica, Ecuador, Peru, Nigeria, Morocco, El Salvador, Zambia, Honduras, Bolivia, Indonesia, Yemen A.R., Senegal, Kenya |
| Low-income | Ghana, Togo, Sudan, Pakistan, Madagascar, Sierra Leone, Haiti, Tanzania, Upper Volta, Burundi, Burma, Nepal, Ethiopia, Bangladesh |
| **Phase 2** ($V1$ rising, $V2$ falling) | |
| Rich | Norway, France, Netherlands, Finland, Spain |
| Upper middle-income | Israel, Uruguay, South Africa, Chile, Argentina, Portugal, Mexico, Malaysia, Iraq |
| Lower middle-income | Turkey, Colombia, Dominican Rep., Guatemala, Nicaragua, Philippines, Thailand, Egypt |
| Low-income | Sri Lanka, India, Zaire, Malawi |
| **Phase 3** (both $V1$ and $V2$ rising) | |
| Rich | Switzerland, Sweden, Denmark, United States, Belgium, Canada, Australia, Austria, United Kingdom, New Zealand, Ireland |
| Upper middle-income | Saudi Arabia, Brazil |
| Lower middle-income | |
| Low-income | Uganda |

*Notes:* The classification of individual countries into phases is based on the sign of the regression coefficient $b$ in Table 6.3. For a few countries the velocity curve, either $V1$ or $V2$, has been horizontal. In these border cases the sign of the regression coefficient has determined the grouping of phase, although the regression coefficient is not significantly different from zero.

*Source:* See Table 6.1 for the grouping of countries according to per capita income.

cording to our hypothesis, for both $V1$ and $V2$, $b_1$ should be negative, $b_2$ and $b_3$ positive. Furthermore, our hypothesis postulates that $b_1$ should be larger in absolute value for $V2$ than for $V1$.

Regressions of equation (6.2) over the period 1952–82 for seventy-four countries for which a complete data set exists are presented in

Table 6.5. *Pooled regressions of the global velocity function, 1952–82: Seventy-four countries*

| Dependent variable | Coefficients of independent variables (t-values in parentheses) | | | | | | |
| | Constant | log($Y/N$) | [log($Y/N$)]$^2$ | $\hat{P}$ | $R^2$ | SEE | DW |
|---|---|---|---|---|---|---|---|
| *log* V1 | | | | | | | |
| OLS dummies | 53.81 | −1.168 | .081 | .002 | .8550 | .0328 | .59 |
| | (13.20)* | (−10.74)* | (11.19)* | (6.01)* | | | |
| C–O dummies | .046 | −.768 | .058 | .001 | .9380 | .0085 | 1.87 |
| | (2.66)* | (−4.30)* | (4.66)* | (3.32)* | | | |
| *log* V2 | | | | | | | |
| OLS dummies | 8.155 | −1.405 | .066 | .001 | .888 | .0353 | .54 |
| | (19.30)* | (−12.46)* | (8.84)* | (2.85)* | | | |
| C–O dummies | .181 | −.469 | .024 | .001 | .9036 | .0080 | 1.80 |
| | (4.91)* | (−2.61)* | (1.91)# | (3.60)* | | | |

*Notes:* The inflation rate, $\hat{P} = \Delta logP_t$, is multiplied by 100.
The correction for serial correlation is the one-step-ahead Cochrane–Orcutt technique. See Kmenta (1971, pp. 512–14).
*Statistically significant at the 5% level.
#Statistically significant at the 10% level.

Table 6.5.[4] Results for both V1 and V2 are included. Results are shown using OLS and, to account for the presence of severe autocorrelation, adjusted with the Cochrane–Orcutt procedure.

The results for both V1 and V2 using OLS conform to our hypothesis. All three independent variables have the postulated signs and are statistically significant. When the data are corrected for the severe autocorrelation observed using OLS, our hypothesis is also well confirmed for both V1 and V2. Finally, the larger (in absolute value) coefficient of per capita income in the V2 than in the V1 regressions (using OLS) conforms with our hypothetical description of the two curves in Chart 6.1 that V2 should decline more than V1 through much of the range.

The presence of severe autocorrelation in the OLS regression may reflect the omission of important explanatory variables. This omission would not be surprising since we use per capita income as a measure

[4] The countries omitted from the original sample of eighty-four due to lack of data are Algeria, Argentina, Ivory Coast, Nicaragua, Senegal, Togo, Sudan, Madagascar, Upper Volta, and Burundi.

of all the different aspects of financial development discussed in previous chapters. The Cochrane–Orcutt adjustment does not account for such an omission. Consequently, we regard the evidence from the charts in this chapter as more informative than the regressions for the presence of a global velocity curve.[5,6]

## 6.4.    Comparisons with other studies

Several cross-country studies of velocity behavior have used IFS data (Ezekiel and Adekunle (1969); Melitz and Correa (1970); Driscoll and Lahiri (1983); Townsend (1983)). However, to our knowledge no study has examined such a long time period or as complete a sample as ours. Ezekiel and Adekunle examined thirty-seven countries for the period 1950–64, Melitz and Correa seventeen countries and Driscoll and Lahiri twelve countries each for the period 1952–67.

A number of aspects of these studies, however, are consistent with our approach. Ezekiel and Adekunle found for their sample of countries that both $V1$ and $V2$ generally declined with the level of per capita income; however, they detected some evidence for rising velocity at very high levels of economic development. Melitz and Correa demonstrated, as we have done in this chapter, that the pattern of velocity across countries is closely related to the level of per capita income, tracing a U-shaped pattern. Driscoll and Lahiri showed that the relative size of the agricultural sector is positively related to velocity $V1$ across countries, consistent with our results in Chapters 4 and 5; that is, as the agricultural sector declines in relative size, velocity falls. Finally, Townsend, using Raymond Goldsmith's (1969) data, showed that the pattern of velocity across countries is positively related to the ratio of private credit to GNP, where GNP is a proxy

---

[5] The inclusion of separate dummy variables for each year to capture time specific shifts, in addition to the country dummies in the global velocity curve, produced results almost identical to these of Table 6.4, as did those in regressions including a time trend as a separate independent variable.

[6] Converting per capita income for each country into U.S. dollars using official exchange rates from the IFS data, as we did, may induce considerable bias. Such a conversion assumes that the basket of goods consumed in each country is identical to that of the United States. Less developed countries tend to consume a basket of goods more heavily weighted toward nontraded services than do advanced countries. Thus, converting per capita income of the less developed country into the currency units of a more advanced country will bias the former's measured income downward (see Balassa (1964)). The use of purchasing power–adjusted exchange rates as in Kravis, Heston, and Summers (1978) may help solve this problem. Considering the crude character of our proxy variable for financial development in equation (6.2), i.e., real per capita income, we did not attempt this procedure.

measure of financial development – a result also consistent with our approach.[7]

## 6.5.    Summary

Our approach suggests that velocity should be falling at the early stages of economic development and rising at later stages. Using a world-wide sample of about eighty countries for the period 1952–1982, we detected a global U-shaped velocity curve similar to the long-run velocity curves for industrialized countries displayed in Chapter 2 and analyzed in Chapter 4. We regard the empirical evidence presented here – based on a data set and on test procedures complementary to those of Chapters 4 and 5 – as additional evidence in favor of our institutional explanation.

Our results also suggest that the traditional explanatory variables of the income velocity of money, that is, real income and interest rates, should be combined with institutional variables when accounting for the global U-shaped patterns.

In today's economically well-integrated world, most countries face the same nominal interest rates on world capital markets (ignoring exchange controls), and most countries since World War II have experienced positive secular growth in real income. Global differences in the behavior of secular velocity – falling, horizontal, and rising trends in velocity in Charts 6.1 through 6.9 – thus have to be accounted for by explanatory variables other than real income and interest rates. We suggest that these alternatives are the institutional variables emphasized in our study. However, the sharply rising trend of velocity $V1$ in a few high-inflation countries may best be explained by expectations of future higher inflation rates.

---

[7] Other studies examining velocity across countries include Doblin (1951), Fleetwood-Jucker (1958), Kaufman and Latta (1966), and Perlman (1970).

*Velocity curves of eighty-four countries in the post–World War II period.
(V1 solid line, V2 dashed line)*

*Source: International Financial Statistics*

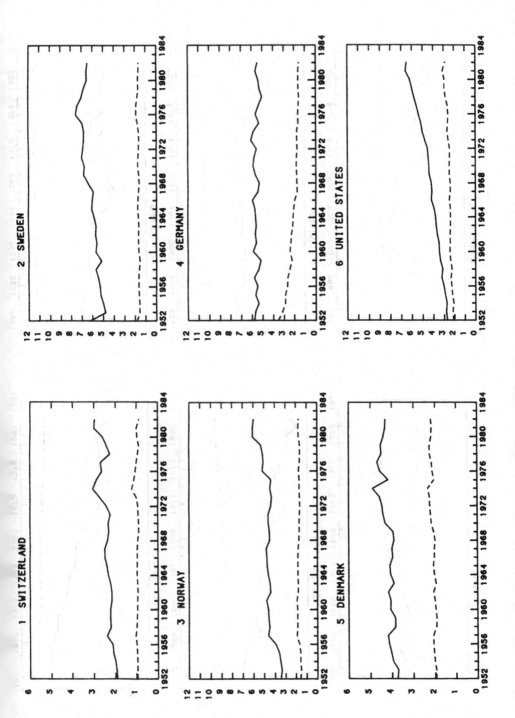

121

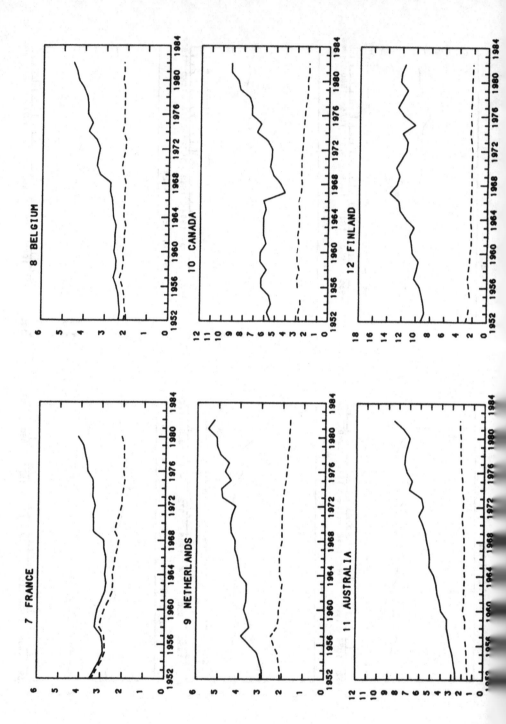

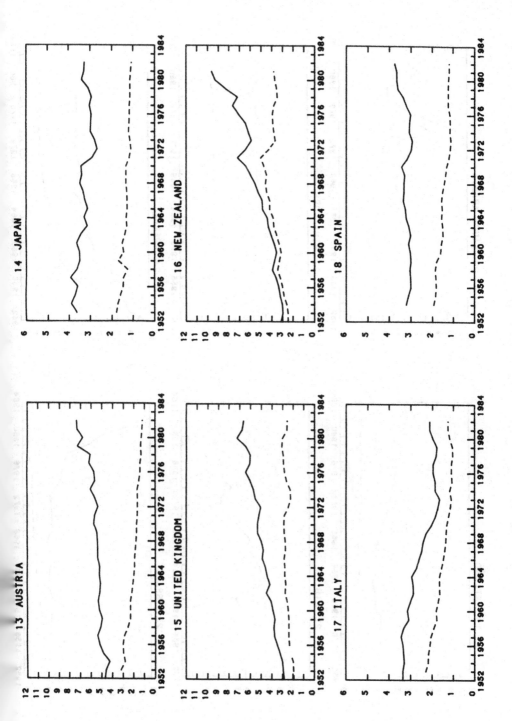

123

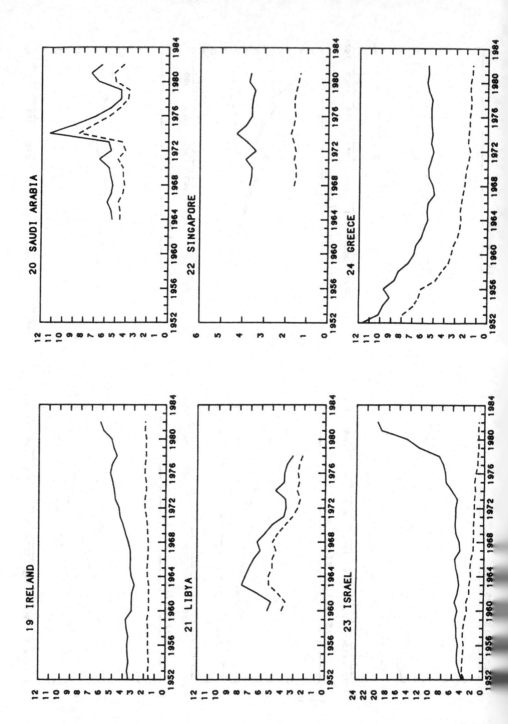

124

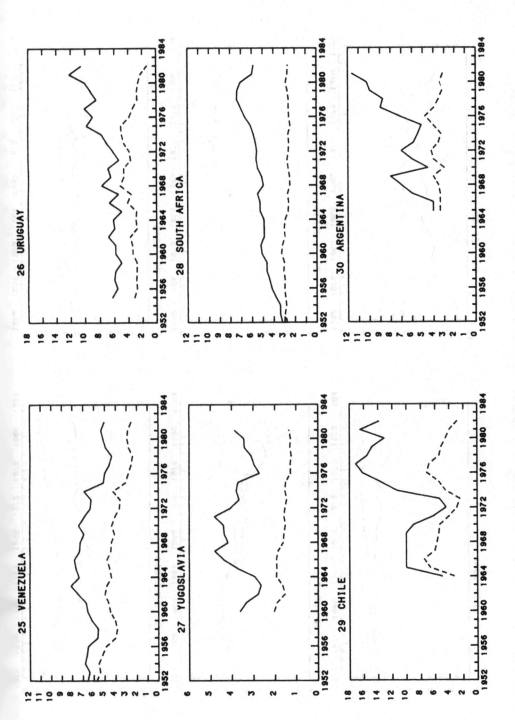

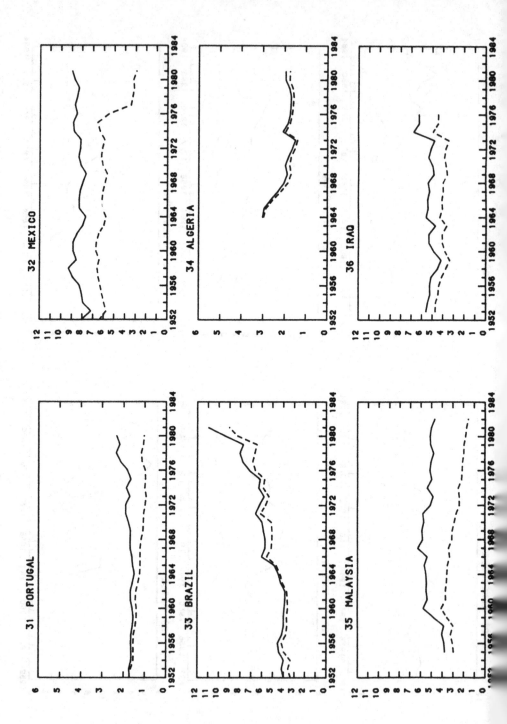

31 PORTUGAL

32 MEXICO

33 BRAZIL

34 ALGERIA

35 MALAYSIA

36 IRAQ

126

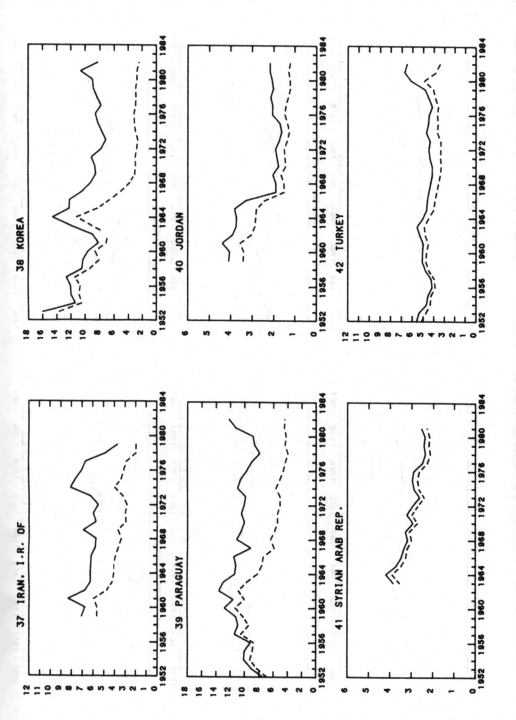

127

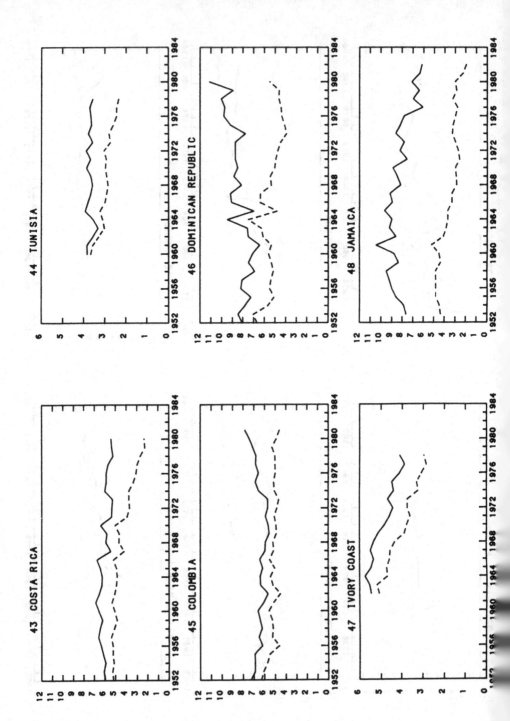

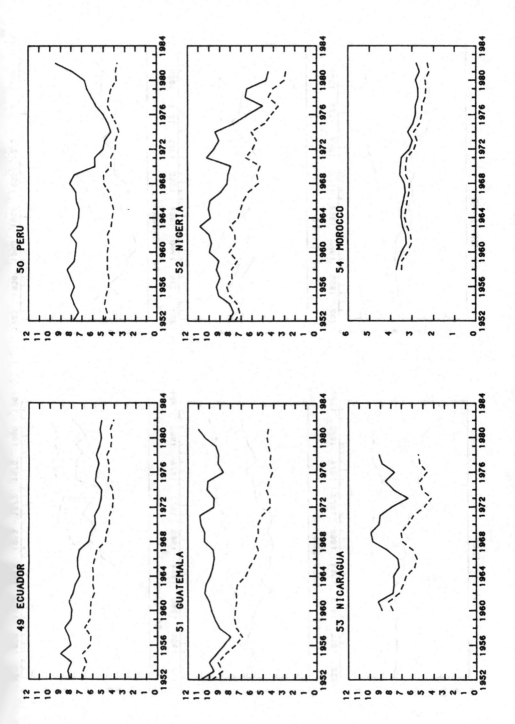

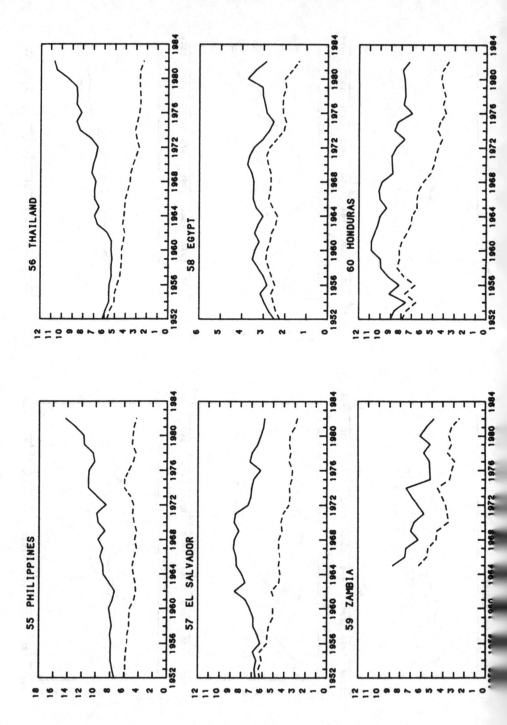

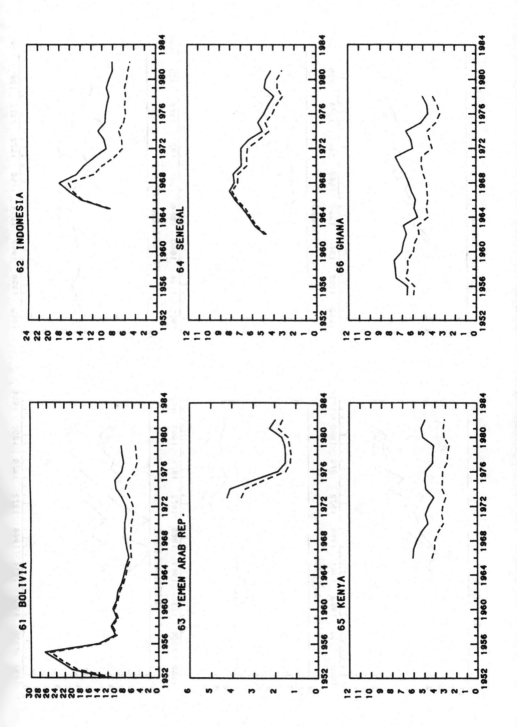

131

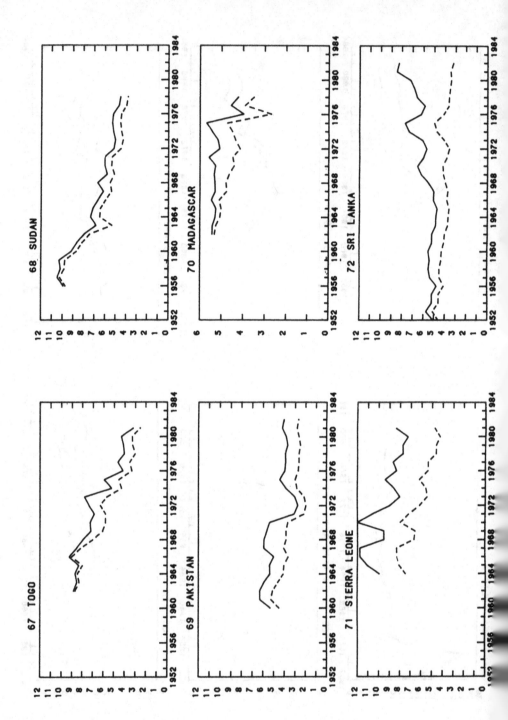

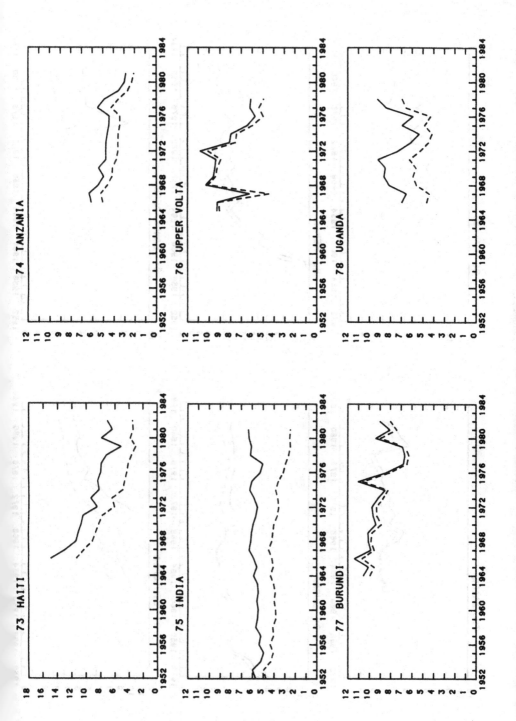

133

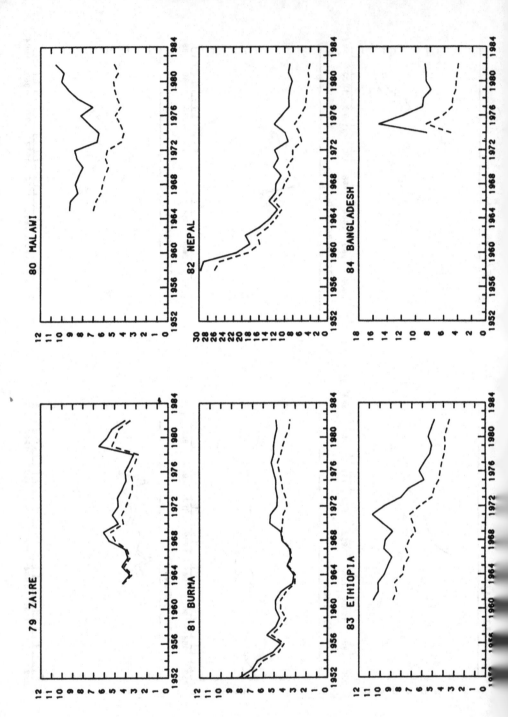

# CHAPTER 7

# The stochastic properties of velocity: Evidence for five countries

## 7.1. Introduction

In the last two decades there has been considerable interest in the stochastic properties of velocity. Since a number of U.S. studies have found that velocity displays the characteristics of a random walk, a question that arises from this evidence on the stochastic nature of velocity is how to reconcile it with the evidence presented in Chapters 4 and 5 – that velocity behavior over the past century is well explained by institutional variables, permanent real income, and the interest rate. An answer to this question is provided in this chapter.

Gould and Nelson (1974) in a seminal article[1] questioned the predictive content of the long-run time series of velocity used by Friedman and Schwartz in *A Monetary History of the United States, 1867–1960* (1963). According to Gould and Nelson, the discussion by Friedman and Schwartz of meaningful patterns in the long-run movement of velocity, and of deviations from trend taken directly from the time series, presumes that future velocity behavior can be extrapolated from past velocity behavior. They examined the stochastic structure of velocity for the period 1869–1960 to determine whether a statistical basis could be found for extrapolative predictions. Zero autocorrelations of the first differences of velocity as well as an insignificant coefficient on the trend term led them to conclude that velocity is a random walk without drift.

Subsequently, Stokes and Neuberger (1979) demonstrated that the Gould and Nelson result is highly period sensitive. They noted that the 1867–1960 period covered by Friedman and Schwartz combines three distinct historical periods: 1867–79 – the Greenback episode; 1940–60 – World War II and the subsequent rise in velocity; and the rest. A reexamination of the evidence for the homogeneous period, 1880–1940, led Stokes and Neuberger to reverse Gould and Nelson's results: Velocity is not a random walk, and the trend has a significant negative coefficient.

Recently, Nelson and Plosser (1982), following a procedure devel-

---

[1] Also see Gould et al. (1978).

135

oped by Dickey and Fuller (1979), developed an approach distinguishing between two classes of time series processes: trend stationary (TS) processes and differenced stationary (DS) processes. A TS process characterizes a time series whose deviations from trend are stationary or self-reversing, whereas a DS process characterizes a nonstationary series that does not revert to trend. A simple example of a DS process is a random walk.[2] The application of tests developed by Nelson and Plosser to U.S. velocity data for the period 1869–1970 found it to be a DS process, consistent with the original Gould and Nelson findings.

In this chapter we apply the tests pioneered for the U.S. case by Gould and Nelson, and by Nelson and Plosser, to the five countries for which we have close to a century of data: the United States, Canada, the United Kingdom, Sweden, and Norway. Our findings for the majority of countries examined here support those of the earlier studies: Velocity over the past century for the majority of the countries in our study is characterized by a random walk without drift.

One implication of a random walk is that since only the current value of velocity can be used to predict that of the next period, past values of velocity should have no predictive power. Alternatively, changes in velocity should be random – that is, future changes cannot be predicted by past changes. However, the fact that velocity displays the characteristics of a random walk does not mean that changes in variables that economic theory views as important determinants of velocity cannot be used to predict future changes. In this chapter we test whether changes in velocity can be explained by past changes in velocity as well as by past changes in a set of variables that can be viewed as potential important determinants of current changes in velocity – the long-run determinants of velocity discussed previously in Chapter 4.

### 7.2.    Is velocity a random walk?

As a simple test for the presence of a random walk, we conduct the type of test suggested by Gould and Nelson (1974). Specifically, the present period's level of velocity is regressed on the previous period's level of velocity as follows:

$$\log V_t = A + B \log V_{t-1} + u_{1t} \tag{7.1}$$

where the constant $A$ is a measure of drift, $B$ is the regression coefficient on lagged velocity, and $u_{1t}$ is a serially uncorrelated error term.

---

[2] For an application of this distinction to recent U.S. velocity behavior, see Haraf (1986).

Table 7.1 reports the results of estimation of equation (7.1) using annual data for the five countries examined in Chapter 4. Unlike in Gould and Nelson, regression (7.1) is expressed in logs rather than levels to avoid the problem of heteroscedacity.[3] Following Gould and Nelson we test the hypotheses that $A$ is not significantly different from zero and $B$ is not significantly different from one. To avoid the problem of bias observed in the use of a standard $t$-distribution in the Gould and Nelson study, we compared the calculated $t$-ratios to the correct distribution suggested by Dickey and Fuller (1979). $t$-tests based on the Dickey and Fuller distribution show that $A$ differs significantly from zero and $B$ is not significantly different from one for all countries except the United States. A joint $F$-test of the hypothesis $A = 0$, $B = 1$ based on a distribution suggested by Dickey and Fuller (1981) confirms the null hypothesis for all countries except the United States.

A key problem with these results is that the distribution of $B$ involves the true value of $A$, which we do not know. The values calculated in Dickey and Fuller are valid only under the maintained hypothesis that the true value of $A$ is zero. Thus the results that the null hypothesis $A = 0$, $B = 1$ is rejected for the United States may reflect that $A$ is different from zero, that $B$ is different from one, or both.[4]

We next conduct the type of test suggested by Nelson and Plosser (1982). The test, designed to ascertain whether the time series pattern of velocity can be characterized as a DS process, is based on the following regression equation:

$$\log V_t = A + B \log V_{t-1} + CT + u_{2t} \tag{7.2}$$

where $T$ is a time trend.

Table 7.2 reports the results of regressions of equation (7.2) for the five countries. The test devised to determine whether equation (7.2) can be characterized as a DS process is $B = 1$, $C = 0$. As in the previous case, we conducted both $t$-tests and joint $F$-tests using the distributions suggested by Dickey and Fuller. With the addition of the time trend, the distribution of the test statistics does not depend on unknown parameters such as the true value of $A$, so interpretation of the statistics is more clear-cut.[5]

Based on $t$-tests, $B$ is not significantly different from one in all five countries, and $C$ is not significantly different from zero in all except Canada and Norway. The joint $F$-tests that $B = 1$, $C = 0$ is not rejected in all cases except the United States, and then only at the 10% level of

[3] See Stokes and Neuberger (1979).
[4] We wish to thank Charles Nelson for bringing this to our attention.
[5] See Dickey and Fuller (1981, pp. 1068–9).

Table 7.1. *Gould and Nelson (1974) tests for a random walk*

$\log V_t = A + B \log V_{t-1} + u_{1t}$    (7.1)

| Country (Period) | Coefficients of independent variables (t-values in parentheses) | | SEE | $\bar{R}^2$ | Durbin h | Q | F (A = 0, B = 1) | F critical | | t (B = 1) | t critical, 5% |
| | A | B | | | | | | 5% | 10% | | |
|---|---|---|---|---|---|---|---|---|---|---|---|
| U.S. (1881–1972) | .038 (2.43)* | .927 (44.89)* | .063 | .957 | 1.02[b] | 30.71[c] | 7.82[d] | 4.71 | 3.86 | -3.51 | -2.89 |
| Canada (1901–75) | .091 (1.85)# | .901 (16.81)* | .071 | .792 | 1.96 | 20.95[c] | 1.72 | 4.86 | 3.94 | -1.85[a] | -2.93 |
| UK (1877–1974) | .031 (1.68)* | .943 (27.52)* | .056 | .886 | .93[b] | 25.90[c] | 1.44 | 4.71 | 3.86 | -1.68[a] | -2.89 |
| Sweden (1881–1974) | .065 (2.18)* | .926 (30.43)* | .066 | .909 | 2.52 | 26.50[c] | 3.21 | 4.71 | 3.86 | -2.42[a] | -2.89 |
| Norway (1881–1939) (1954–74) | .030 (1.51) | .941 (28.86)* | .079 | .913 | 1.80 | 53.39 | 1.67 | 4.71 | 3.86 | -1.81[a] | -2.89 |

* Statistically different from zero at the 5% level.

# Statistically different from zero at the 10% level.

[a] Not statistically different from one at the 5% level (using Dickey and Fuller (1979)).

[b] Rejection of first-order serial correlation at the 5% level.

[c] Rejection of higher-order serial correlation at the 5% level.

[d] Rejection of $H_0$: $A = 0$, $B = 1$ at the 5% level (using Dickey and Fuller (1981)).

Table 7.2. Nelson and Plosser (1982) tests for a DS process

log $V_t = A + B \log V_{t-1} + CT + u_{2t}$   (7.2)

| Country (Period) | Coefficients of independent variables (t-values in parentheses) | | | SEE | $\bar{R}^2$ | Q | F $(B=1, C=0)$ | F critical (Dickey & Fuller) | | t $(B=1)$ | t critical, 5% |
| | A | B | C | | | | | 5% | 10% | | |
| --- | --- | --- | --- | --- | --- | --- | --- | --- | --- | --- | --- |
| U.S. (1881–1972) | .058 | .914 | −.0002 | .063 | .956 | 30.57[c] | 6.26[d] | 6.49 | 5.47 | −2.54[a] | −3.45 |
| | (1.40) | (26.91)* | (−.51) | | | | | | | | |
| Canada (1901–75) | .089 | .872 | .0007 | .069 | .798 | 22.63[c] | 3.47 | 6.49 | 5.47 | −2.33[a] | −3.50 |
| | (1.84)# | (15.88)* | (1.85)# | | | | | | | | |
| UK (1877–1974) | 0.30 | .942 | .00003 | .056 | .885 | 25.86[c] | 1.40 | 6.49 | 5.47 | −1.67[a] | −3.45 |
| | (1.43) | (27.33)* | (.15) | | | | | | | | |
| Sweden (1881–1974) | .046 | .931 | .0003 | .066 | .909 | 27.36[c] | 3.71 | 6.49 | 5.47 | −2.10[a] | −3.45 |
| | (1.37) | (30.47)* | (1.24) | | | | | | | | |
| Norway (1881–1939) | .003 | .943 | .0006 | .078 | .916 | 58.17 | 3.40 | 6.49 | 5.47 | −1.77[a] | −3.45 |
| (1954–74) | (.12) | (29.35)* | (1.85)# | | | | | | | | |

Notes: Same as in Table 7.1, except

[a] Rejection of $H_0$: $B = 1$, $C = 0$ at the 10% level (using Dickey and Fuller (1981)).

significance. These results suggest that velocity follows a DS process in all five countries. It follows a random walk without drift for all countries except Canada and Norway, where it follows a random walk with a drift.[6]

Finally, to determine whether the stochastic process of velocity is sensitive to the monetary regime, we split our data sample for the five countries into two regimes: the gold standard, encompassing the years up to 1914; and managed money, the subsequent period. This demarcation is admittedly rough, since these countries were on a gold exchange standard for a portion of the interwar period, and were all part of the gold based Bretton Woods fixed exchange rate system over virtually the whole post–World War II period covered in this study. However, in all five countries the extent to which national money supplies were managed increased considerably after 1914.

Under the gold standard, according to Klein (1975), the money supply (in the United States) displayed the properties of a stationary series – with a tendency to revert to its trend level. This finding reflected the tendency under the gold standard for gold flows to be self-reversing. Under managed money, according to Leijonhufvud (1984), the money supply process (in the United States) is a nonstationary series characterized by a random walk in rates of changes.

In Table 7.3 we present the results of Nelson and Plosser types of regressions for these two subperiods for our five countries. Based on the Dickey and Fuller distributions, both the $t$- and $F$-tests indicate that during the gold standard period the random walk hypothesis is rejected for the United States but not for the other countries.[7] In the period of managed money all five countries are characterized by a DS process.

These results suggest that for at least one country – the United States – the nature of the monetary regime may have influenced the velocity process. Under the gold standard, the predictable nature of the money supply regime may have made velocity predictable. For the other countries velocity may have been unpredictable because theirs were more open economies subject to both real and nominal shocks originating abroad. Under managed money, for all five countries, the

---

[6] Evidence of significant serial correlation for Norway as judged by the Box Pierce $Q$ statistics may call into question the findings for that country. The period covered includes a large gap in the data for World War II, when data were unavailable. However, a similar regression run over the period 1880–1939 yielded similar coefficients and test statistics, and a high value for the $Q$ statistic.

[7] For Canada, the small number of observations for the gold standard period would make the results unreliable.

Table 7.3. Tests for a DS process by monetary regimes: The gold standard and managed money

$$\log V_t = A + B \log V_{t-1} + CT + u_{2t} \quad (7.2)$$

| Country (Period) | Coefficients of independent variables (t-values in parentheses) A | B | C | SEE | $\bar{R}^2$ | Q | F (B = 1, C = 0) | F critical 5% | 10% | t (B = 1) | t critical, 5% |
|---|---|---|---|---|---|---|---|---|---|---|---|
| U.S. (1881–1913) | .443 (3.07)* | .650 (6.63)* | -.006 (-2.48)* | .044 | .962 | 11.22[c] | 10.46[d] | 7.24 | 5.91 | -3.57 | -3.55 |
| (1914–72) | .025 (.48) | .905 (16.51)* | .0003 (.57) | .071 | .830 | 20.35[c] | 2.02 | 6.73 | 5.61 | -1.73[a] | -3.50 |
| Canada (1901–13) | .773 (2.30)* | .327 (1.14) | -.017 (-2.22)* | .044 | .831 | 1.92[c] | 2.77 | 7.24 | 5.91 | -2.34[a] | -3.60 |
| (1914–75) | .108 (2.00)# | .816 (10.90)* | .001 (2.02)* | .073 | .799 | 15.36[c] | 3.22 | 6.73 | 5.61 | -2.46[a] | -3.50 |
| UK (1877–1913) | .143 (2.49)* | .715 (5.94)* | .001 (1.65) | .026 | .823 | 18.08[c] | 2.93 | 7.24 | 5.91 | -2.36[a] | -3.55 |
| (1914–74) | -.011 (-.31) | .913 (19.29)* | .0008 (1.48) | .067 | .886 | 19.62[c] | 2.04 | 6.73 | 5.61 | -1.85[a] | -3.50 |
| Sweden (1881–1913) | .207 (1.19) | .838 (7.30)* | -.003 (-1.06) | .049 | .959 | 15.73[c] | 1.45 | 7.24 | 5.91 | -1.41[a] | -3.55 |
| (1914–74) | .090 (2.01)* | .726 (7.91)* | .002 (2.49)* | .071 | .860 | 25.60[c] | 4.45 | 6.73 | 5.61 | -2.98[a] | -3.50 |
| Norway (1881–1913) | .166 (1.33) | .810 (6.90)* | -.003 (-1.26) | .037 | .970 | 12.36[c] | 2.05 | 7.24 | 5.91 | -1.62[a] | -3.55 |
| (1914–39) (1955–74) | -.091 (-1.70)# | .745 (7.94)* | .003 (2.63)* | .093 | .894 | 38.13 | 3.86 | 6.73 | 5.61 | -2.71[a] | -3.50 |

Notes: Same as in Table 7.1, except
[d] Rejection of $H_0$: $B = 1$, $C = 0$ at the 5% level (using Dickey and Fuller (1981)).

more stochastic nature of the money supply process may also have influenced the velocity process.

## 7.3.    Are changes in velocity predictable?

Evidence that velocity displays the characteristics of a random walk in the majority of countries examined here does not mean that velocity is a will-o'-the-wisp, that is, that it merely reflects random walks in nominal income and money, and hence that the relationship between money and income is totally unpredictable. Indeed there is a large body of evidence to the contrary (Friedman and Schwartz (1982); Poole (1986)). Rather, the random walk suggests that there are numerous forces that systematically affect velocity, and that it is impossible without prior information to predict which set of forces is paramount.[8] Thus, for example, an acceleration in money growth will initially cause velocity to fall (below its trend), but then as holders of cash balances adjust their actual holdings to the original desired level, velocity will eventually rise and may even overshoot (Friedman and Schwartz (1982)). If such a pattern is at work, changes in velocity would display negative serial correlation following a burst of monetary growth. Alternatively, a shock to aggregate demand raising nominal income without any increase in money growth would, if it persisted, raise velocity for several periods in a row and, as a consequence, velocity would display positive serial correlation.

The historical record suggests that the two types of disturbances are equally frequent. When, for example, a rise in velocity is observed, the rise by itself provides no predictive information as to whether velocity is likely to rise further or decline. Thus past changes in velocity cannot be used to predict future changes; however, there is no reason why prior information on other variables that systematically affect velocity may not aid in predicting future changes.

In what follows, we test whether successive past changes in the determinants of velocity isolated in this study are significant in explaining future changes in velocity. Initially, we estimate two regression equations:

$$\Delta \log V_t = A + B_1 \Delta \log V_{t-1} + u_{3t} \tag{7.3}$$
$$\Delta \log V_t = A + B_1 \Delta \log V_{t-1} + B_2 \Delta \log V_{t-2} + u_{4t} \tag{7.4}$$

The results are presented in Table 7.4. An implication of a random walk is that $A = B_1 = 0$ in equation (7.3) and that $A = B_1 = B_2 = 0$ in equation (7.4). As can be seen in Table 7.4, based on joint $F$-tests the null hypothesis is accepted for all countries for equation (7.3), but

[8] See Poole (1986).

Table 7.4. *Changes in velocity regressed on successive past changes in velocity*

$$\Delta\log V_t = A + B_1 \Delta\log V_{t-1} + u_{3t} \qquad (7.3)$$
$$\Delta\log V_t = A + B_1 \Delta\log V_{t-1} + B_2 \Delta\log V_{t-2} + u_{4t} \qquad (7.4)$$

| Country (Period) | Coefficients of independent variables (t-values in parentheses) | | | SEE | $\bar{R}^2$ | Durbin $h$ or (t-value)$^c$ | $Q$ | $F$ ($A=0$, $B_1=0$, $B_2=0$) | $F$ critical | |
| | $A$ | $B_1$ | $B_2$ | | | | | | 5% | 10% |
|---|---|---|---|---|---|---|---|---|---|---|
| **U.S. (1883–1972)** | | | | | | | | | | |
| (3) | .009 (−1.26) | .114 (1.12) | | .065 | .0029 | .53$^b$ | 26.56$^c$ | 1.72 | 3.10 | 2.37 |
| (4) | −.009 (−1.25) | 1.127 (1.19) | .002 (.02) | .065 | −.006 | (.89)$^b$ | 25.84$^c$ | 1.20 | 2.71 | 2.15 |
| **Canada (1903–75)** | | | | | | | | | | |
| (3) | .001 (.13) | .157 (1.35) | | .072 | .0111 | (.83)$^b$ | 17.73$^c$ | .92 | 3.13 | 2.38 |
| (4) | .001 (.12) | .173 (1.45) | −.099 (−.83) | .073 | .007 | (.05)$^b$ | 17.06$^c$ | .84 | 2.74 | 2.17 |
| **UK (1879–1974)** | | | | | | | | | | |
| (3) | .001 (.25) | .061 (.59) | | .057 | −.0068 | (−1.68)$^b$ | 27.14$^c$ | .21 | 3.09 | 2.37 |
| (4) | .0007 (.12) | .049 (.48) | .174 (1.68)$^{\#}$ | .056 | .012 | (1.07)$^b$ | 26.00$^b$ | 1.07 | 2.71 | 2.15 |

## Table 7.4. (cont.)

$$\Delta \log V_t = A + B_1 \Delta \log V_{t-1} + u_{3t} \qquad (7.3)$$
$$\Delta \log V_t = A + B_1 \Delta \log V_{t-1} + B_2 \Delta \log V_{t-2} + u_{4t} \qquad (7.4)$$

| Country (Period) | Coefficients of independent variables ($t$-values in parentheses) | | | SEE | $\bar{R}^2$ | Durbin $h$ or ($t$-value)[c] | $Q$ | $F$ ($A = 0$, $B_1 = 0$, $B_2 = 0$) | $F$ critical | |
| --- | --- | --- | --- | --- | --- | --- | --- | --- | --- | --- |
| | $A$ | $B_1$ | $B_2$ | | | | | | 5% | 10% |
| **Sweden (1883–1974)** | | | | | | | | | | |
| (3) | −.004 (−.64) | .234 (2.26)* | | .067 | .0427 | 5.84 | 21.72[c] | 2.85 | 3.10 | 2.37 |
| (4) | .004 (−.58) | .282 (2.70)* | −.196 (−1.87)# | .066 | .071 | (−.18)[b] | 23.61[c] | 3.13[d] | 2.71 | 2.15 |
| **Norway (1883–1939)** **(1955–74)** | | | | | | | | | | |
| (3) | −.002 (−.17) | .175 (1.54) | | .080 | .0177 | 11.14 | 54.38 | 1.22 | 3.21 | 2.38 |
| (4) | −.002 (−.28) | .252 (2.39)* | −.431 (−4.08)* | .074 | .19 | .91[b] | 18.61[c] | 6.50[d] | 2.73 | 2.17 |

*Notes:* Same as in Table 7.1, except

[a]Rejection of $H_0$: $A = 0$, $B_1 = 0$, $B_2 = 0$, or $H_0$: $A = 0$, $B_1 = 0$, at the 5% level.

[c]When the statistic could not be computed, the value of the coefficient of $e_{t-1}$ in the regression of $e_t$ on $e_{t-1}$ plus all the independent variables is reported.

when a second lagged term is added in equation (7.4) the hypothesis is rejected for Sweden and Norway. The presence of significant coefficients on both lagged changes in velocity for these countries suggests that a more complicated autoregressive process may be at work.

Finally, equation (7.5) includes as additional regressors to those in equation (7.4) changes in the long-run determinants of velocity isolated in Chapter 4. Inclusion of these additional independent variables will enable us to ascertain whether prior changes in velocity's long-run determinants can aid in predicting future changes in velocity.[9]

$$\Delta \log V_t = A + B_1 \Delta \log V_{t-1} + B_2 \Delta \log V_{t-2} + C_1 \Delta \log \left(\frac{Y}{PN}\right)^p_{t-1}$$
$$+ C_2 \Delta \log \left(\frac{Y}{PN}\right)^p_{t-2} + D_1 \Delta i_{t-1} + D_2 \Delta i_{t-2}$$
$$+ E_1 \Delta \log \text{cycle}_{t-1} + E_2 \Delta \log \text{cycle}_{t-2} \tag{7.5}$$
$$+ F_1 \Delta \log \left(\frac{LNA}{L}\right)_{t-1} + F_2 \Delta \log \left(\frac{LNA}{L}\right)_{t-2}$$
$$+ G_1 \Delta \log \left(\frac{C}{M}\right)_{t-1} + G_2 \Delta \log \left(\frac{C}{M}\right)_{t-2}$$
$$+ H_1 \Delta \log \left(\frac{TNBFA}{TFA}\right)_{t-1} + H_2 \Delta \log \left(\frac{TNBFA}{TFA}\right)_{t-2}$$
$$+ J_1 \Delta \log s_{\hat{y}(t-1)} + J_2 \Delta \log s_{\hat{y}(t-2)} + u_{5t}$$

where $(Y/PN)^p$ stands for per capita permanent income, $i$ the long-term bond yield, cycle the ratio of measured to permanent per capita income, $LNA/L$ the ratio of the labor force in nonagricultural pursuits to the total labor force, $C/M$ the currency–money ratio, $TNBFA/TFA$ the ratio of total nonbank financial assets to total financial assets, and $s_{\hat{y}}$ a six-year moving standard deviation of real per capita income.

Table 7.5 presents the results of regressions of equation (7.5). For each country, significant coefficients (based on $t$-tests of individual coefficients and on the sum of the coefficients) on a number of the lagged independent variables are detected. Thus, of the traditional determinants of velocity, significant (at least at the 10% level) lagged changes can be found in permanent income for every country; in the cycle variable for the United Kingdom, Sweden, and Norway; and in the interest rate for Norway. Of the institutional variables, significant lagged changes can be detected in $LNA/L$ for the United States and United Kingdom, and in $C/M$ for Sweden and Norway.

These results combined with rejection of the null hypothesis $F(A=0, B_i=0, C_i=0, \ldots, J_i=0)$ and a considerable improvement in $\bar{R}^2$ in every

---

[9] For a similar testing procedure see Hall's (1978) approach to the permanent income hypothesis.

Table 7.5. *Changes in velocity regressed on successive past changes in velocity and successive past changes in the determinants of velocity*

$$\Delta \log V_t = A + B_1 \Delta \log V_{t-1} + B_2 \Delta \log V_{t-2} + C_1 \Delta \log\left(\frac{Y}{PN}\right)^p_{t-1} + C_2 \Delta \log\left(\frac{Y}{PN}\right)^p_{t-2} + D_1 \Delta i_{t-1} + D_2 \Delta i_{t-2}$$

$$+ E_1 \Delta \log \text{cycle}_{t-1} + E_2 \Delta \log \text{cycle}_{t-2} + F_1 \Delta \log\left(\frac{LNA}{L}\right)_{t-1} + F_2 \Delta \log\left(\frac{LNA}{L}\right)_{t-2} + G_1 \Delta \log\left(\frac{C}{M}\right)_{t-1} + G_2 \Delta \log\left(\frac{C}{M}\right)_{t-2} \quad (7.5)$$

$$+ H_1 \Delta \log\left(\frac{TNBFA}{TFA}\right)_{t-1} + H_2 \Delta \log\left(\frac{TNBFA}{TFA}\right)_{t-2} + J_1 \Delta \log s_{y(t-1)} + J_2 \Delta \log s_{y(t-2)} + u_{5t}$$

| | Coefficients of independent variables and t-values for sum of coefficients (t-values in parentheses) | | | | | | | | | | | |
|---|---|---|---|---|---|---|---|---|---|---|---|---|
| Country (Period) | $A$ | $B_1$ | $B_2$ | $C_1$ | $C_2$ | $t_\Sigma$ | $D_1$ | $D_2$ | $t_\Sigma$ | $E_1$ | $E_2$ | $t_\Sigma$ |
| U.S. (1883–1972) | .037 | −1.24 | .056 | −.706 | −.241 | −2.56* | −.235 | .506 | .18 | .406 | .056 | 1.55 |
| | (1.78)* | (−.61) | (.30) | (−1.46) | (−.46) | | (−.26) | (−.58) | | (1.64) | (.27) | |
| Canada (1903–75) | .018 | −.178 | .084 | 1.615 | −1.591 | .59 | −3.957 | .856 | −.88 | .151 | .110 | .57 |
| | (.88) | (−.77) | (.37) | (2.18)* | (−2.27)* | | (−1.46) | (.28) | | (.42) | (−.39) | |
| UK (1879–1974) | −.007 | −.009 | .108 | −.707 | .272 | −1.91# | .226 | −.668 | −.41 | .381 | .884 | 3.80* |
| | (−.81) | (−.07) | (.85) | (−2.36)* | (.89) | | (.32) | (−.95) | | (1.67)# | (3.79)* | |
| Sweden (1883–1974) | .016 | .337 | −.533 | −.178 | −.321 | −1.84# | −.144 | 9.936 | 1.39 | −.517 | .313 | −.53 |
| | (.85) | (1.79)# | (−2.97)* | (−.52) | (−.97) | | (−.02) | (1.45) | | (−1.74)# | (1.17) | |
| Norway (1883–1939, 1955–74) | −.003 | −.196 | −.205 | −.220 | −.244 | −2.22* | 7.881 | −2.383 | 1.49 | .278 | −.983 | −1.13 |
| | (−.24) | (−.94) | (−1.17) | (−.71) | (−.76) | | (3.27)* | (−.96) | | (.63) | (−2.40)* | |

| Country (Period) | $F_1$ | $F_2$ | $t_\Sigma$ | $G_1$ | $G_2$ | $t_\Sigma$ | $H_1$ | $H_2$ | $t_\Sigma$ | $J_1$ | $J_2$ | $t_\Sigma$ |
|---|---|---|---|---|---|---|---|---|---|---|---|---|
| U.S. (1883–1972) | -1.898 | -2.976 | -1.76* | -.116 | -.007 | -.99 | -.314 | -.047 | -.81 | -.029 | .014 | -.36 |
| | (-.67) | (-1.06) | | (-1.02) | (-.06) | | (-.50) | (-.07) | | (-1.03) | (.47) | |
| Canada (1903–75) | -1.209 | -.891 | -.68 | .054 | -.245 | -.92 | -.031 | -.225 | -.92 | -.024 | -.008 | -.82 |
| | (-.23) | (-.17) | | (.29) | (-1.31) | | (-.12) | (-.87) | | (-.68) | (-.43) | |
| UK (1879–1974) | 9.674 | 1.880 | 2.08* | -1.43 | .099 | -.26 | .181 | -.620 | -.86 | -.007 | -.0003 | -.25 |
| | (1.94)# | (.40) | | (-1.18) | (.77) | | (.51) | (-1.57) | | (-.35) | (-.02) | |
| Sweden (1883–1974) | 1.561 | -2.381 | -.51 | .329 | .379 | 2.78* | .969 | -.899 | .09 | -.043 | .010 | -1.16 |
| | (.53) | (-.83) | | (1.82)# | (2.19)* | | (.87) | (-.81) | | (-2.07)* | (.51) | |
| Norway (1883–1939, 1955–74) | .933 | -.380 | .87 | .506 | .291 | 2.80 | -.195 | .985 | 1.43 | -.026 | -.021 | -1.52 |
| | (.85) | (-.37) | | (2.74)* | (1.53) | | (-.18) | (.91) | | (-1.13) | (-.98) | |

| Country (Period) | SEE | $\bar{R}^2$ | Durbin $h$ or ($t$-value)$^e$ | $Q$ | $F$ ($A = 0$, $B_i = 0$, $C_i = 0$, $\ldots$, $J_i = 0$) | F critical 5% | F critical 10% |
|---|---|---|---|---|---|---|---|
| U.S. (1883–1972) | .060 | .147 | (.67)$^b$ | 31.08$^c$ | 1.99$^d$ | 1.78 | 1.55 |
| Canada (1903–75) | .070 | .070 | (1.91)$^b$ | 21.94$^c$ | 1.26 | 1.82 | 1.60 |
| UK (1879–1974) | .050 | .221 | (-.82)$^b$ | 26.08$^c$ | 2.53$^d$ | 1.75 | 1.56 |
| Sweden (1883–1974) | .062 | .182 | (-.29)$^b$ | 19.81$^c$ | 2.16$^d$ | 1.77 | 1.56 |
| Norway (1883–1939, 1955–74) | .063 | .397 | (.17)$^b$ | 25.16$^c$ | 3.89$^d$ | 1.80 | 1.58 |

Notes: Same as in Table 7.1, except

[d] Rejection of $H_0$: $A = 0, B_i = 0, C_i = 0, \ldots, J_i = 0$ at the 5% level.

[f] The $t_\Sigma$ reported after each pair of coefficients is the $t$-value of the sum of the two coefficients.

country – compared to the equations in Table 7.4 including only lagged changes in velocity as regressors – suggest that prior knowledge of changes in velocity's determinants improves predictions of future changes in velocity.[10]

## 7.4.    Conclusions

In sum, the results over the past century for the five countries in our study, with application of the approaches of Gould and Nelson, and Nelson and Plosser, confirm for all five their characterization of the behavior of velocity as a random walk. For the gold standard subperiod, velocity displays a random walk for all countries except the United States, but for the period of managed money, velocity is a random walk in all countries. These results suggest, at least for the United States, that the monetary regime may be of importance. The fact that velocity behavior in that country becomes unpredictable after the demise of the gold standard may be a consequence of the switch to a more unpredictable monetary regime.

An implication of the random walk hypothesis is that past changes in velocity cannot be used to predict future changes. Our tests of this implication were confirmed for three countries but not for Sweden or Norway. This result may reflect a more complicated autoregressive process in these two countries.

Finally, we demonstrated that although for the majority of the five countries future changes in velocity cannot be predicted by past changes in velocity alone, changes in the determinants of velocity isolated in this study can in every country significantly improve predictions of future changes in velocity. Thus changes in velocity are better predicted given prior information, and the random walk hypothesis is consistent with our institutional approach.

These results point to the limitations on the use of simple univariate time series models such as the random walk to explain the evolution of important economic variables such as velocity, since these models run the risk of omitting such key factors as the long-run determinants of velocity isolated in this study.

---

[10] As a test of the monetarist hypothesis that velocity changes can be predicted by past accelerations in money growth (Taylor (1976); Friedman and Schwartz (1982)), we also experimented with lagged accelerations in money growth as additional explanatory variables in the regressions explaining velocity change. We obtained a significant (at the 5% level) negative coefficient for a two-year lagged acceleration in money growth for the United States and a significant negative coefficient for a one-year lagged acceleration for Norway, confirming Taylor's results. However, for the other countries this variable was insignificant.

# CHAPTER 8

# Conclusions and implications

## 8.1. Major conclusions

Chapter 2 presents annual evidence on the secular behavior of the income velocity of money using a broad money definition for twelve advanced countries from approximately the mid-1870s to the mid-1970s. For the majority of these countries velocity displays a U-shaped pattern that declines from the late nineteenth century to just after World War II, when it begins a secular rise. For the Scandinavian countries the turnaround occurred in the 1920s. Germany, Italy, and Japan, where velocity continues to fall in the post–World War II period, are three exceptions to this pattern.

Chapter 2 also surveys a number of current theories of long-run velocity behavior. The literature lists several determinants of the decline in velocity, including permanent income and interest rates (including the own rate of return on money), monetization, and the spread of commercial banking. The determinants of its rise include technological improvements in the payments process and the development of money substitutes. No one theory explains both the secular decline and rise of velocity, nor has an attempt been made to account for the entire long-run pattern.

Chapter 3 presents a framework to explain the U-shaped secular behavior of velocity. That framework, which is inspired by the work of Knut Wicksell, stresses the influence of institutional factors. According to our approach, the process of monetization accounts for the downward trend in velocity. This process reflects the spread of the money economy, and of commercial banking. Financial sophistication and improved economic stability account for the upward trend. Financial sophistication refers both to the emergence of money substitutes and to the development of methods of economizing on cash balances. Improved economic stability encompasses many aspects of the modern welfare state as well as stabilization policies.

According to our approach, velocity is influenced by both sets of institutional variables, but the monetization effect first dominates, causing velocity to fall. Later, the influence of financial development and improved stability are stronger than the monetization process,

149

causing velocity to rise. The relative strength of these two sets of forces determines the dating of the turning point of velocity. Finally, we argue that these institutional explanatory variables either are additional to or supersede the standard determinants of velocity, including real income and interest rates.

In Chapter 4 we test our approach to the long-run behavior of velocity using annual data for approximately 100 years for five countries: the United States, Canada, the United Kingdom, Sweden, and Norway. For each country we propose empirical counterparts for the institutional variables. We add these variables to a standard regression of velocity on permanent income and interest rates. Finally, we pool the data for the five countries and perform similar tests for the pooled data.

We use several institutional variables: (1) as a measure of the monetization process, the share of the labor force in nonagricultural pursuits; (2) as a measure of the spread of commercial banking, the currency–money ratio; (3) as a measure of financial development, the ratio of total nonbank financial assets to total financial assets; (4) as a measure of the influence of growing economic stability, a six-year moving standard deviation of the annual percentage change in real per capita income; and (5) as an alternative measure of improved stability, total government expenditures, both including and excluding defense expenditures, as shares of national income.

Our results show that for virtually every country inclusion of the institutional variables significantly improves a benchmark regression of velocity on permanent income, interest rates, and a cyclical variable. In addition, in the majority of cases the institutional variables, with the exception of both measures of economic stability, are correctly signed and statistically significant. Finally, introduction of institutional variables lowers the permanent income elasticity of the demand for money for each of the five countries. This result suggests that the use of permanent income in earlier studies masks the influence of the institutional factors we isolate in this study.

Further evidence is provided by pooling the data for the five countries and performing regressions similar to those for each country taken in isolation. The pooling procedure treats the five countries as part of one entity and assumes that the common behavior of velocity is explained by common economic determinants. The results of the pooled regressions are similar and even stronger than those for the individual countries. The majority of the institutional variables represent significant determinants of common velocity. In addition, we test for similarities and differences among the five countries of the underlying benchmark determinants of velocity as well as of our institutional variables. For the entire period few significant differences emerge between institutional variables across the five countries. Moreover, significant differences between the permanent income variables are reduced when we introduce the institutional variables. This finding is consistent with our earlier conclusion that permanent income may be a proxy for these variables.

For the pooled data, periods of falling velocity were distinguished from periods of rising velocity. In sympathy with our hypothesis, the monetization variables are of relatively greater importance in periods of falling velocity, and financial sophistication of greater importance in periods of rising velocity. Moreover, it appears as though the difference between institutional variables declined in the later period of rising velocity, suggesting possible convergence over time of the institutional framework in the five countries.

Finally, we compare velocity movements during the gold standard period and the subsequent managed money period. Growing similarity between the institutional variables over time, which produces a convergence of velocity movement, suggests that the influence of institutional variables on "common" velocity occurs independent of the monetary standard.

Chapter 5 is a case study of Sweden during the pre–World War I period. The institutional details of three aspects of monetization are examined: the rise of commercial banking, changes in wage contracts and in labor markets, and changes in transaction arrangements in the goods markets. The latter two aspects capture the increased use of money. Empirical counterparts of these three processes are entered in the velocity function. The results are consistent with those for the five countries and the pooled sample. The monetization process exerted a significant influence on Swedish velocity. When real income is added as an additional explanatory variable, there is no major improvement in fit, whereas the interest rate is generally significant.

Chapter 6 presents evidence for our approach drawn from data for over eighty countries in the post–World War II period. Dividing the sample of countries into four major groupings by level of economic development, we discern a U-shaped global velocity curve, with lower-income countries exhibiting falling velocity trends, middle-income countries having a relatively flat trend, and high-income countries a rising trend. In addition, a pooled regression across seventy-four countries over the last three decades produces results consistent with a global U-shaped velocity curve.

In sum, our results confirm the role of institutional factors as deter-

minants of the long-run behavior of velocity. Not only do these factors explain the behavior of velocity over time within advanced countries but they also explain present-day differences in velocity behavior
between advanced and less developed economies.

In Chapter 7 we consider the recent literature on the stochastic
properties of velocity. Earlier findings concluded that velocity for the
United States displays the characteristics of a random walk without
drift. With application of our long-run data set of five countries, this
result is confirmed for all countries. When we break the entire period
into the gold standard and managed money subperiods, we find that
velocity in the United States during the gold standard period did not
display the properties of a random walk, whereas for the other four
countries it did. For the period of managed money, velocity was a
random walk.

One implication of a random walk is that past changes in velocity
cannot be used to predict future changes. However, this does not mean
that past changes in variables that economic theory deems important
determinants of velocity cannot be used to predict future changes. We
find that past changes in the institutional and traditional determinants of velocity isolated in this study can be used to predict future
changes in velocity. Thus the evidence on the stochastic behavior of
velocity is consistent with our approach.

A number of studies have also followed the approach taken in this
book, based on Bordo and Jonung (1981) and Jonung (1983), provid-
ing additional evidence for several countries and different historical
periods on the importance of institutional variables as determinants
of the long-run trend of velocity.[1]

## 8.2.     Implications

Our study has important implications for both monetary theory and
policy. First, our evidence that institutional factors account for much
of the long-run movements of velocity explained in many other studies by real income (permanent income or wealth) suggests that earlier
specifications of the long-run demand for money may have been se-
riously misspecified. The results of our study downplay real income
as a central determinant of velocity. Most likely, this measure has served
as a proxy variable for institutional developments not considered by
most other researchers. Our study suggests that a proper specification

---

[1] See Capie and Bali (1985) for the United Kingdom, and for earlier centuries Lindert
(1985). Riley and McCusker (1983) discuss the relationship between declining velocity and the monetization process. See also Bordo (1986).

of the long-run demand function should incorporate the institutional forces of monetization and financial development.

Second, our extensive evidence of regularity in the behavior of velocity over time and space and of the importance of institutional factors in explaining this regularity may have value for policy makers. Recent attempts to target monetary aggregates presuppose a stable and predictable evolution of velocity. Accounting for institutional factors, such as those discussed in this study, in money demand functions may help to avoid the type of problems policy makers have experienced from time to time of unexplained shifts in money demand. Our results suggest that attention should be paid to the long-run behavior of velocity and its institutional determinants when monetary strategies are being formulated.

In short, we believe that the evidence marshalled in this study warrants serious attention to the institutional determinants of velocity and the demand for money.

# Appendix 1: Data sources

## 1A.  Data sources for the velocity series in Chapter 2

**Chart 2.1  United States**

*National income* 1870–1975. NNP in current prices. 1870–1909,
R. Gallman unpublished data underlying "Gross National Product in
the United States, 1834–1909," in *Output, Employment, and Productivity
in the United States After 1800*. Studies in Income and Wealth Volume
30 by the Conference on Research in Income and Wealth, NBER,
New York, 1966. 1910–46, S. Kuznets NNP variant III from *Capital
in the American Economy*, Princeton, NJ, 1961. 1947–75, Department
of Commerce. All the data were kindly supplied by the NBER.

*Money supply* 1870–1975. $M2$, the sum of currency held by the public
plus total deposits (demand deposits plus time deposits excluding large
certificates of deposit). Annual average data revised July 18, 1977,
kindly supplied by Anna J. Schwartz of the NBER. $M1$, the sum of
currency and demand deposits, 1915–60, can only be separated from
$M2$ beginning in 1915. M. Friedman and A. J. Schwartz (1963), *A
Monetary History of the United States, 1867–1960*, Princeton, NJ. 1961–
75, kindly supplied by A. J. Schwartz.

**Chart 2.2  Canada**

*National income* 1870–1975. GNP at market prices. For 1870 to 1900
we used Firestone's benchmark series for GNP at constant prices, which
we then inflated by his implicit price deflator on a 1949 equal 100
base; O. J. Firestone (1958), *Canada's Economic Development, 1867–1953*,
Bowes and Bowes, London. We then interpolated between the benchmarks to derive the.annual series. For 1900 to 1925 we used Ankli's
series; R. Ankli (January 1976), "Canadian GNP Estimates, 1900–
1925," unpublished paper, Guelph University. For 1926 to 1975 we
used Series 13-531 from the *Canada Year Book*.

*Money supply* 1870–1975. $M2$, the sum of currency held by the public
plus total deposits (sum of demand deposits and savings deposits).
The series is dated as of the end of the year. 1870–1913, C. A. Curtis

(1931), *Statistical Contributions to Economic History,* vol. 1, Macmillan, Toronto. *Currency* consists of Bank note circulation (Curtis, p. 20) plus Dominion notes held by the public, M. C. Urquhart and K. A. H. Buckley (1965), *Historical Statistics of Canada,* Cambridge University Press, Toronto, Series H.15. 1870, was estimated by multiplying total Dominion notes in 1870 by the average ratio of Dominion notes held by the public to total Dominion notes for 1871–81. No data were available to us for coinage held by the public. *Demand Deposits,* Curtis (p. 22). *Time Deposits,* ibid., p. 33, called Deposits by the Public After Notice or on a Fixed Day in Canada. *Total Deposits,* ibid., p. 22. From the sum of currency plus deposits we subtracted an item called *Notes of and Cheques on Other Banks,* ibid., p. 40. 1913–25, all the data comes from a memorandum by G. Freeman (December 15, 1959), *Memorandum Currency and Chartered Bank Deposits 1913–25,* Bank of Canada. 1926–1971, the data comes from a Bank of Canada Memorandum (1972), *"Canadian Currency and Chartered Bank Deposits 1926 to Date".* 1972–5, *Bank of Canada Review,* January–June 1977.

**Chart 2.3   United Kingdom**

*National income* 1870–1975. NNP in current market prices. 1870–1953, C. Feinstein (1972), *National Income, Expenditure, and Output of the United Kingdom, 1855–1965,* Cambridge University Press, Table 1, col. 13, p. 14. 1954–75, United Kingdom, Central Statistical Office (1976), *National Income and Expenditure.*

*Money supply* 1870–1975. *M*2. 1870–1914, M. D. Bordo (1981), "The U.K. Money Supply, 1870–1914," *Research in Economic History,* vol. 6, pp. 107–25. 1915–66, D. K. Sheppard (1971), *The Growth and Role of U.K. Financial Institutions, 1880–1967,* London, Methuen and Co.; 1967–75, Bank of England Official Series (*M*3), seasonally adjusted (this series was the closest approximation to Sheppard's data); *Bank of England Quarterly Bulletin,* various issues. The series is dated as of the end of the year.

**Chart 2.4   Sweden**

*National income* 1870–1975. GDP in current prices. 1870–1955, O. Johansson (1967), *The Gross Domestic Product of Sweden and its Composition, 1861–1955,* Almqvist och Wiksell, Stockholm. 1956–75, S.O.S. Series N.

*Money supply* 1871–1975. *M*2 annual averages of monthly data. *M*2 defined as the sum of currency held by the public plus demand deposits plus time deposits in commercial banks. 1871–1971, L. Jonung (1975), *Studies in the Monetary History of Sweden*, Appendix, UCLA Ph.D. dissertation. 1972–5, *Riksbankens årsbok* (various years) *(Annual Report of the Riksbank)*.

### Chart 2.5   Norway

*National income* 1870–1974. GDP in current prices. *Historisk Statistikk* (1968) and *Statistical Yearbook for Norway*, Oslo (various issues).

*Money supply* 1870–1974. M2 annual averages of quarterly data. M2 defined as the sum of currency held by the public (notes and coins outside banks) plus total demand deposits (demand deposits in commercial banks, savings banks, Post Giro, and Postal Savings Bank) plus total time deposits (time deposits in commercial banks, savings banks, and postal savings). Source and definitions, J. T. Klovland (1978), *Quantitative Studies in the Monetary History of Norway*, unpublished Ph.D. dissertation at the Norwegian School of Economics and Business Administration, Bergen.

### Chart 2.6   Denmark

*National income* 1870–1974. GDP at factor cost, current prices. 1870–1970, S. A. Hansen (1972–74), *Økonomisk vaekst i Danmark*, B II Table 3, G. A. D. Copenhagen. 1970–4, *Statistisk Arbog* (1976) *(Statistical Yearbook for Denmark)*, Table 390.

*Money supply* 1870–1974. M2 definition. Currency, 1870–1900, B. R. Mitchell (1975), *European Historical Statistics 1750–1970*, Macmillan, London, Table H.1. 1900–74, *Credit Market Statistics*, Copenhagen, (various issues). Deposits 1870–1974, *Credit Market Statistics* (various issues).

### Chart 2.7   Finland

*National income* 1900–75. NDP at market prices. 1900–26, A. Suvanto (1974), "Permanent Income, Inflation Expectations and the Demand for Money in Finland," University of Helsinki Working papers, Appendix. 1927–56, K. Larna (1959), *The Money Supply, Money Flows and Domestic Product in Finland 1910–1956*, Helsinki, Appendix Table 7. 1957–75 *Statistical Yearbook of Finland* (various issues).

*Money supply* 1900–75. M2 definition. Currency 1900–36, *Finlands Bank;* 1936–75, *Bank of Finland Yearbook*. Deposits 1900–75, *Unitas Fören-*

*ingsbanken i Finland* (various years) and *Statistical Yearbook for Finland,* Helsinki.

## Chart 2.8 Germany

*National income* 1870–1975. NNP at market prices. 1870–1938, W. Hoffman, (1965), *Das Wachstum der Deutsches Wirtschaft seit der Mitte des 19 Jahrhundert.* Berlin, Springer Verlag, Table 248. 1950–75, *Statistisches Jahrbuch* (1976), Table 26.

*Money supply* 1870–1975. M2 definition. 1870–1913, R. H. Tilly (1973), "Zeitreihen Zum Geldumlauf in Deutschland, 1870–1913," *J. für Nationalekonomie und Statistik,* Band 87, Table 6, p. 347. 1925–38, *Deutsches Geld und Bankwesen in Zahlen 1876–1975* (1976), Herausgeber: Deutsche Bundesbank, Verlag: Fritz Knapp Gmbh. Frankfurt am Main, pp. 14 and 18.

## Chart 2.9 Holland

*National income* 1910–74. NNP. Data supplied by M. M. G. Fase of the Netherlands Bank.

*Money supply* 1900–74. M2 definition. *75 jaar statistick van nederland.* Central bureau voor de statistick (1976).

## Chart 2.10 Italy

*National income* 1870–1975. NNI. 1870–1936, a simple average of "Income" from F. Spinelli (1980). "The Demand for Money in the Italian Economy, 1867–1965," *Journal of Monetary Economics,* vol. 6, no. 1 (January), 83–104, and "Total Net National Income," (Tav 135) from *Statistiche Storiche dell'Italia 1861–1975* (1976), Instituto Centrale de Statistica, Roma, p. 180. 1937–75, ibid.

*Money supply* 1870–1975. M2 definition. 1870–1937, F. Spinelli (1980), "The Demand for Money in the Italian Economy 1867–1965." 1938–65, a simple average of Spinelli and data in *Statistiche Storiche dell'Italia, 1861–1975,* Tables 94 and 95. 1966–75, *Statistiche Storiche dell'Italia 1861–1975,* Tables 94 and 95.

## Chart 2.11 Japan

*National income* 1975–82. GDP. Data provided by the Bank of Japan.

*Money supply* 1875–1982. *M*2 definition. Data provided by the Bank of Japan.


### Chart 2.12   Australia

*National income* 1870–1972. GDP. 1870–1939, N. G. Butlin (1962), *Australian Domestic Product, Investment and Borrowing, 1861–1938/39.* Cambridge University Press. 1939–48, *National Income and Expenditure Papers,* Canberra. 1949–72, *Australian National Accounts,* Canberra (various years).

*Money supply* 1870–1972. *M*2 definition. 1870–1945, *Australian Banking and Monetary Statistics 1817–1945,* (1971), Reserve Bank of Australia. 1945–70, *Australian Banking and Monetary Statistics 1945–1970,* (1971), Reserve Bank of Australia. 1971–7, N. Butlin, *A Preliminary Annual Data Base (1900–1974).*


### Chart 2.13   France

*National income* 1870–1969. GNP. M. Saint Marc (1983), *Histoire Monetaire de la France 1800–1980.* Presse Universitaire de France, Paris.

*Money supply* 1870–1969. *M*1 definition. Ibid.


### 1B.     Data sources for the regressions in Chapter 4

This data is available on request from the authors.


### United States

1.  *National income* 1870–1975. See Appendix 1A.
2.  *Implicit price deflator* 1870–1975. 1929 equal 100. Sources same as in item 1.
3.  *Real income* 1870–1975. NNP derived as in item 1 in constant 1929 *equal* 100 dollars.
4.  *Population* 1870–1975. 1870–1957, U.S. Department of Commerce (1975), *Historical Statistics.* 1958–69, U.S. Department of Commerce, *Current Population Reports, Population Estimates.* 1970–5, U.N. *Demographic Yearbook.*
5.  *Real per capita permanent income* 1870–1975. Expected per capita NNP, 1929 prices. Data kindly supplied by Anna J. Schwartz, NBER.

6. *Money supply* 1870–1975. See Appendix 1A.
7. *Long-term interest rate* ($r_l$) 1870–1975. Basic yield ten years maturity on corporate bonds. Extension of Macauley's railroad bond rate. Data supplied by NBER.
8. *Short-term interest rate* ($r_s$) 1870–1975. Prime commercial paper rate on 4–6 months bills. Data source same as item 7 above.
9. *Own-rate of return on money* ($r_m$) 1870–1972. Worksheets underlying Klein (1977).
10. *Total nonbank financial assets/total financial assets* 1870–1975. 1870–1963, benchmarks, R. Goldsmith (1969), *Financial Structure and Development*, Yale, Appendix Table D-33, and R. Goldsmith (1958), *Financial Intermediaries in the American Economy since 1900*, Table 10, p. 73, NBER, New York. We then linearly interpolated between Goldsmith's benchmarks to produce an annual series. 1964–1975, annual data derived from the sources underlying Goldsmith's tables.
11. *Total private nonbank financial assets/total private financial assets* 1870–1975. Source same as item 10 above, less assets of Federal Reserve Banks, Postal Savings System, Government Lending Institutions, federal pension, retirement and social security funds, and state and local pension and retirement funds.
12. *Number of commercial banks* 1870–1975. 1870–1895, sum of national and nonnational banks, *Historical Statistics* (1975). 1896–1970, number of all commercial banks, ibid. 1971–5, *Federal Reserve Bulletin* (various issues).
13. *Number of commercial bank branches* 1900–75. 1900–20, linear interpolations between quinquennial benchmarks. 1921–75, annual data. 1900–1970, *Historical Statistics* (1975). 1971–75, *Federal Reserve Bulletin*.
14. *Share of labor force in nonagricultural pursuits* 1870–1975. Employed nonagricultural civilian labor force divided by total employed civilian labor force. 1870–1947, interpolated between census years. 1948–1975, annual data. U.S. Department of Commerce (1975), *Historical Statistics* Tables D17 and D18, p. 127. 1971–5, U.S. Department of Labor (1977), *Handbook of Labor Statistics*, BLS Bulletin 1905, Table 1, p. 22.

## Canada

1. *National income* 1870–1975. See Appendix 1A.
2. *Implicit price deflator* 1870–1975. We used the same data series

as in item 1, connecting the various sections to a 1949 *equal* 100 base.

3. *Real income* 1870–1975. We used GNP as derived in item 1 in constant 1949 *equal* 100 dollars.

4. *Population* 1870–1975. Urquhart and Buckley (1965), Series A.1. 1956–75, *Bank of Canada Review*, August 1977.

5. *Real per capita permanent income* 1900–75. We adjusted per capita real income, item 3 divided by item 4, using Friedman's (1957) weights and accounting for the long-term growth rate of real per capita income 1900–75 of 2.14%. The formula used was

$$\left(\frac{Y}{PN}\right)_t^p = \frac{\beta}{\beta - \alpha}\left[w_1\left(\frac{Y}{PN}\right)_t + w_2\left(\frac{Y}{PN}\right)_{t-1}^p\right].$$

Taking $\left(\frac{Y}{PN}\right)1899 = \left(\frac{Y}{PN}\right)_t^p 1899 = \left(\frac{Y}{PN}\right)_{t-1}^p$

we generated the series using $\alpha = .021431$ and $\beta = .4$. This produced the algorithm:

$$\left(\frac{Y}{PN}\right)_t^p = 1.0566\left[.32968\left(\frac{Y}{PN}\right)_t + .67032\left(\frac{Y}{PN}\right)_{t-1}^p\right]$$

M. Friedman (1957), *A Theory of the Consumption Function*, Princeton, pp. 146–7.

6. *Money supply* 1870–1975. See Appendix 1A.

7. *Long-term bond yield* ($r_l$) 1870–1975. Government of Canada long-term bond yield (annual averages). 1870–1913, E. P. Neufeld (1972), *The Financial System of Canada*, Table 15.2, Macmillan, Toronto. 1919–70, *ibid.*, Table 15.3. 1971–76, *Bank of Canada Review*. There is a gap in Neufeld's data from 1914 to 1918. We filled this gap by regressing the Government of Canada bond yield on the Province of Ontario bond yield from 1900–13 and then using the regression equation to predict the GOC yields for the missing years.

8. *Short-term interest rate* ($r_s$) 1934–75. Three-month Treasury Bill rate, annual average of monthly data. Bank of Canada (1977), *Selected Canadian and International Interest Rates*, mimeo.

9. *The own-rate of return on money* ($r_m$) 1935–75. Following the approach used by Klein (1974), we constructed the variable $r_m = (1 - H/M_2)r_s$, where $H$, the stock of high-powered money, is the sum of currency held by the public and chartered bank

reserves (chartered bank holdings of Bank of Canada notes
and deposits). Source same as item 7 above.

10. *Total nonbank financial assets/total financial assets* 1870–1975.
1870–1968, Neufeld (1972), Appendix Table A. 1969–75 we
updated Neufeld's data following the sources suggested in his
Appendix Table A.

11. *Bank branches in Canada* 1870–1975. 1870–1959, Urquhart and
Buckley (1965), Series H 294. 1870–89, we interpolated between quinquennial benchmark years. 1960–75, *Canada Yearbook.*

12. *Share of labor force in nonagricultural pursuits* 1881–1975. 1881–
1910, Urquhart and Buckley (1965), Series C-2. 1911–61,
*Statistics Canada,* Census of 1961, Series 3.1, Table 3. 1971
data obtained with kind permission of Statistics Canada Census Division. We interpolated linearly between the ten census
years. 1972–4, total labor force from Statistics Canada, *The
Labour Force,* December 1975, Table 31, p. 57. Nonagricultural labor force from Statistics Canada (1974), *Historical Labour Force Statistics,* p. 402. 1975 estimated by a linear regression of the percentage of the labor force in nonagricultural
pursuits on a time trend.

### United Kingdom

1. *National income* 1870–1975. See Appendix 1A.

2. *Implicit price deflator* 1870–1975. 1970 *equal* 100. Sources same
as in item 1.

3. *Real income* 1870–1975. NNP derived as in item 1 in constant
1970 *equal* 100 dollars.

4. *Population* 1870–1975. 1870–1965, Feinstein (1972), Table 55,
col. 1966–75, CSO *Annual Statistical Abstract.*

5. *Real per capita permanent income* 1870–1975. We adjusted per
capita real income, item 3 divided by item 4, using Friedman's
(1957) weights and accounting for the long-term growth rate
of real per capita income 1870–1975 of 1.14% per annum.
The formula used was

$$\left(\frac{Y}{PN}\right)^p_t = 1.0293 \left[ .32968\left(\frac{Y}{PN}\right)_t + .67032\left(\frac{Y}{PN}\right)^p_{t-1} \right]$$

6. *Money supply* 1870–1975. See Appendix 1A.

7. *Long-term interest rate* ($r_l$) 1870–1975. Rate of interest on con-

sols (2.5%). 1870–1966, Sheppard (1971), Table A.3.7. 1967–75, Central Statistical Office, *Annual Abstract of Statistics*, various issues.

8. *Short-term interest rate* ($r_s$) 1870–1975. Rate of interest on three-month bank bills. 1870–1966, Sheppard (1971). 1967–75, CSO, *Annual Abstract of Statistics*.

9. *Own-rate of return on money* ($r_m$) 1870–1975. As for Canada, we followed the approach used by Klein (1974) and constructed $r_m = (1 - H/M_2)r_s$, where $H$, the stock of high-powered money, consists of currency held by the public plus reserves of the commercial banks. This data came from the same sources as the money supply (item 1).

10. *Total nonbank financial assets/total financial assets* 1870–1975. 1870–1963, linear interpolations between R. Goldsmith's benchmarks, Goldsmith (1969), Appendix, Table D-10. 1964–75, annual data from the sources underlying Goldsmith's data.

11. *Total private nonbank financial assets/total private financial assets* 1870–1975. Source same as for item 10 above less assets of Bank of England, Post Office Savings Banks, National Insurance Funds, the Birmingham Municipal Bank, Superannuation Funds, and Local Authorities Funds.

12. *Number of bank branches* 1870–1975. 1870–80, annual estimates derived from S. Nishimura (1977), "The Estimates of Bank Deposits in the U.K. 1870–1930," unpublished paper, Hosei University. 1881–1950, annual data from Sheppard (1971), Table A.1.1. 1951–75, annual data from *Bankers Almanac and Yearbook* (various issues).

13. *Share of labor force in nonagricultural pursuits* 1870–1975. 1870–1937, linear interpolations between decennial benchmarks. B. R. Mitchell and P. Deane (1962), *Abstract of British Historical Statistics*, Cambridge University Press, Cambridge, p. 60. 1938–68, annual data from U.K. Department of Employment and Productivity, *British Labour Statistics, Historical Abstract 1886–1968*, pp. 218–19. 1969–75, *Annual Abstract of Statistics*, 1976, p. 149.

**Sweden**

1. *National income* 1870–1974. See Appendix 1A.
2. *Implicit price deflator* 1870–1974. 1913 equal 100. Source same as in item 1.

3. *Real income* 1870–1975. GDP derived as in item 1 in constant 1913 equal 100 kronor.
4. *Population* 1870–1974. 1870–1955, O. Johansson (1967). 1956–75, *Statistisk årsbok för Sverige* (various issues).
5. *Real per capita permanent income* 1870–1974. We adjusted per capita real income, item 3 divided by item 4, using Friedman's (1957) weights and accounting for the long-term growth rate of real per capita income 1870–1974 of 2.5% per annum. The formula used was

$$\left(\frac{Y}{PN}\right)^p_t = 1.06664 \left[.32968\left(\frac{Y}{PN}\right)_t + .67032\left(\frac{Y}{PN}\right)^p_{t-1}\right]$$

6. *Money supply* 1871–1975. See Appendix 1A.
7. *Long-term interest rate* ($r_l$) 1870–1975. Effektiv medelränta på totala statsskulden (effective average return on the total government debt). 1860–1973, SAF:s beräkningar. 1974–5, *Riksgäldskontorets årsbok*, 1975–6.
8. *Total nonbank financial assets/total financial assets* 1880–1975. 1880–1963, linear interpolations between R. Goldsmith's benchmarks. Goldsmith (1969), Appendix, Table D-29. 1964–75, annual data from *Riksbankens årsbok*.
9. *Number of bank offices* 1870–1975. (End of year) commercial banks. 1870–1911, S. Brisman (1934), *Sveriges Affärsbanker*, vol. II, Stockholm, pp. 219–20. 1912–53, SM Serie E, *Uppgifter om bankerna*. 1954–68, SOS, *Uppgifter om bankerna*. 1961–71, SOS, *Bankaktiebolagen, Postbanken, Fondkommissionärerna och Fondbörsen*. 1972–5, SOS, *Bankaktiebolagen, Postbanken, Fondkommissionärerna, Fondbörsen och VPC*.
10. *Share of labor force in nonagricultural, fishing, and forestry pursuits* 1870–1975. 1870–1960, B. R. Mitchell (1975), *European Historical Statistics 1750–1970*, Macmillan, London, Table C1, p. 162. 1940 and 1962–75, *I.L.O. Yearbook*. Remaining years interpolated.

**Norway**

1. *National income* 1870–1974. See Appendix 1A.
2. *Implicit price deflator* 1870–1974. 1961 *equal* 100. Sources same as in item 1.
3. *Real income* 1870–1974. GDP derived as in item 1 in constant 1961 equal 100 kronor.

4. *Population* 1870–1974. *Historisk Statistikk* (1968), Oslo, and *Statistical Yearbook for Norway.*

5. *Real per capita permanent income* 1870–1974. We adjusted per capita réal income, item 3 divided by item 4, using Friedman's (1957) weights and accounting for the long-term growth rate of real per capita income 1870–1974 or 2.19% per annum. The formula used was

$$\left(\frac{Y}{PN}\right)_t^p = 1.05780 \left[.32968\left(\frac{Y}{PN}\right)_t + .67032\left(\frac{Y}{PN}\right)_{t-1}^p\right]$$

6. *Money supply* 1870–1974. See Appendix 1A.

7. *Long-term interest rate* ($r_l$) 1870–1975. Long-term bond yield (15 years). J. T. Klovland (1976), "Obligasjonsrenten i Norge 1852–1976," *Statsøkonomisk Tidskrift,* vol. 90.

8. *Total nonbank financial assets/total financial assets* 1880–1975. 1880–1963, linear interpolations between R. Goldsmith's benchmarks, Goldsmith (1969), Appendix, Table D-21. 1964–75, annual data from the sources underlying Goldsmith's data.

9. *Number of banks* 1870–1974. Commercial banks and savings banks. 1870–1966, *Historisk Statistikk* (1968). 1966–74, *Credit Market Statistics* (various issues).

10. *Share of labor force in nonagriculture, fishing, and forestry pursuits* 1875–1975. 1875–1950, linear interpolations between benchmark years from B. R. Mitchell (1975), *European Historical Statistics 1750–1970,* London, p. 159, Table C1. 1957–75, *I.L.O. Yearbook* (various issues). Remaining years interpolated.

## 1C.    Data sources for the regressions in Chapter 4, Appendix B

**United States**

Notes

TGE: Total government expenditure (federal government) including interest payments on the public debt.
Interest: Interest payments on the public debt.
Defense: National defense expenditures.

Sources

1870–1970: All data from *U.S. Historical Statistics* (1975), Series Y 457–465, p. 1114.
The national defense expenditures were obtained by addition of the columns 458, 459, 460, 1971–75: All data from *Sta-*

*tistical Abstract of the U.S.* (1976), Sec. 8, Table No. 377, p. 231.

## Canada

Notes

TGE: Total government expenditure (federal government) including interest payments on the public debt.
Interest: Interest payments on the public debt.
Defense: National defense expenditures.

Sources

1870–1960: All data from M. C. Urquhart and K. A. Buckley (1965), *Historical Statistics of Canada,* Series G26-44, pp. 200–3.
1960–1975: Years ended March 31, *Canada Yearbook* (various years).
TGE and defense:
1961: 1963–4 Issue, pp. 984–5.
1962–4: 1965 Issue, pp. 975–6.
1965–6: 1967 Issue, pp. 1040–1.
1967: 1969 Issue, pp. 1060–1.
1968–9: 1970/1 Issue, p. 149.
1970–1: 1972 Issue, p. 1146.
1972: 1975 Issue, p. 790.
1973–5: 1976/7 Issue, p. 970.
From 1961 to 1971, defense figures were taken from the row entitled "Defense Expenditures." From 1972 to 1975, from the row entitled "Protection of Persons and Property" (which includes national defense).

Interest:

Figures taken from the column "Interest Paid on Debt"
1961–9: 1970/1 Issue, p. 1151.
1970–1: 1972 Issue, p. 1148.
1972–5: 1978/9 Issue, p. 820.

## United Kingdom

Notes

TGE: Total government expenditure (central government) including interest payments on the public debt.

Interest: Interest payments on the public debt.
Defense: National defense expenditures.

Sources

1870–1939: All data from B. R. Mitchell and P. Deane (1962) *Abstract of British Historical Statistics,* Cambridge University Press, Chapter XIV, Table 4, except national defense expenditure 1914–18 from Alan T. Peacock and J. Wiseman (1961), *The Growth of Public Expenditure in the United Kingdom,* NBER, Princeton University Press, Table A-15, p. 184.

1940–75: *Annual Abstract of Statistics,* Central Statistical Office.

1940–45: *Annual Abstract of Statistics* (1938–49), Table 263, p. 237.

1946–9: *Annual Abstract of Statistics* (#92, 1955), Table 278, p. 243.

1950–8: *Annual Abstract of Statistics* (#98, 1961), Table 283, p. 241.

1959–68: *Annual Abstract of Statistics* (#107, 1970), Table 299, p. 282. Defense expenditures refer to military expenditures figures from Table 319, p. 297 (same issue).

1969–75: *Annual Abstract of Statistics* (#117, 1981), Table 14.5, p. 349. Defense expenditures refer to the military expenditures figures from Table 14.18, p. 360 (same issue).

**Sweden**

Notes

TGE: Total Government Expenditure not including interest payments on the national debt.

Sources

1870–1912: O. Johansson (1967), *Gross Domestic Product of Sweden,* Almqvist och Wiksell, Stockholm.

1913–75: A. Forsman (1980), En teori om staten och de offentliga utgifterna, Almqvist och Wiksell, Uppsala.

**Norway**

Notes

TGE: Total Government Expenditure (central government) including interest payments on the public debt.
Interest: Interest payments on the public debt.

Sources

1870–1900: Tabell IX in *Langtidslinjer i norsk ekonomi,* Samfunnsekonomiske Studier N. 16, Statistisk Sentralbyrå, Oslo, 1956.

1900–29: Tabell 8, Nasjonalregnskap, Statistisk Sentralbyrå, Oslo, 1953.

1930–60: Tabell 27, Nasjonalregnskap, Statistisk Sentralbyrå, Oslo, 1968.

1961–75: Tabell 243 and 251 in *Historisk Statistikk,* Oslo, 1978.

**1D.** **Data sources for the exchange rates used in converting permanent income into dollars for the pooled regressions in Chapter 4**

*United Kingdom (annual averages, dollars per pound)* 1870–1975. M. Friedman and A. J. Schwartz (1982), *Monetary Trends of the United States and United Kingdom.* Chicago, University of Chicago Press, Table 4-A-2.

*Canada (annual averages, dollars per Canadian dollars)* 1900–1975. 1900–60, M. Urquhart and K. Buckley (1965), *Historical Statistics of Canada,* Toronto, Macmillan. 1961–75, Board of Governors, Federal Reserve System, *Annual Statistical Digest* (various issues).

*Sweden (annual average cents per krona)* 1870–1975. *Annual Report of the Bank of Sweden* (various issues).

*Norway (annual average cents per krone)* 1870–1975. *Annual Report of the Bank of Norway* (various issues).

# REFERENCES

Adie, D. (1971), "The English Money Stock, 1834–1844," *Explorations in Economic History*, vol. 9, no. 2, pp. 111–43.

Arango, S., and Nadiri, M. I. (1981), "Demand for Money in Open Economies," *Journal of Monetary Economic*, vol. 7, no. 1, January, pp. 69–89.

Back, P. (1961), *En klass i uppbrott* [A class in movement], Svenska Lantarbetar-sörbundet, Stockholm.

Bagge, G.; Lundberg, E.; and Svennilson, I. (1933), *Wages in Sweden*, vol. 1, P. S. King and Son Ltd., London.

(1935), *Wages in Sweden*, vol. 2, P. S. King and Son Ltd., London.

Balassa, B. (1964), "The Purchasing Power Parity Doctrine: A Reappraisal," *Journal of Political Economy*, vol. 72, pp. 548–96.

Barkai, H. (1973), "The Macroeconomies of Tsarist Russia in the Industrialization Era: Monetary Developments, the Balance of Payments, and the Gold Standard," *Journal of Economic History*, vol. 33, March, pp. 339–71.

Baumol, W. (1952), "The Transactions Demand for Cash: An Inventory Theoretic Approach," *Quarterly Journal of Economics*, vol. 66, November, pp. 545–56.

Bordo, M. D. (1986), "Explorations in Monetary History: A Survey of the Literature," *Explorations in Economic History*, vol. 23, no. 4, October, pp. 339–415.

Bordo, M. D., and Choudhri, E. U. (1982), "Currency Substitution and the Demand for Money: Some Evidence for Canada," *Journal of Money, Credit, and Banking*, vol. 14, no. 1, pp. 48–67.

Bordo, M. D., and Jonung, L. (1981), "The Long Run Behavior of the Income Velocity of Money: A Cross Country Comparison of Five Advanced Countries, 1870–1975," *Economic Inquiry*, vol. 19, pp. 96–116.

Brisman, S. (1931), "Den stora reformperioden, 1860–1904" [The period of great reforms, 1860–1904], part 3 in *Sveriges Riksbank* [The Bank of Sweden], vol. 4, The Bank of Sweden, Stockholm.

(1934), *Sveriges affärsbanker* [Sweden's commercial banks], Fritzes Bokhandel, Stockholm.

Brittain, B. (1981), "International Currency Substitution and the Apparent Instability of Velocity in Some Western European Economies and in the United States," *Journal of Money, Credit, and Banking*, vol. 13, no. 2, May, pp. 135–55.

Brunner, K., and Meltzer, A. H. (1963), "Predicting Velocity: Implications for Theory and Policy," *Journal of Finance*, vol. 18, May, pp. 319–54.

168

(1967), "Economies of Scale in Cash Balances Reconsidered," *Quarterly Journal of Economics*, vol. 81, August, pp. 422–36.

(1971), "The Uses of Money: Money in the Theory of an Exchange Economy," *American Economic Review*, vol. 60, pp. 784–805.

Cagan, P. (1956), "The Monetary Dynamics of Hyperinflation, in M. Friedman (ed.), *Studies in the Quantity Theory of Money*, pp. 25–117, University of Chicago Press, Chicago.

(1965), *Determinants and Effects of Changes in the Stock of Money, 1875–1960*, NBER, New York.

Cagan, P., and Schwartz, A. (1975), "Has the Growth of Money Substitutes Hindered Monetary Policy?," *Journal of Money, Credit, and Banking*, vol. 7, May, pp. 137–60.

Cameron, R. (1967), *Banking in the Early Stages of Industrialization*, Oxford University Press, London.

(1972), *Banking and Economic Development*, Oxford University Press, London.

Capie F., and Webber, A. (1985), *A Monetary History of the U.K., 1870–1982*, vol. 1: *Data Sources Methods*, Allen and Unwin, London.

Capie, F., and Rodrik-Bali, G. (1985), "The Money Adjustment Process in the United Kingdom, 1870–1914," *Economica*, vol. 52, pp. 117–22.

Carr, J. L., and Darby, M. R. (1981), "The Role of Money Supply Shocks in the Short-Run Demand for Money," *Journal of Monetary Economics*, vol. 8, September, pp. 183–99.

Chandavarkar, A. G. (1977), "Monetization of Developing Economies," *IMF Staff Papers*, vol. 24, November, pp. 665–721.

Chow, G. (1966), "On the Long-Run and Short-Run Demand for Money," *Journal of Political Economy*, vol. 74, April, pp. 111–31.

Clower, R. W. (1969), "Introduction," *Monetary Theory*, pp. 7–21, Penguin Modern Readings, London.

Collins, M. (1983), "Long Term Growth of the English Banking Sector and Money Stock, 1844–80," *Economic History Review*, vol. 36, no. 3, pp. 274–94.

Cuddington, J. T. (1983), "Currency Substitution, Capital Mobility, and Money Demand," *Journal of International Money and Finance*, vol. 2, no. 2, August, pp. 111–34.

Darby, M. (1972), "The Allocation of Transitory Income among Consumers' Assets," *American Economic Review*, vol. 62, no. 5, December, pp. 928–41.

Deane, P. (1972), "New Estimates of Gross National Product for the United Kingdom, 1830–1914," *Review of Income and Wealth*, vol. 14, no. 2, June, pp. 95–112.

Dickey, D. A., and Fuller, W. A. (1979), "Distribution of the Estimators for Autoregressive Time Series with a Unit Root," *Journal of the American Statistical Association*, vol. 74, June, pp. 427–31.

(1981), "Likelihood Ratio Statistics for Autoregressive Time Series with a Unit Root," *Econometrica*, vol. 49, no. 4, July, pp. 1057–72.

Doblin, E. M. (1951), "The Ratio of Income to Money Supply: An International Survey," *Review of Economics and Statistics*, vol. 33, pp. 201–13.

Driscoll, M. J., and Lahiri, A. K. (1983), "Income Velocity of Money in Agricultural Developing Economies," *Review of Economics and Statistics*, vol. 65, no. 3, August, pp. 393–401.

Easton, S. (1984), "Real Output and the Gold Standard Years, 1830–1913," in M. D. Bordo and A. J. Schwartz (eds.), *A Retrospective on the Classical Gold Standard, 1821–1931*, pp. 513–38, University of Chicago Press, Chicago.

Ejdestam, J.; Hedin, N.; and Nygren, E. (1965), *Bilder ur lanthandelns historia* [Pictures from the history of the country store], 2d ed., A. B. Hakon Swenson, Västerås.

Ezekiel, H., and Adekunle, J. O. (1969), "The Secular Behavior of Income Velocity: An International Cross-Section Study," *IMF Staff Papers*, vol. 16, no. 2, July, pp. 224–239.

Fase, M. M. A., and Kure, J. B. (1975), "The Demand for Money in Thirteen European and Non European Countries: A Tabular Survey," *Kredit und Kapital*, vol. 3, pp. 410–19.

Feige, E., and Pearce, D. (1977), "Substitutability between Money and Near Monies: A Survey of the Time Series Evidence," *Journal of Economic Literature*, vol. 15, no. 2, June, pp. 439–69.

Fisher, D. (1978), *Monetary Theory and the Demand for Money*, Martin Robertson, Oxford.

Fisher, I. (1911), *The Purchasing Power of Money*, A. M. Kelly, New York, 1971.

Fleetwood-Jucker, E. E. (1958), "The Key Role of the Velocity of Circulation of Money and Credit," *Oxford Economic Papers*, vol. 10, No. 3, October, pp. 240–315.

Friedman, M. (1956), "The Quantity Theory of Money: A Restatement" in M. Friedman (ed.), *Studies in the Quantity Theory of Money*, pp. 3–21, University of Chicago Press, Chicago.

——— (1957), *A Theory of the Consumption Function*, NBER, New York.

——— (1959), "The Demand for Money: Some Theoretical and Empirical Results," *Journal of Political Economy*, vol. 67, no. 4, August, pp. 327–51.

——— (1971), *A Theoretical Framework for Monetary Analysis*, NBER, New York.

Friedman, M., and Schwartz, A. J. (1963), *A Monetary History of the United States, 1867–1960*, Princeton University Press, Princeton, NJ.

——— (1970), *Monetary Statistics of the United States*, NBER, New York.

——— (1982), *Monetary Trends in the United States and the United Kingdom*, NBER-University of Chicago Press, Chicago.

Gårdlund, T. (1942), *Industrialismens samhälle* [The society of industrialization], Tiden, Stockholm.

Garvy, G. (1959), *Deposit Velocity and Its Significance*, Federal Reserve Bank of New York, New York.

Garvy, G., and Blyn, M. (1970), *The Velocity of Money*, Federal Reserve Bank of New York, New York.

Gasslander, O. (1956), *Bank och industriellt genombrottt* [Banking and industrial development], vol. 1, Gen.-stab:s lit. anst. Stockholm.

Goldfeld, S. M. (1973), "The Demand for Money Revisited," *Brookings Papers on Economic Activity*, vol. 3, no. 2, pp. 577–638.

Goldsmith, R. (1969), *Financial Structure and Development*, Yale University Press, New Haven, CT.

(1985), *Comparative National Balance Sheets: A Study of Twenty Countries, 1668–1978*, University of Chicago Press, Chicago.

Goodhart, C. A. E. (1982), "Monetary Trends in the United States and the United Kingdom: A British Review," *Journal of Economic Literature*, vol. 20, December, pp. 1540–51.

Gould, J. P., and Nelson, C. R. (1974), "The Stochastic Structure of the Velocity of Money," *American Economic Review*, vol. 64, no. 2, June, pp. 405–18.

Gould, J. P.; Nelson, C. R.; Miller, M.; and Upton, C. W. (1978), "The Stochastic Properties of Velocity and the Quantity Theory of Money," *Journal of Monetary Economics*, vol. 4, no. 2, April, pp. 220–48.

Graves, P. (1978), "New Evidence on Income and Velocity of Money," *Economic Inquiry*, vol. 16, January, pp. 53–68.

Gurley, J., and Shaw, E. (1960), *Money in a Theory of Finance*, Brookings Institution, Washington, D.C.

Hafer, R., and Hein, S. (1982), *Financial Innovations and the Interest Elasticity of Money Demand: Some Historical Evidence*, Research Paper No. 82-011, Federal Reserve Bank of St. Louis, St. Louis, MO.

Hall, R. E. (1978), "The Stochastic Implications of the Life Cycle–Permanent Income Hypothesis: Theories and Evidence," *Journal of Political Economy*, vol. 86, pp. 971–87.

Haraf, W. S. (1986), "The Recent Behavior of Velocity: Implications for Alternative Monetary Rules," *The Cato Journal*, vol. 6, no. 2, Fall, pp. 641–62.

Hedin, L. E. (1967), "Swedish Railroads, 1860–1914," *Economy and History*, vol. 10, pp. 3–37.

Hegeland, H. (1951), *The Quantity Theory of Money*, Gumpert, Gothenburg.

Hicks, J. R. (1967), *Critical Essays in Monetary Theory*, Oxford University Press, Oxford.

Holtrop, M. W. (1929), "Theories of the Velocity of Circulation of Money in Earlier Economic Literature," *Economic Journal*, (Economic History Series no. 4), January, pp. 503–24.

Huffman, W., and Lothian, J. (1984), "The Gold Standard and the Transmission of Business Cycles, 1873–1932," in M. D. Bordo and A. J. Schwartz (eds.), *A Retrospective on the Classical Gold Standard, 1821–1931*, pp. 455–511, University of Chicago Press, Chicago.

Isaksen, A. J. (1975), *The Demand for Money in Norway*, Bank of Norway, Oslo.

Johansson, O. (1967), *The Gross Domestic Product of Sweden and Its Composition, 1861–1955*, Almqvist och Wiksell, Stockholm.

Johnson, H. G. (1969), "Inside Money, Outside Money, Income, Wealth, and Welfare in Monetary Theory," *Journal of Money, Credit, and Banking*, vol. 1, no. 1, February, pp. 30–45.

Jonung, L. (1975), "Studies in the Monetary History of Sweden," Ph.D. diss., University of California, Los Angeles.

(1978a), "The Long-Run Demand for Money: A Wicksellian Approach," *Scandinavian Journal of Economics*, vol. 80, pp. 216–30.

(1978b), "The Legal Framework and the Economics of Private Bank Notes in Sweden, 1831–1901," in G. Skogh (ed.), *Law and Economics – Report from a Symposium in Sweden*, pp. 185–201, University of Lund, Lund.

(1983), "Monetization and the Behaviour of Velocity in Sweden, 1871–1913," *Explorations in Economic History*, vol. 20, pp. 418–39.

(1984), "Swedish Experience under the Classical Gold Standard, 1873–1914," in M. D. Bordo and A. J. Schwartz (eds.), *The Classical Gold Standard in Retrospective*, pp. 361–99, NBER-University of Chicago Press, Chicago.

Jörberg, L. (1972), *A History of Prices in Sweden, 1732–1914*, part 2, Gleerup, Lund.

Judd, J.; and Scadding, J. (1982), "The Search for a Stable Money Demand Function: A Survey of the Post-1973 Literature," *Journal of Economic Literature*, vol. 20, pp. 993–1023.

Kaufman, G. G., and Latta, C. M. (1966), "The Demand for Money: Preliminary Evidence from Industrial Countries," *Journal of Financial and Quantitative Analysis*, vol. 1, no. 3, September, pp. 75–89.

Khan, M. (1980), "Monetary Shocks and the Dynamics of Inflation," *IMF Staff Papers*, vol. 27, no. 2, June, pp. 250–84.

Klein, B. (1973), "Income Velocity, Interest Rates, and the Money Supply Multiplier," *Journal of Money, Credit, and Banking*, vol. 5, pp. 656–68.

(1974), "Competitive Interest Payments on Bank Deposits and the Long-Run Demand for Money," *American Economic Review*, vol. 64, pp. 931–49.

(1975), "Our New Monetary Standard: The Measurement and Effects of Price Uncertainty, 1880–1973," *Economic Inquiry*, vol. 13, no. 4, pp. 461–84.

(1977), "The Demand for Quality Adjusted Cash Balances: Price Uncertainty in the U.S. Demand for Money Function," *Journal of Political Economy*, vol. 85, no. 4, August, pp. 691–716.

Klovland, J. T. (1983), "The Demand for Money in Secular Perspective: The Case of Norway, 1867–1980," *European Economic Review*, vol. 22, no. 2, July, 193–218.

Kmenta, J. (1971), *Elements of Econometrics*, Macmillan, New York.

Komlos, J. "Financial Innovation and the Demand for Money in Austria-Hungary," *Journal of European Economic History*. In press.

Kravis, I.; Heston, A. W.; and Summers, R. (1978), "Real GNP per Capita for More Than One Hundred Countries," *Economic Journal*, vol. 88, June, pp. 215–42.

Laidler, D. (1966), "The Rate of Interest and the Demand for Money – Some Empirical Evidence," *Journal of Political Economy*, vol. 74, December, pp. 545–55.

⎯⎯⎯ (1971), "The Influence of Money on Economic Activity: A Survey of Some Current Problems," in G. Clayton, J. G. Gilbert, and R. Sedgewick (eds.), *Monetary Theory and Policy in the 1970's*, pp. 73–135, Oxford University Press, Oxford.

⎯⎯⎯ (1980), "The Demand for Money in the United States – Yet Again," in K. Brunner and A. H. Meltzer (eds.), *On the State of Macroeconomics*, pp. 219–71, Carnegie Rochester Conference on Public Policy, vol. 12, North Holland, Amsterdam.

⎯⎯⎯ (1982), *Monetarist Perspectives*, Harvard University Press, Cambridge, MA.

⎯⎯⎯ (1984), "The Buffer Stock Notion in Monetary Economics," *Conference Proceedings Supplement to the Economic Journal*, vol. 94, March, pp. 17–34.

⎯⎯⎯ (1985), *The Demand for Money: Theories and Evidence*, 3d ed., Harper and Row, New York.

Latané, H. (1954), "Cash Balances and the Interest Rate: A Pragmatic Approach," *Review of Economics and Statistics*, vol. 36, November, pp. 456–60.

⎯⎯⎯ (1969), "Income Velocity and Interest Rates: A Pragmatic Approach," *Review of Economics and Statistics*, vol. 62, November, pp. 445–9.

Leijonhufvud, A. (1984), "Inflation and Economic Performance," in B. N. Siegel (ed.), *Money in Crisis: The Federal Reserve, the Economy, and Monetary Reform*, pp. 19–36, Pacific Institute for Public Policy Research, San Francisco.

Lieberman, C. (1977), "The Transactions Demand for Money and Technological Change," *Review of Economics and Statistics*, August, pp. 307–13.

⎯⎯⎯ (1980), "The Long-Run and Short-Run Demand for Money, Revisited," *Journal of Money, Credit, and Banking*, vol. 12, no. 1, February, pp. 43–57.

Lindert, P. (1985), "English Population, Wages, and Prices, 1541–1913," *Journal of Interdisciplinary History*, vol. 15, no. 4, pp. 609–34.

Lybeck, J. A. (1975), "Issues in the Theory of the Long-Run Demand for Money," *Scandinavian Journal of Economics*, vol. 77, pp. 193–206.

Macesich, G. (1962), "The Demand for Currency and Taxation in Canada," *Southern Economic Journal*, vol. 29, pp. 33–6.

Mayer, T. (1982), "Monetary Trends in the United States and the United Kingdom: A Review Article," *Journal of Economic Literature*, vol. 20, December, pp. 1528–39.

Mayor, T. H., and Pearl, L. R. (1984), "Life Cycle Effects, Structural Change, and Long-Run Movements in the Velocity of Money," *Journal of Money, Credit, and Banking*, vol. 16, no. 2, May, pp. 175–84.

McKinnon, R. I. (1982), "Currency Substitution and Instability in the World Dollar Standard," *American Economic Review*, vol. 72, no. 3, June, pp. 320–33.

Melitz, J., and Correa, H. (1970), "International Differences in Income Velocity," *Review of Economics and Statistics*, vol. 52, no. 1, February, pp. 12–17.

Meltzer, A. H. (1963), "The Demand for Money: The Evidence from the Time Series," *Journal of Political Economy*, June, pp. 219–46.

Miles, M. (1978), "Currency Substitution, Flexible Exchange Rates, and Monetary Independence," *American Economic Review*, vol. 68, no. 3, June, pp. 428–36.

Nelson, C. R., and Plosser, C. (1982), "Trends and Random Walks in Macroeconomic Time Series: Some Evidence and Implications," *Journal of Monetary Economics*, vol. 2, no. 2, September, pp. 139–52.

Nurkse, R. (1944), *International Currency Experience*, League of Nations, Geneva; reprinted by Arno Press, New York, 1978.

Patterson D., and Shearer, R. (1985), "The Money Supply in Mid–Nineteenth Century Canada: Estimates and Their Implications," mimeo., University of British Columbia.

Perlman, M. (1970), "International Differences in Liquid Assets Portfolios," in D. Meiselman (ed.), *The Varieties of Monetary Experience*, pp. 299–337, University of Chicago Press, Chicago.

Poole, W. (1986), "A Random Walk down Velocity Lane," *Memorandum to the Shadow Open Market Committee*, March, mimeo, University of Rochester.

Riley, J., and McCusker, J. (1983), "Money Supply, Economic Growth, and the Quantity Theory of Money: France, 1650–1778," *Explorations in Economic History*, vol. 20, no. 3, July, pp. 274–93.

Roley, V. V. (1985), "Money Demand Predictability," *Journal of Money, Credit, and Banking*, vol. 17, no. 4, part 2, November, pp. 611–41.

Saint Marc, M. (1983), *Histoire Monetaire de la France, 1800–1980*, Presses Universitaire de France, Paris.

Sandberg, L. G. (1978), "Banking and Economic Growth in Sweden before World War I," *Journal of Economic History*, vol. 38, pp. 650–80.

Schwartz, A. J. (1975), "Monetary Trends in the United States and the United Kingdom, 1878–1970: Selected Findings," *Journal of Economic History*, vol. 35, pp. 138–59.

(1985), "The Service Flows of Money: A Historical Perspective," mimeo, NBER, New York.

Selden, R. (1956), "Monetary Velocity in the United States," in M. Friedman (ed.), *Studies in the Quantity Theory of Money*, pp. 179–257, University of Chicago Press, Chicago.

Smith, W. (1960), "Debt Management in the United States," *Employment, Growth, and Price Levels*, Study Paper No. 19, JEC. 86th Cong., 2d Session, January 21, 1960, pp. 116–74.

Snyder, C. (1924), "New Measures of the Equation of Exchange," *American Economic Review*, vol. 14, March, pp. 699–713.

Sommarin, E. (1942), *Vårt sparbanksväsen, 1834–1892* [Our savings bank system, 1834–1892], Gleerup, Lund.

Stauffer, R. F. (1978), "A Reinterpretation of Velocity Trends in the United

States, 1900–1920," *Journal of Money, Credit, and Banking*, vol. 10, no. 1, February, pp. 105–11.

Stokes, H., and Neuberger, H. (1979), "A Note on the Stochastic Structure of the Velocity of Money: Some Reservations," *American Economist*, vol. 23, Fall, pp. 62–4.

Taylor, D. (1976), "Friedman's Dynamic Models: Empirical Tests," *Journal of Monetary Economics*, vol. 2, pp. 531–8.

Timberlake, R. (1974), "Denominational Factors in Nineteenth Century Currency Experience," *Journal of Economic History*, vol. 34, September, pp. 835–50.

Tobin, J. (1956), "The Interest-Elasticity of Transactions Demand for Cash," *Review of Economics and Statistics*, vol. 38, no. 3, August, pp. 241–7.

(1965), "The Monetary Interpretation of History," *American Economic Review*, vol. 55, no. 3, June, pp. 464–85.

(1985), "Neoclassical Theory in America: J. B. Clark and Fisher," *American Economic Review*, vol. 75, no. 6, December, pp. 28–38.

Townsend, J. C. (1983), "Financial Structure and Economic Activity, *American Economic Review*, vol. 73, no. 45, December, pp. 895–911.

Utterström, G. (1957), *Jordbrukets arbetare* [Workers in agriculture], Tiden, Stockholm.

Warburton, C. (1949), "The Secular Trend in Monetary Velocity," *Quarterly Journal of Economics*, vol. 63, February, pp. 68–91.

Wicksell, K. (1935), *Lectures on Political Economy*, vol. 2, Routledge and Sons, London.

(1936), *Interest and Prices*, Macmillan, London.

# Author index

177

# Subject index

Printed in the United States
by Baker & Taylor Publisher Services